PRINCE

M000014274

BIRDS

OF NORTH AMERICA AND GREENLAND

PRINCETON ILLUSTRATED CHECKLISTS

Birds of Eastern Africa, by Ber van Perlo

Birds of Southern Africa, by Ber van Perlo

Birds of Southern South America and Antarctica, by Martín R. de la Peña and Maurice Rumboll

Birds of Western and Central Africa, by Ber van Perlo

Birds of Mexico and Central America, by Ber van Perlo

Birds of South America: Non-Passerines: Rheas to Woodpeckers, by Francisco Erize, Jorge R. Rodriguez Mata, and Maurice Rumboll

Birds of Europe, Russia, China, and Japan: Passerines: Tyrant Flycatchers to Buntings, by Norman Arlott

Birds of Europe, Russia, China, and Japan: Non-Passerines: Loons to Woodpeckers, by Norman Arlott

Birds of the West Indies, by Norman Arlott

Birds of North America, by Norman Arlott

Birds of Hawaii, New Zealand, and the Central and West Pacific, by Ber van Perlo

Birds of North America and Greenland, by Norman Arlott

PRINCETON ILLUSTRATED CHECKLISTS

BIRDS

OF NORTH AMERICA AND GREENLAND

Written and illustrated by
NORMAN ARLOTT

Princeton University Press
Princeton and Oxford

DEDICATION

I would like to dedicate this book to my esteemed friend Steve Graham, who took me on my first real birding trip in the USA.

Published in the United States, Canada, and the Philippine Islands by Princeton University Press, 41 William Street, Princeton, New Jersey 08540

nathist.press.princeton.edu

Published by arrangement with HarperCollins Publishers Ltd

Originally published in English by HarperCollins Publishers Ltd under the title *Birds of North America and Greenland*

First published 2011

Library of Congress Control Number 2011926110
ISBN 978-0-691-15140-3

Edited and designed by D & N Publishing, Baydon, Wiltshire

Colour reproduction by Dot Gradations Ltd, UK
Printed and bound in Hong Kong by Printing Express Ltd

10 9 8 7 6 5 4 3 2 1

CONTENTS

Acknowledgements   8
Introduction   8
Area and Species Covered   9
Plates   9
Nomenclature   9
Identification   9
Distribution Maps   9
Map of the Region   10
Bird Topography   11

Species Descriptions and Colour Plates
1   Ducks and Geese   12
2   Geese and Swans   14
3   Ducks   16
4   Ducks   18
5   Ducks   20
6   Ducks   22
7   Ducks   24
8   Chachalaca and Gamebirds   26
9   Gamebirds   28
10 Gamebirds   30
11 Divers (Loons)   32
12 Grebes   34
13 Albatrosses and Fulmar   36
14 Petrels   38
15 Shearwaters   40
16 Shearwaters and Storm-petrels   42
17 Storm-petrels   44
18 Frigatebirds, Tropicbirds, Boobies and Gannet   46
19 Pelicans, Cormorants and Anhinga   48
20 Bitterns, Night-herons and Herons   50
21 Egrets and Herons   52
22 Ibises, Spoonbills, Storks and Flamingo   54
23 Vultures, Condor and Eagles   56
24 Caracara, Osprey, Kites and Harrier   58
25 Hawks   60
26 Hawks   62
27 Falcons   64
28 Rails and Crakes   66
29 Gallinules, Coots, Limpkin and Cranes   68
30 Jacana, Avocet, Stilts, Oystercatchers and Thick-knee   70

31	Plovers	72
32	Plovers	74
33	Shanks and Sandpipers	76
34	Willet, Tattlers and Sandpipers	78
35	Curlews	80
36	Dowitchers, Godwits and Ruff	82
37	Turnstones, Surfbird and *Calidris* Sandpipers	84
38	*Calidris* Sandpipers	86
39	*Calidris* Sandpipers	88
40	Snipe, Woodcock, Phalaropes and Pratincole	90
41	Gulls	92
42	Gulls	94
43	Gulls	96
44	Terns	98
45	Terns	100
46	Skuas	102
47	Auks	104
48	Auks	106
49	Pigeons and Doves	108
50	Doves	110
51	Hoopoe, Anis, Cuckoos and Roadrunner	112
52	Owls	114
53	Owls	116
54	Nightjars and Nighthawks	118
55	Swifts	120
56	Hummingbirds	122
57	Hummingbirds	124
58	Parakeets, Trogons and Kingfishers	126
59	Wryneck and Woodpeckers	128
60	Woodpeckers	130
61	Sapsuckers, Flickers and Woodpeckers	132
62	Becard and Tyrant Flycatchers	134
63	Tyrant Flycatchers	136
64	Tyrant Flycatchers	138
65	Tyrant Flycatchers	140
66	Tyrant Flycatchers, Tityra and Shrikes	142
67	Vireos	144
68	Vireos	146
69	Jays	148
70	Nutcracker, Crows and Ravens	150
71	Larks, Pipits and Accentor	152
72	Wagtails and Dipper	154
73	Martins and Swallow	156

74 Swallows   158
75 Verdin, Bushtit and Chickadees   160
76 Titmice, Brown Creeper and Nuthatches   162
77 Wrens   164
78 Old World Warblers and Gnatcatchers   166
79 Kinglets, Wrentit and Old World Flycatchers   168
80 Thrushes   170
81 Thrushes   172
82 Thrushes   174
83 Mockingbirds and Thrashers   176
84 Catbird, Starling, Mynas, Bulbul, Waxwings and
    Silky Flycatchers   178
85 American Warblers   180
86 American Warblers   182
87 American Warblers   184
88 American Warblers   186
89 American Warblers   188
90 American Warblers   190
91 Bananaquit, Tanagers, Grassquits and Seedeater   192
92 Towhees and American Sparrows   194
93 American Sparrows   196
94 American Sparrows and Lark Bunting   198
95 American Sparrows and Juncos   200
96 Dickcissel, Old World Sparrows, Longspurs and Buntings   202
97 Buntings, Cardinal and Pyrrhuloxia   204
98 Grosbeaks, *Passerina* Buntings and Blue Bunting   206
99 Bobolink, Meadowlarks and American Blackbirds   208
100 American Orioles   210
101 Grackles and Cowbirds   212
102 Finches   214
103 Finches   216
104 Finches   218

Further Reading   220
Index   221

ACKNOWLEDGEMENTS

Bird books take a relatively short time to paint and write, but the knowledge that enables them to be completed is gained over many, many years. I well remember that my passion started as a very young boy bird nesting (now, quite rightly, frowned upon) with my father. That passion has since been enhanced by being fortunate enough to be in the field with and inspired by some well known and not so well known 'birders'. In particular, I must mention the following who have encouraged me and allowed me to pick their brains over the years: the late John G. Williams, the late Eric Hosking, the late Crispin Fisher, Robert Gillmor, the late Basil Parsons, Brian Leflay and Moss Taylor. This book could not have gone ahead without the help of the staff at the British Museum at Tring, especially Mark Adams and Robert Prŷs-Jones. Namrita and David Price-Goodfellow deserve special praise for their skill, and patience, in putting together the various component parts of this book. Without publishers there would not be a book, so it gives me great pleasure to thank everyone at HarperCollins, particularly Myles Archibald and Julia Koppitz. Lastly, but definitely not least, I thank friends and family who have had to put up with my various mood changes whilst trying to sort out some of the more difficult aspects of putting this book together, my wife Marie probably enduring more than most.

INTRODUCTION

The format of this book follows that of my Palearctic and West Indies volumes. Although primarily an illustrated checklist, space would not allow me to produce the ultimate field guide. However, it is hoped that within these pages I have given a helpful nudge towards what to look for when searching for new birds as well as being a reminder of birds seen.

Most of the text in this book is based on the type of notes I make before embarking on a field trip to a new area, and hopefully they will, along with the illustrations, help to identify most birds encountered. Obviously the use of more in-depth tomes will be required for some of the trickier species (*see* Further Reading).

I can only hope that with this work I have been able to add to the pleasure of anticipation or memory, and perhaps even added some extra piece of knowledge about the birds of this huge region.

Plumage variation of the Great Horned Owl, the most widespread owl of North America.

AREA AND SPECIES COVERED

The USA, Canada and Greenland are covered, which is not strictly the complete Nearctic, but for various reasons it was deemed better to stay within these three countries.

I have endeavoured to include every species recorded in the region, apart from non-established introductions, and many of the major subspecies. Each has been depicted in breeding plumage, and non-breeding plumage when it differs significantly. To keep the book to a manageable size no juvenile plumages have been illustrated, although, when thought necessary and room permits, a short passage has been included in 'Field notes'.

I have needed to tweak the recommended order in places in order to aid plate composition; hopefully this will not cause too much aggravation.

PLATES

The abbreviations and symbols used on the plates are as follows:
♂ = male; ♀ = female; br = breeding; n-br = non-breeding.

NOMENCLATURE

I have headlined the English names that I believe are those used by most birders in the field, which means I have in many cases reverted to 'old school' names rather than some of the more modern interpretations. However, most of these 'new' names, along with other well-used names, are included in parentheses.

IDENTIFICATION

It is hoped that the illustrations will be all that is needed to identify a specific bird, but quite obviously with some of the trickier species more information is needed, hence the need for Field Notes, Voice and Habitat.

FIELD NOTES: Because of the need to keep text to a minimum this section rarely mentions those aspects of a bird that should be obvious from the illustrations, e.g. wing bars, bill shape etc. It is used mainly to point to a bird's habits or to mention facets of identification that are hidden in a standing or perched bird.

VOICE: Probably the first sign of a bird's presence. The descriptions are shown in *italics*. Where space has allowed I have included different interpretations of the same song. Although difficult to produce an accurate reproduction of bird songs or calls in the written word, this section is worth studying in order to get a feel for what is often the most important area of bird identification.

HABITAT: The main habitat preferences mentioned are those in which a species breeds; wintering habitats are also included if appropriate.

DISTRIBUTION: Mainly general, so should be read in conjunction with the maps.

DISTRIBUTION MAPS

Distribution maps are shown for all species except vagrants and those that have been recently introduced. They should only be used as a rough guide to where a species can be found at different times of the year. Red ▬ areas indicate where a species may be found in the summer on its breeding grounds; blue ▬ shows where it is found in winter when not breeding; and purple ▬ areas are where a species is a year-round resident. Paler versions of each colour show distributions at sea.

MAP OF THE REGION

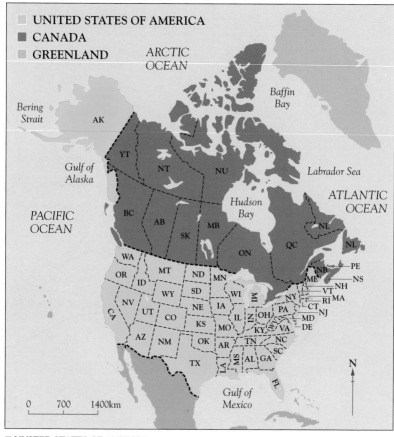

UNITED STATES OF AMERICA
CANADA
GREENLAND

ARCTIC OCEAN

Baffin Bay

Bering Strait

AK

Gulf of Alaska

YT

NT

NU

Labrador Sea

PACIFIC OCEAN

BC

AB

SK

MB

Hudson Bay

ON

QC

ATLANTIC OCEAN

NL

NL

WA

OR

ID

MT

ND

MN

WY

SD

WI

NE

IA

MI

PE

NB

ME

NH

VT

RI MA

NY

CT

NJ

PA

MD

DE

NV

UT

CO

CA

AZ

NM

KS

OK

MO

IL

IN

OH

KY

WV

VA

NC

TN

SC

TX

LA

MS

AL

GA

FL

Gulf of Mexico

N

0   700   1400km

UNITED STATES OF AMERICA

AK	Alaska	IA	Iowa	MI	Michigan	NM	New Mexico	TN	Tennessee
AL	Alabama	ID	Idaho	MN	Minnesota	NV	Nevada	TX	Texas
AR	Arkansas	IL	Illinois	MO	Missouri	NY	New York	UT	Utah
AZ	Arizona	IN	Indiana	MS	Mississippi	OH	Ohio	VA	Virginia
CA	California	KS	Kansas	MT	Montana	OK	Oklahoma	VT	Vermont
CO	Colorado	KY	Kentucky	NC	North Carolina	OR	Oregon	WA	Washington
CT	Connecticut	LA	Louisiana	ND	North Dakota	PA	Pennsylvania	WI	Wisconsin
DE	Delaware	MA	Massachusetts	NE	Nebraska	RI	Rhode Island	WV	West Virginia
FL	Florida	MD	Maryland	NH	New Hampshire	SC	South Carolina	WY	Wyoming
GA	Georgia	ME	Maine	NJ	New Jersey	SD	South Dakota		

CANADA

AB	Alberta	MB	Manitoba	NB	New Brunswick	NS	Nova Scotia	QC	Quebec
BC	British Columbia	NU	Nunavut	NL	Newfoundland and Labrador	ON	Ontario	SK	Saskatchewan
		NT	Northwest Territories			PE	Prince Edward Island	YT	Yukon Territory

BIRD TOPOGRAPHY

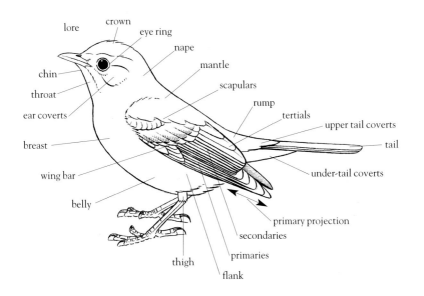

lore
crown
eye ring
nape
mantle
scapulars
rump
tertials
upper tail coverts
tail
chin
throat
ear coverts
breast
wing bar
belly
under-tail coverts
primary projection
secondaries
primaries
thigh
flank

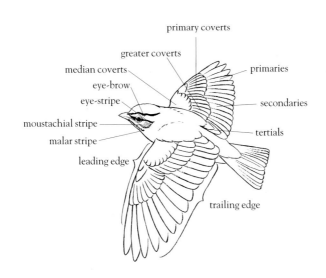

primary coverts
greater coverts
median coverts
eye-brow
eye-stripe
primaries
secondaries
moustachial stripe
malar stripe
leading edge
tertials
trailing edge

1 DUCKS AND GEESE

1 FULVOUS WHISTLING-DUCK (FULVOUS TREE DUCK)
Dendrocygna bicolor 45–53cm FIELD NOTES: Generally in small flocks. In flight shows white horseshoe shape on upper tail coverts. Juvenile duller, more greyish. VOICE: A whistling *k-weeoo*, also a harsh *kee*. HABITAT: Freshwater areas with extensive emergent vegetation, also on pastureland. DISTRIBUTION: Resident on Texas and Louisiana coast. Scattered records on W and E coasts as well as inland.

2 BLACK-BELLIED WHISTLING-DUCK (BLACK-BELLIED or RED-BILLED TREE DUCK) *Dendrocygna autumnalis* 48–53cm FIELD NOTES: In flight shows bold white wing bar on upperwing. Juvenile duller with a grey bill. VOICE: A high-pitched, chattering whistle. HABITAT: Freshwater marsh, shallow lakes and coastal lagoons. DISTRIBUTION: Resident in S Texas, summers in S Arizona.

3 BEAN GOOSE *Anser fabalis* 66–84cm FIELD NOTES: Juvenile more scaly on back. Shown are a taiga form and a tundra form (fig 3b) *A. f. rossicus*. Another tundra form, *A. f. serrirostris*, is larger. VOICE: A *wink-wink* and a deep, nasal *hank-hank*, also typical goose cackling. HABITAT: Usually open country. DISTRIBUTION: Vagrant to the Aleutians and W Alaska.

4 LESSER WHITE-FRONTED GOOSE *Anser erythropus* 53–66cm FIELD NOTES: Juvenile lacks white at the base of bill and has an unmarked belly. VOICE: In flight utters a squeaky *kyu-yu-yu*. HABITAT: Usually occurs in open areas. DISTRIBUTION: Vagrant from N Europe.

5 WHITE-FRONTED GOOSE (GREATER WHITE-FRONTED GOOSE)
Anser albifrons 64–78cm FIELD NOTES: Juvenile lacks white at base of bill and has an unmarked belly. Greenland race *A. a. flavirostris* (fig 5b) has orange bill. VOICE: Typical goose cackling. In flight, utters a musical *lyo-lyok*. HABITAT: Summers on tundra, winters on grassland, usually near coasts. DISTRIBUTION: Breeds in W Canada, W Greenland and Alaska. Winters primarily on W and Gulf coasts.

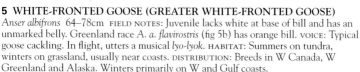

6 PINK-FOOTED GOOSE *Anser brachyrhynchus* 60–75cm FIELD NOTES: In flight shows light grey forewing, not as pale as Greylag Goose. Juvenile duller with scaly back. VOICE: A *wink-wink* and a high-pitched *ahng-ahng-ahng*, also a constant cackling from flocks in flight. HABITAT: Breeds on rocky areas in Arctic tundra. Winters in estuaries and on pastures. DISTRIBUTION: Summers in E Greenland. Vagrant elsewhere.

7 GREYLAG GOOSE *Anser anser* 75–90cm FIELD NOTES: In flight shows a distinctive pale grey forewing. VOICE: In flight, gives a deep, honking *aahng-ahng-ung*. HABITAT: Salt marsh, stubble and grassland. DISTRIBUTION: Vagrant to Greenland.

8 BARNACLE GOOSE *Branta leucopsis* 58–71cm FIELD NOTES: Unmistakeable. Juvenile duller. VOICE: Flight notes likened to the yelping of a pack of dogs. HABITAT: Breeds on high Arctic coastal areas, winters on coastal grasslands. DISTRIBUTION: Summers E Greenland. Vagrants recorded in NE North America.

9 CACKLING GOOSE *Branta hutchinsii* 55cm FIELD NOTES: Small. Recently split from Canada Goose. VOICE: High-pitched cackling. HABITAT: Breeds in coastal tundra, winters on coastal and inland grasslands. DISTRIBUTION: Summers in Arctic Canada and Alaska, winters on the Gulf coast.

10 CANADA GOOSE *Branta canadensis* 90–100cm FIELD NOTES: Common. Often gregarious. Variable, some birds very dark. VOICE: A varied, musical honk. HABITAT: Lakes, ponds and various types of grassland. DISTRIBUTION: Throughout North America. Northern breeders migrate south.

11 BRENT GOOSE (BRANT) *Branta bernicla* 55–66cm FIELD NOTES: Juveniles lack white neck marks. Variable, 'Black Brant' *B. b. nigricans* (fig 11b) and 'Pale-bellied Brent Goose' (fig 11c) *B. b. hrota* shown. VOICE: A rolling, gargling *raunk-raunk-raunk*. HABITAT: Breeds in tundra, winters on coasts and nearby marshes. DISTRIBUTION: Summers in Arctic Canada and Alaska, winters along Pacific and Atlantic coasts.

2 GEESE AND SWANS

1 SNOW GOOSE (BLUE GOOSE) *Chen (Anser) caerulescens* 65–84cm
FIELD NOTES: Gregarious, large winter flocks. Smaller 'Lesser Snow Goose' has longer, heavier bill than Ross's Goose. Juvenile white morph has crown, hind-neck, back and wings grey, the latter with feathers edged white. Juvenile dark (blue) morph all over dark slaty-brown. VOICE: In flight utters a nasal, cackling *la-luk*, said to resemble the barking of a small dog. HABITAT: Breeds on tundra, winters on marshes. DISTRIBUTION: Summers in NW Greenland and from N Alaska east to Baffin Island. Migrates across North America to winter primarily on Pacific, Atlantic and Gulf coast areas.

2 ROSS'S GOOSE *Chen (Anser) rossii* 53–66cm FIELD NOTES: Often joins with flocks of Snow Geese. Dainty bill. Juvenile white morph has pale greyish hind-crown, nape and scapulars. VOICE: In flight utters a grunt-like *kug* and a weak cackling *kek-ke-gak*. HABITAT: Breeds on tundra, winters on marshes and agricultural land. DISTRIBUTION: Summers in Arctic Canada, migrates south to winter in California, New Mexico and on the W Gulf coast.

3 EMPEROR GOOSE *Chen (Anser) canagica* 66–89cm FIELD NOTES: Juvenile overall dark grey flecked paler with a white eye ring. White tail with black tail coverts (blue morph of Snow and Ross's Goose have w hite tail coverts). VOICE: In flight gives a hoarse, high-pitched *kla-ha kla-ha* or a shrill *yang-yang*. HABITAT: Summers on coastal tundra lakes, lagoons and marshes. Winters along rocky seashores and on coastal mudflats. DISTRIBUTION: Breeds on W coast of Alaska, winters on the Aleutians with vagrants recorded on Pacific coast.

4 MUTE SWAN *Cygnus olor* 125–155cm FIELD NOTES: In flight, wings make a distinctive musical throbbing noise. Juvenile dull brownish grey, bill lacks the frontal knob and is greyish pink with black areas as adult. VOICE: Utters various hisses, grunts and snorts. HABITAT: Lakes, ponds, estuaries and sheltered coastal bays. DISTRIBUTION: NE USA.

5 TUNDRA SWAN (WHISTLING SWAN) *Cygnus columbianus* 115–140cm
FIELD NOTES: Short necked. Gregarious, often in very large flocks. Juvenile pale greyish brown, bill pink, paler at base. Bewick's Swan *C. c. bewickii* (fig 5b) is a rare vagrant from Europe. VOICE: In flight gives a yelping *wow-wow-wow*. HABITAT: Summers among marshy tundra ponds, winters on coastal marshes, flooded land and pastures. DISTRIBUTION: Breeds W and N coastal Alaska and Arctic Canada. Winters mainly along Pacific and Atlantic coastal areas.

6 TRUMPETER SWAN *Cygnus buccinator* 150–180cm FIELD NOTES: Long neck. Dark, long bill. Head and neck sometimes stained yellowish. Juvenile greyish brown, slightly darker on head, bill pink with black base. VOICE: A deep, bugling *ko-hoh*. HABITAT: Summers on marshes, lakes and ponds, winters on tidal estuaries. DISTRIBUTION: Breeds in Alaska and in isolated pockets in SW Canada and NW America. Alaskan birds migratory, wintering in the west from S Alaska to Washington, with scattered records over much of the USA.

7 WHOOPER SWAN *Cygnus cygnus* 140–165cm FIELD NOTES: Long neck. Elongated, yellow bill patch. Juvenile greyish brown, slightly darker than juvenile Tundra Swan, bill pink, paler at base. VOICE: Various honking and bugling calls. In flight utters a deep *hoop-hoop-hoop*. HABITAT: Summers by pools, lakes and rivers. Winters on flooded pastures, farmland and occasionally on coastal inlets and bays. DISTRIBUTION: Vagrant, recorded from Greenland and scattered locations in North America. May have bred in Alaska.

dark morph

dark morph

3

white morph

2

white morph

1

♀

4

5b

♂

5

6

7

3 DUCKS

1 EURASIAN WIGEON (WIGEON) *Anas penelope* 45–50cm FIELD NOTES:
Female usually more russet on head than American Wigeon. In flight, male shows
large white patch on upperwing and grey underwing. VOICE: Male gives a clear,
whistling *wheeooo*, the female a growling *krrr*. HABITAT: Coastal marshes with nearby
wet grassland. DISTRIBUTION: Regular winter visitor mainly to E and W coasts.

2 AMERICAN WIGEON (BALDPATE) *Anas americana* 45–50cm FIELD NOTES:
Gregarious, in winter often in very large flocks. Grazes more than most other ducks.
Male upperwing pattern similar to Wigeon, underwing has a white central area.
VOICE: Male gives a distinct throaty whistle *wiw-weew*. Female has a growling
rred. HABITAT: Breeds by small lakes and marshes, winters on freshwater and coastal
marshes. DISTRIBUTION: Summers over much of Alaska, Canada and N USA, migrates
south to winter over all S US states as well as coasts of the Pacific and Atlantic.

3 FALCATED DUCK (FALCATED TEAL) *Anas falcata* 48–54cm
FIELD NOTES: May occur among Pintail and/or Wigeon flocks. Feeds mainly by dabbling
or up-ending. Generally shy and wary. VOICE: Male has a short, low whistle followed by
a wavering *uit-trr*. Female has a gruff quack. HABITAT: Water meadows, lakes, rivers and
sometimes coastal estuaries. DISTRIBUTION: Vagrant, recorded from the Aleutians and
the Pacific coast; many records may refer to escapes.

4 GADWALL *Anas strepera* 46–55cm FIELD NOTES: In flight, both male and female
show white patch on secondaries of upperwing. Usually found in small groups, and can
be quite wary. VOICE: Usually fairly silent. Male gives a sharp *ahrk*, also a low whistle.
Female has a mechanical Mallard-like *quack*. HABITAT: Lowland freshwater lakes and
marshes, with extensive fringe vegetation. Winters in similar types and less frequently
on estuaries. DISTRIBUTION: Breeds over much of C and W North America, winters
over much of S North America, on W coast from Alaska southward and on E coast
north to Nova Scotia.

5 AMERICAN BLACK DUCK (BLACK DUCK) *Anas rubripes* 53–61cm
FIELD NOTES: Gregarious, forms large winter flocks. In flight shows striking white
underwing. Feeds by dabbling and up-ending. VOICE: Very similar to Mallard. HABITAT:
Rivers, marshes, ponds and coastal bays. DISTRIBUTION: Occurs over much of E North
America, northern breeders migrate to E USA. Introduced to scattered localities in
W North America.

6 MALLARD *Anas platyrhynchos* 50–65cm FIELD NOTES: The well-known duck of
city lakes and ponds. Feeds by dabbling and up-ending. 'Mexican Mallard' *A. p. diazi*
(fig 6b) occurs from Arizona to Texas. VOICE: The male utters a rasping *kreep*. The
females *quack-quack-quack* is probably one of the best known of all bird calls. HABITAT:
Virtually any river, lake, pond or estuary. DISTRIBUTION: Breeds over much of boreal
and temperate Canada south through much of the USA except SE. Northern birds
migrate south in winter to occur all over the USA.

7 MOTTLED DUCK (FLORIDA DUCK) *Anas fulvigula* 53–61cm
FIELD NOTES: Yellow bill. Pale sides of head and neck contrast with brown body.
All habits and actions similar to Mallard although occurs usually in smaller groups.
VOICE: Similar to Mallard. HABITAT: Coastal and inland marshes. DISTRIBUTION: Florida
and the Gulf coast.

8 SPOT-BILLED DUCK (CHINESE SPOTBILL) *Anas poecilorhyncha zonorhyncha*
58–63cm FIELD NOTES: Yellow-tipped bill. White underwing. Shy and wary, feeds,
mostly in evenings or mornings, by dabbling, up-ending and grazing. VOICE: Almost
indistinguishable from Mallard. Generally silent. HABITAT: Well vegetated, shallow
freshwater lakes and marshes. DISTRIBUTION: Vagrant, recorded from E North
America.

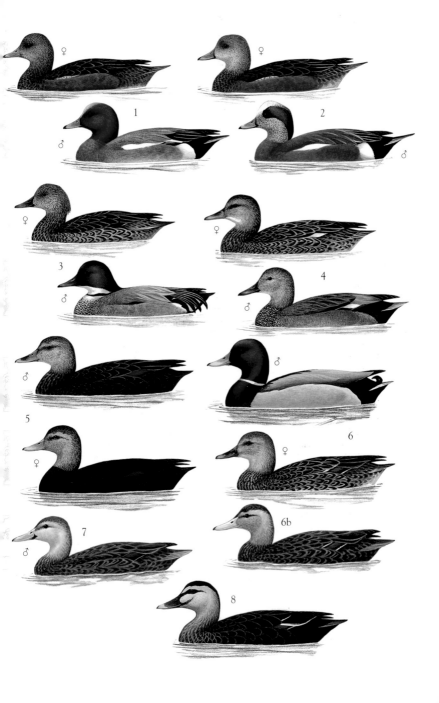

4 DUCKS

1 BLUE-WINGED TEAL *Anas discors* 37–41cm FIELD NOTES: Female has distinctive pale oval area at base of bill. In flight, both sexes show a pale blue forewing. VOICE: Male utters a thin *tsee-tsee*. Female has a high-pitched *quack*. HABITAT: Open country with shallow lakes and pools, in winter also on larger lakes and coastal lagoons. DISTRIBUTION: Summers over much of North America, winters along Atlantic coast, south from Carolina, Gulf coast and on California coast.

2 CINNAMON TEAL *Anas cyanoptera* 38–48cm FIELD NOTES: Female similar to female Blue-winged Teal but generally warmer brown. In flight, wing pattern as Blue-winged Teal. VOICE: Male utters a rattling *gredek-gredek*. Female gives a high-pitched *quack*. HABITAT: Marshes, shallow freshwater lakes and ponds with emergent vegetation. DISTRIBUTION: W North America from S Canada, migrates to winter in Texas and California. Vagrant elsewhere.

3 SHOVELER (NORTHERN SHOVELER) *Anas clypeata* 44–52cm FIELD NOTES: 'Heavy' bill. Upperwing of male shows pale blue forewing, female upperwing duller. VOICE: Male utters a hollow *sluk-uk*, female a quacking *gak-gak-gak- ga-ga*. HABITAT: Freshwater lakes and marshes with emergent vegetation. In winter also on more open water. DISTRIBUTION: Summers from Alaska and W Canada through WC USA. Winters in S USA.

4 WHITE-CHEEKED PINTAIL (BAHAMA PINTAIL or DUCK) *Anas bahamensis* 41–51cm FIELD NOTES: Female similar to male but head pattern less sharp and tail slightly shorter. VOICE: Male utters a low whistle. Female has a descending series of quacks. HABITAT: Freshwater and saltwater pools, creeks and estuaries. DISTRIBUTION: Vagrant, recorded from Florida and Gulf coast.

5 PINTAIL (NORTHERN PINTAIL) *Anas acuta* 51–56cm (breeding male 61–65cm) FIELD NOTES: Long neck and tail make for an elongated look in flight. VOICE: Male utters a mellow *proop-proop*. Female has a series of weak quacks. HABITAT: Breeds in wet pastures and marshy watersides, post breeding also occurs on lakes and coastal lagoons, mudflats and estuaries. DISTRIBUTION: Summers from Alaska, Canada and most of W and C USA. Winters over much of the S USA and on E and W coasts.

6 BAIKAL TEAL (FORMOSA TEAL) *Anas formosa* 39–43cm FIELD NOTES: Non-breeding male shows 'shadow' of distinctive breeding head pattern. VOICE: Male utters a *wot-wot-wot*, often persistently. Females give a low *quack*. HABITAT: Fresh and brackish-water areas. DISTRIBUTION: Vagrant, recorded from Alaska and W coast of North America.

7 GARGANEY *Anas querquedula* 37–41cm FIELD NOTES: In flight, upperwing of male shows pale grey forewing, at a distance can look white winged. Female upperwing mostly dull grey. VOICE: Male utters a rattling *knerek*, female a high nasal *quack*. HABITAT: Lakes and marshes and sheltered coastal waters. DISTRIBUTION: Vagrant, scattered records over much of USA and S Canada.

8 GREEN-WINGED TEAL *Anas carolinensis* 34–38cm FIELD NOTES: Often forms large winter flocks. Flight is rapid with much twisting and turning. Recently split from Eurasian Teal (*see below* for difference), the female is virtually identical. VOICE: Males utter a soft, high-pitched *preep-preep*. Females rather silent although often give a nasal *quack* when alarmed. HABITAT: Breeds on freshwater lakes and pools with fringing vegetation. In winter also on salt marshes, estuaries and sheltered coastal bays. DISTRIBUTION: Summers in Alaska, much of Canada, away from Arctic areas, and W USA. Winters over most of the USA.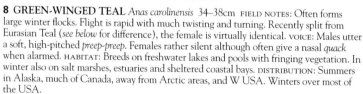

9 COMMON or EURASIAN TEAL (TEAL) *Anas crecca* 34–38cm FIELD NOTES: Yellow-lined, green face patch, no white breast stripe. Actions and habits as Green-winged Teal. VOICE: Similar to Green-winged Teal. HABITAT: As Green-winged Teal. DISTRIBUTION: Vagrant, to Greenland and E and W coasts of North America.

5 DUCKS

1 CANVASBACK *Aythya valisineria* 48–61cm FIELD NOTES: Sloping forehead. In flight, upperwing of male very pale. VOICE: Displaying male utters a squeaky hooting. Female utters a low *krrr....* HABITAT: Prairie marshes, winters on lakes, coastal lagoons, sheltered bays and estuaries. DISTRIBUTION: W North America, winters in S USA and along E and W coasts of North America.

2 POCHARD (COMMON or EUROPEAN POCHARD) *Aythya ferina* 42–49cm FIELD NOTES: Bill dark at base and tip. Upperwing of both sexes show a pale grey wing bar. VOICE: Generally silent. HABITAT: Lakes with surrounding vegetation, winters mainly on open lakes. DISTRIBUTION: Vagrant, most records from the Aleutians and Pribilofs.

3 REDHEAD *Aythya americana* 45–56cm FIELD NOTES: Steep forehead. Black-tipped bill. In flight, upperwing of both sexes show pale grey secondaries. VOICE: Displaying males utter a distinct mewing. Females have a harsh *squak.* HABITAT: Freshwater lakes and marshes, also on coastal waters in winter. DISTRIBUTION: Mainly in prairies of USA and Canada, also in C Alaska. Migrates south to winter in S USA and along E coast of North America.

4 RING-NECKED DUCK *Aythya collaris* 37–46cm FIELD NOTES: Peaked head. In flight, from above, both sexes show a grey wing bar. VOICE: Displaying male utters a low whistle. Females give a soft rolling *trrr.* HABITAT: Freshwater lakes and pools, in winter also on larger lakes and locally on brackish lagoons and coastal bays. DISTRIBUTION: Across S Canada and adjacent N states of the USA, migrates south to winter along E and W coasts and in S USA.

5 TUFTED DUCK *Aythya fuligula* 40–47cm FIELD NOTES: In flight, upperwing of both sexes has a distinct, wide white wing bar. VOICE: Generally silent. Female may utter a gruff growl. HABITAT: Freshwater lakes, ponds, rivers, sheltered coastal bays and lagoons. DISTRIBUTION: Vagrant, regular on the W and E coasts of North America, less often in Greenland.

6 LESSER SCAUP *Aythya affinis* 38–46cm FIELD NOTES: In flight, upperwing of both sexes show white secondaries. Less rounded head than Greater Scaup. VOICE: Displaying male utters a weak whistle. Female has a weak growl. HABITAT: Freshwater lakes and pools, winters on lakes, coastal lagoons, sheltered bays and estuaries. DISTRIBUTION: Alaska, W Canada and the prairie states of the USA, winters on all coasts and inland in the S and E USA.

7 GREATER SCAUP (SCAUP) *Aythya marila* 40–51cm FIELD NOTES: In flight, upperwing of both sexes show a wide, white wing bar. Rounded head. VOICE: Displaying male utters a soft cooing and whistling. Female gives a harsh *karr karr.* HABITAT: Tundra lakes, winters along shallow inshore coastal waters, estuaries and locally on inland lakes. DISTRIBUTION: Alaska and Canada, migrates over most of North America to winter on E and W coasts.

8 WOOD DUCK (CAROLINA WOOD DUCK) *Aix sponsa* 43–51cm FIELD NOTES: Eclipse male similar to female but with a shadowy version of breeding head pattern. VOICE: Male gives a squeaky whistle, female a sharp *cr-r-ek cr-r-ek.* HABITAT: Wooded pools, lakes and rivers, in winter also on brackish marshes. DISTRIBUTION: Resident in W and SE USA; summer breeders in NE USA and S Canada migrate to winter in Florida and the Gulf coast.

9 HARLEQUIN DUCK *Histrionicus histrionicus* 38–45cm FIELD NOTES: Eclipse male similar to female but with white breast stripe, scapulars and tertials. VOICE: Displaying male utters a high-pitched whistle. Female has various harsh calls. HABITAT: Torrent rivers; winters along rocky coasts. DISTRIBUTION: Alaska south through the Rockies, in NE Canada and S Greenland. In winter, western birds move to nearby W coast, north-eastern birds move to E coast, south to Maine. The Greenland birds are resident.

6 DUCKS

1 EIDER (COMMON EIDER) *Somateria mollissima* 50–71cm FIELD NOTES: In flight, male shows black primaries and secondaries. Variable; races shown are *S. m. dresseri* occurring NE North America, *S. m. v-nigra* (fig 1b) occurring in NW North America, *S. m. sedentaria* (fig 1c) occurring in the Hudson Bay area and *S. m. borealis* (fig 1d) from Arctic Atlantic to Greenland. VOICE: Male utters a crooning *ahOOoo*, female a grating *krr*. HABITAT: Coastal shores, winters on inshore waters. DISTRIBUTION: Coasts from British Columbia, Alaska, Arctic Canada and NE Canada south to Maine in the USA. Winters on Pacific coast south to Vancouver and Atlantic coast south to Carolina.

2 KING EIDER *Somateria spectabilis* 47–63cm FIELD NOTES: In flight, male upperwing is black with a white forewing patch. VOICE: Male utters a deep croon. Female has a wooden *gogogogogo....* HABITAT: Coastal and inland tundra, winters on open sea and coastal bays. DISTRIBUTION: Arctic coasts of Canada, Alaska and Greenland. Winters on Pacific coast south to British Columbia and on the E coast south to New England.

3 SPECTACLED EIDER (FISCHER'S EIDER) *Somateria fischeri* 52–57cm FIELD NOTES: In flight, male shows black primaries and secondaries. VOICE: Male gives a weak crooning. Females utter a harsh croak. HABITAT: Coastal tundra, winters at sea. DISTRIBUTION: N and W Alaska, winters in the Bering Sea.

4 STELLER'S EIDER *Polysticta stelleri* 43–47cm FIELD NOTES: Male has a white upper forewing, black primaries and secondaries, the latter with white trailing edge. VOICE: Generally silent. Females have various barking or whistling calls. HABITAT: Pools among coastal tundra, winters on inshore coastal waters. DISTRIBUTION: N and W coasts of Alaska, winters mainly from S Alaska and the Aleutians.

5 SURF SCOTER *Melanitta perspicillata* 45–66cm FIELD NOTES: Big bill, square head shape. Gregarious. VOICE: Displaying males utter a low gurgling. Females give a harsh croak. HABITAT: Lakes, pools and rivers, winters in coastal waters. DISTRIBUTION: Alaska, NW Canada and NE Canada. Winters on all North American coasts.

6 WHITE-WINGED SCOTER *Melanitta deglandi* 51–58cm FIELD NOTES: In flight, both sexes show white secondaries. Gregarious. VOICE: Displaying male utters a thin whistle. Both sexes give a harsh croak. HABITAT: Lakes and large pools, winters on inshore waters and occasionally on inland lakes. DISTRIBUTION: Alaska and W Canada. Winters on E and W coasts of North America.

7 BLACK SCOTER *Melanitta americana* 44–54cm FIELD NOTES: Regularly in very large numbers mixed with other scoters. Often seen flying low over the sea in long undulating lines. VOICE: Males gives a slurred *peeeew* and a whistled *cree*. HABITAT: Tundra lakes and pools. Winters mainly on inshore coastal waters. DISTRIBUTION: Alaska, NW and NE Canada. Winters on all North American coasts.

8 MUSCOVY DUCK *Cairina moschata* 66–84cm FIELD NOTES: In flight, both sexes show large white forewing and underwing. Domestic forms may have various white patches or are mostly white with a red face. VOICE: Usually silent. Male may give a low hiss, female a weak *quack*. HABITAT: Wooded lakes, pools, marshes and rivers. DISTRIBUTION: Vagrant, recorded from Texas. Feral populations established in parts of the USA.

7 DUCKS

1 LONG-TAILED DUCK (OLDSQUAW) *Clangula hyemalis* 36–47cm (Breeding male 48–60cm) FIELD NOTES: Unmistakeable. VOICE: Males utter a yodelling *ow-ow-owlee...calcoocaloo*. Females deliver weak quacks. HABITAT: Tundra pools. Winters at sea. DISTRIBUTION: Canadian Arctic, Alaska and coastal Greenland. Winters coastally from Aleutians to California and in the east, south to North Carolina.

2 BUFFLEHEAD *Bucephala albeola* 32–39cm FIELD NOTES: In flight, male's white head and white upperwing distinctive, female has white secondary patch. VOICE: Usually silent. Males utter a growl, female guttural notes. HABITAT: Woodland pools. Winters on lakes, rivers and coastal waters. DISTRIBUTION: Alaska and Canada east to Hudson Bay. Winters over much of the USA, coastal Alaska and Canada.

3 GOLDENEYE (COMMON GOLDENEYE) *Bucephala clangula* 42–50cm FIELD NOTES: Male upperwing has large white patch, female has same patch but split by 2 black bars. VOICE: Displaying male utters strange whistles and dry notes. Female gives a purring *braa*. HABITAT: Forest lakes and pools. Winters on lakes and coastal waters. DISTRIBUTION: Most of North America south to the Great Lakes. Winters throughout USA, along NW Pacific coast and NE coast to Nova Scotia.

4 BARROW'S GOLDENEYE *Bucephala islandica* 42–53cm FIELD NOTES: Upperwing of both sexes shows large, white patch split by a thin, black bar. VOICE: Displaying male utters a soft *ka-KAA*. Female has low growling notes. HABITAT: Forest lakes. Winters on lakes, rivers and coastal waters. DISTRIBUTION: SW Greenland, N Labrador, Alaska and W Canada, south to Wyoming and N California. Winters along Pacific coast and coast of NE Canada south to Long Island.

5 HOODED MERGANSER *Lophodytes cucullatus* 42–50cm FIELD NOTES: Unmistakeable. VOICE: Generally silent. Displaying male utters a frog-like *crrroooooo*. HABITAT: Forest lakes and rivers, in winter also on larger lakes and coastal lagoons. DISTRIBUTION: S Alaska, W Canada south to Montana and Oregon, also S and C Canada, south to the Great Plains and locally into the Mississippi Valley. Winters SE USA and along Pacific coast to Alaska.

6 SMEW *Mergellus albellus* 38–44cm FIELD NOTES: Upperwing of both sexes shows a white wing patch. VOICE: Generally silent. HABITAT: Lakes, pools and rivers in wooded areas, winters on lakes and coastal waters. DISTRIBUTION: Vagrant, recorded from Alaska, the Aleutians and E and W coasts.

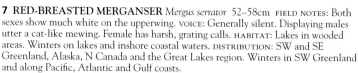

7 RED-BREASTED MERGANSER *Mergus serrator* 52–58cm FIELD NOTES: Both sexes show much white on the upperwing. VOICE: Generally silent. Displaying males utter a cat-like mewing. Female has harsh, grating calls. HABITAT: Lakes in wooded areas. Winters on lakes and inshore coastal waters. DISTRIBUTION: SW and SE Greenland, Alaska, N Canada and the Great Lakes region. Winters in SW Greenland and along Pacific, Atlantic and Gulf coasts.

8 GOOSANDER (COMMON MERGANSER) *Mergus merganser* 58–72cm FIELD NOTES: Upperwing of male shows large white patch, female's is less extensive. VOICE: Displaying males give a twanging *uig-a*. Females have various harsh notes. HABITAT: Lakes and rivers in wooded areas. Winters mostly on freshwater lakes. DISTRIBUTION: Alaska, most of Canada, south of Arctic, and W USA. Winters over much of the USA.

9 RUDDY DUCK *Oxyura jamaicensis* 35–43cm FIELD NOTES: Sociable. VOICE: Usually silent. Display sounds made by tapping bill against inflated chest. HABITAT: Marshes and ponds. In winter also on brackish and sheltered coastal waters. DISTRIBUTION: W USA and Canada, isolated populations in the east. Winters in all coastal areas and inland in S and W USA.

10 MASKED DUCK *Nomonyx dominica* 30–36cm FIELD NOTES: Upperwing of both sexes shows a large white patch. VOICE: Male utters a loud *kuri-kuroo*. Female gives low hisses and clucks. HABITAT: Well-vegetated pools and marshes. DISTRIBUTION: Vagrant, scattered records mainly in SE USA.

♀ br

♀ n-br

♂ br

1

♂ n-br

♀

♂

♀

3

♂

2.

♀

4

♀

♂

5

♂

♀

6

♀

7

♂

♂

8

♂

♀

8

♂
n-br

♀ br

♀

9

10

♂ br

♂

8 CHACHALACA AND GAMEBIRDS

1 PLAIN CHACHALACA *Ortalis vetula* 56cm FIELD NOTES: Forages in trees and on the ground. Bare skin of throat greyish when not breeding. VOICE: A raucous *kuh-kuh-ruh* or *cha-cha-lac* and a low *krrr krrr krrr....* HABITAT: Tall chaparral thickets. DISTRIBUTION: S Texas.

2 WILD TURKEY *Meleagris gallopavo* Male 100–125cm; Female 76–95cm FIELD NOTES: Unmistakeable. Western birds have pail tips to tail and rump feathers. VOICE: Well-known 'gobbling', a liquid *cluk-cluk* and a yelping *keeow keeow keeow*. HABITAT: Deciduous and mixed woods with extensive clearings. DISTRIBUTION: Over much of the USA, away from most of the Rockies.

3 DUSKY GROUSE *Dendragapus obscurus* 47–57cm FIELD NOTES: Wary. Male displays with fanned tail and exposed purplish neck sacs. Female as Sooty Grouse female. Originally combined with Sooty Grouse and called Blue Grouse. VOICE: A series of low hoots. HABITAT: Mainly conifer forests and forest edge. DISTRIBUTION: Interior of W USA and W Canada.

4 SOOTY GROUSE *Dendragapus fuliginosus* 47–57cm FIELD NOTES: Male displays with fanned tail and exposed yellow neck sacs. Originally combined with Dusky Grouse and called Blue Grouse. VOICE: A series of low hoots. HABITAT: Mainly conifer forests and forest edge. DISTRIBUTION: Pacific, from Alaska south to California.

5 SPRUCE GROUSE *Falcipennis canadensis* 38–43cm FIELD NOTES: Male displays with tail fanned. Females vary from grey to rufous. VOICE: Low hoots during display. HABITAT: Coniferous forests. DISTRIBUTION: Boreal Alaska, Canada, NW and NE USA. Franklins Grouse *F. c. franklinii* (fig 5b) occurs in NW USA, W Canada and SE Alaska.

6 WILLOW GROUSE (WILLOW PTARMIGAN) *Lagopus lagopus* 37–42cm FIELD NOTES: In flight shows white wings and black outer tail feathers. VOICE: A guttural *go-back go-back go-back ak-ak-ak* and an accelerating laugh. HABITAT: Tundra with low, dense vegetation. DISTRIBUTION: N and westernmost Canada and Alaska.

7 WHITE-TAILED PTARMIGAN *Lagopus leucurus* 32cm FIELD NOTES: In flight shows white wings. VOICE: A rapid *pik pik pik pik pikKEEA* and various clucking calls. HABITAT: Barren, rocky tundra. DISTRIBUTION: W mountain areas from Alaska and scattered locations south to N New Mexico.

8 PTARMIGAN (ROCK PTARMIGAN) *Lagopus mutus* 43–36cm FIELD NOTES: In flight shows white wings and black outer tail feathers. *L. m. evermanni* (fig 8b) is one of the darkest races and occurs on the Aleutians in grassy lowlands. VOICE: A dry *ARR-arr-kakarr* and a grating *kar-r-rk*. HABITAT: High rocky slopes and barren rocky tundra. DISTRIBUTION: Alaska, Arctic and W Canada.

1

2

♀

♂

3

4

♀

♂

5

5b

♂

♀ rufous

♀ grey

♂

6

♂ n-br

♀ br

♂ br

♀ br

♂ br

♂ n-br

7

8

♀ br

♂ br

♂ n-br

8b

♂ br

9 GAMEBIRDS

1 RUFFED GROUSE *Bonasa umbellus* 43cm FIELD NOTES: Male displays with tail fanned and expanded ruff. VOICE: Drumming sounds produced by beating open wings. Various hissing calls. HABITAT: Open areas in dense woodlands. DISTRIBUTION: Boreal Alaska and Canada, NE USA and mountain areas in NW USA.

2 GREATER SAGE GROUSE *Centrocercus urophasianus* Male 66–76cm; Female 48–58cm FIELD NOTES: Displaying male fans tail, fluffs out neck feathers, inflates neck sacs and raises thin head plumes. VOICE: 2 wing-swishing sounds followed by 2 hooting or popping sounds. HABITAT: Sagebrush plains. DISTRIBUTION: W N America, south from SE Alberta and SW Saskatchewan to N Colorado, Nevada and NE California.

3 GUNNISON SAGE GROUSE *Centrocercus minimus* Male 55–64cm; Female 45–50cm FIELD NOTES: Displaying male looks similar to Greater Sage Grouse, but head plumes are more prominent. VOICE: 9 low-pitched hooting sounds and 3 weak wing-swishes. HABITAT: Sagebrush plains. DISTRIBUTION: SW Colorado and SE Utah in W USA.

4 SHARP-TAILED GROUSE *Tympanuchus phasianellus* 38–48cm FIELD NOTES: Male displays with head down, tail cocked, wings spread and purplish neck sac inflated. VOICE: Various hoots, coos, barks and gobbling sounds. HABITAT: Grassland, sagebrush and successional stages of forests. DISTRIBUTION: Alaska, N, W and C Canada to E Quebec and south around Great Lakes area and the US prairies.

5 LESSER PRAIRIE-CHICKEN *Tympanuchus pallidicinctus* 38–41cm FIELD NOTES: During display inflates reddish neck sacs. Female pinnae short. VOICE: A bubbling hoot and a descending clucking. HABITAT: Dry grasslands, often mixed with dwarf shrubs. DISTRIBUTION: SE Colorado, SW Kansas, Oklahoma, E New Mexico and NW Texas.

6 GREATER PRAIRIE-CHICKEN *Tympanuchus cupido* 41–47cm FIELD NOTES: During display inflates yellow-orange neck sacs. Female pinnae short. Coastal Texas race smaller and warmer coloured. VOICE: Similar to Lesser Prairie-chicken, but generally lower-pitched. HABITAT: Prairie mixed with cropland. DISTRIBUTION: Remnant prairie areas of NC USA.

7 PHEASANT (RING-NECKED PHEASANT) *Phasianus colchicus* Male 66–89cm; Female 53–63cm FIELD NOTES: 2 main forms, Ring-necked and Green-necked, both very variable. Race *P. c. versicolor* (Green Pheasant) (fig 7b) often considered a full species. VOICE: A harsh *korkk korrk KO OK korkk-kok*, often followed by wing-whirring. HABITAT: Farmland, open woodland and woodland edge. DISTRIBUTION: Widespread across N USA and parts of S Canada (Introduced).

10 GAMEBIRDS

1 HIMALAYAN SNOWCOCK *Tetraogallus himalayensis* 58–62cm
FIELD NOTES: Usually encountered in pairs or small parties. VOICE: A high-pitched *shi-er shi-er*, a deeper *wai-wain-guar-guar*; when flushed, utters an accelerating *kuk kuk kuk....* HABITAT: Grassy patches on mountain slopes and sparsely vegetated scree. DISTRIBUTION: Ruby Mountains in NE Nevada (Introduced).

2 CHUKAR *Alectoris chukar* 32–34cm FIELD NOTES: Usually in small parties. VOICE: A *chuck chuck chuck* or *chuck chuck chuck chuckARR chuckARA*; when flushed, may utter a *wit-too-wittoo-witoo*. HABITAT: Mountain slopes and semiarid hills with scattered bushes. DISTRIBUTION: W mountain areas, south from British Columbia (Introduced).

3 PARTRIDGE (GREY PARTRIDGE) *Perdix perdix* 29–31cm FIELD NOTES: Often in small parties. VOICE: A harsh, squeaky *kiERRR R-R-R-ik*; when flushed, utters a rapid *skip skip kip kip-ip-ip-ip*. HABITAT: Farmland and open grassland. DISTRIBUTION: Across N America in the USA–Canada border states (Introduced).

4 MONTEZUMA QUAIL *Cyrtonyx montezumae* 21–23cm FIELD NOTES: Shy and wary, generally stays in cover. May dust-bathe in the open on dry tracks. VOICE: A descending, buzzing whistle; also a twittering *whi-whi whi-hu* given in alarm. HABITAT: Open woodland with dense grass. DISTRIBUTION: SE Arizona, SW and C New Mexico and SW Texas.

5 SCALED QUAIL *Callipepla squamata* 22–29cm FIELD NOTES: Generally runs for cover when disturbed. After breeding, forms small to large coveys. VOICE: A hoarse, repeated *rrehh*, a dry, nasal *chow-chowk chow-chowk...* and a *pey-cos pey-cos*. HABITAT: Dry brushy grasslands. DISTRIBUTION: CS USA.

6 GAMBEL'S QUAIL *Callipepla gambeli* 23–27cm FIELD NOTES: No scaling on belly. Often in large parties after breeding. VOICE: A loud *ka-kya ka kah-ha*, a querulous *chi-ca-go-go*; also grunts, cackles and chattering calls. HABITAT: Arid desert scrub. DISTRIBUTION: SW USA.

7 CALIFORNIA QUAIL *Callipepla californica* 24–28cm FIELD NOTES: Scaled belly. Often in large non-breeding groups. VOICE: A loud crowing *ka-kwa* and *ka ka-kwah*; also a loud *chi-ca-go*; also cackles, chuckles and grunts. HABITAT: Grassland, brushland and open woodlands. DISTRIBUTION: Pacific coastal areas from SW British Columbia to California.

8 MOUNTAIN QUAIL *Oreortyx pictus* 24–29cm FIELD NOTES: Often in small parties. VOICE: A loud, repeated *plu-ark*; also a series of *cle* notes and squealing twitter when flushed. HABITAT: Montane chaparral. DISTRIBUTION: Mountain areas of W USA.

9 NORTHERN BOBWHITE *Colinus virginianus* 21–26cm FIELD NOTES: Variable. The nominate occurs over most of E USA, *C. v. floridanus* (fig 9b) from Florida and *C. v. ridgwayi* (fig 9c) from SW Arizona. VOICE: Male gives a rising *bob-WHITE* or *bob-bob-WHITE*, female answers with a thin *a-loie-a-hee*. Various other sounds, including a raucous squealing. HABITAT: Variable, including open or semi-open country, farmland and woodland edge. DISTRIBUTION: Much of E USA; also isolated populations in NW USA

11 DIVERS (LOONS)

1 RED-THROATED DIVER (RED-THROATED LOON) *Gavia stellata*
53–69cm FIELD NOTES: Juvenile as winter adult but with greyish face and neck.
VOICE: Male utters a rolling, growling *oorroo-uh oorroo-uh*, the female a slightly longer,
higher pitched *aarroo aarroo aarroo*. Also a barking and mewing. In flight gives a goose-
like *kah kah kah kah kah*. HABITAT: By lakes and pools or marine inlets, winters on
shallow coastal waters and sometimes on inland lakes. DISTRIBUTION: Breeds in coastal
and tundra areas of Alaska, Canada and Greenland, winters on E and W coasts of USA
and inland on the Great Lakes.

2 BLACK-THROATED DIVER (BLACK-THROATED or ARCTIC LOON)
Gavia arctica 58–73cm FIELD NOTES: Usually shows white on rear of flanks. Often
winters in small groups. Juvenile very similar to winter adult but with slight scaling
on back. VOICE: A loud, mournful *clowee-cok-clowee-cok-clowee*, a snoring *knarr-knorr-
knarr-knorr* and a gull-like *aaah-owww*. HABITAT: By large, deep lakes; winters in coastal
waters. DISTRIBUTION: NW Alaska.

3 PACIFIC DIVER (PACIFIC LOON) *Gavia pacifica* 56–66cm FIELD NOTES: Very
similar to Black-throated Diver, but flanks uniformly dark. In non-breeding, often
shows a dark 'chin strap'. VOICE: A loud, mournful *ooalee-koo ooalee-koo ooalee-koo*; also
a yodelling *o-lo-lee* and various growls and croaks. HABITAT: By freshwater tundra lakes,
winters in coastal waters. DISTRIBUTION: Breeds in Alaska and the Canadian Arctic,
winters on the W coast of Canada and the USA.

4 GREAT NORTHERN DIVER (GREAT NORTHERN or COMMON LOON)
Gavia immer 69–91cm FIELD NOTES: Juvenile as winter adult but with pale scaly
fringes on back. VOICE: A wailing *a-a-whoo-kwee-wheeooo-kwee-wheeooo*, a manic-
laughing *ho-yeyeyeyeyeye*, a drawn-out howl and a low moan. HABITAT: By large lakes;
winters off coasts and less so on inland lakes. DISTRIBUTION: Breeds throughout most of
Canada, coastal areas of W and S Greenland. Winters mainly on the coasts of Canada
and the USA.

**5 YELLOW-BILLED DIVER (YELLOW-BILLED LOON, WHITE-BILLED
DIVER)** *Gavia adamsii* 76–91cm FIELD NOTES: Juvenile like winter adult but with
pale scaly fringes on back. VOICE : Very similar to Great Northern Diver but louder
and harsher. HABITAT: Breeds by tundra lakes and rivers, winters mainly at sea.
DISTRIBUTION: Breeds in the W Canadian Arctic, winters mainly on the W coast of
Canada and S coast of Alaska.

12 GREBES

1 LEAST GREBE *Tachybaptus dominicus* 23–26cm FIELD NOTES: Usually stays near thick shoreline vegetation, feeds primarily by diving for aquatic insects, amphibians or small fish. In flight, upperwing has a white patch on inner primaries and secondaries. Juvenile as non-breeding adult but face pale with dark streaks. VOICE: A nasal *teen* or *weeek*, also a buzzy, descending *vvvvvvvvvvvv*. HABITAT: Freshwater lakes, ponds and ditches, all with thick vegetation. DISTRIBUTION: Resident, but local in S Texas.

2 PIED-BILLED GREBE *Podilymbus podiceps* 30–38cm FIELD NOTES: Feeds mainly by diving for aquatic insects, amphibians, crustaceans and fish. When disturbed, often swims with body mostly or partially submerged. Juvenile similar to non-breeding adult but with dark streaks on the side of the head. VOICE: A far-carrying, hollow cackle, starting fast, then slower and ending with a mournful wail. HABITAT: In breeding season frequents shallow, well-vegetated freshwater lakes, ponds and rivers. In winter often on larger water bodies as well as sheltered coastal areas. DISTRIBUTION: Breeds throughout the USA (not Alaska) and much of S Canada, leaves central and northern areas in winter.

3 SLAVONIAN GREBE (HORNED GREBE) *Podiceps auritus* 31–38cm FIELD NOTES: Non-breeding birds have white cheeks. In flight, upperwing shows white on secondaries and on inner forewing. VOICE: An accelerating trill, also a far-carrying, rattling *joarrh*. HABITAT: Vegetated lakes and ponds in breeding areas and mainly sheltered coastal areas in winter. DISTRIBUTION: Summers over much of W Canada, C Alaska, NC and NW USA. Winters on Pacific coast, south to California, Atlantic coast and Gulf coast.

4 BLACK-NECKED GREBE (EARED GREBE) *Podiceps nigricollis* 28–34cm FIELD NOTES: Non-breeding birds have dark cheeks. In flight, upperwing shows white secondaries. Gregarious, especially in wintering areas. VOICE: A flute-like *poo-eeet* and a vibrant, trilled *tssrrrroooo-eep*. HABITAT: Shallow ponds and lakes with fringing vegetation, winters on coasts and large lakes. DISTRIBUTION: Summers in SW Canada and much of the W USA. Winters mainly on Pacific coast and Gulf coast, rarer on Atlantic coast.

5 RED-NECKED GREBE *Podiceps grisegena* 40–50cm FIELD NOTES: In flight, upperwing shows large white areas on secondaries and forewing. Juvenile duller with darkish face stripes. VOICE: Wailing, braying and squeaking noises, also a grating *cherk- cherk-cherk*. HABITAT: Lakes with surrounding vegetation, winters on more open waters including estuaries and sheltered coastal waters. DISTRIBUTION: Summers in C Alaska, W Canada and NW USA. Winters on Pacific coast south to California and on Atlantic coast south to Florida.

6 WESTERN GREBE *Aechmophorus occidentalis* 51–74cm FIELD NOTES: Dark eye surround on breeding birds, in winter note dull yellowish bill. In flight, upperwing shows white on secondaries and inner primaries. VOICE: A 2-note *kreed-kreet*. Also various creaking or high-pitched calls. HABITAT: Summers on freshwater lakes with surrounding reeds. Winters mainly on coastal waters, less so on large inland lakes. DISTRIBUTION: Summers in SW and SC Canada, W and NC USA. Winters along Pacific coast.

7 CLARK'S GREBE *Aechmophorus clarkii* 51–74cm FIELD NOTES: Paler than Western Grebe, especially on the flanks. White eye surround on breeding birds, in winter note bright yellow bill. In flight, upperwing very similar to Western Grebe, although shows more white in primaries. VOICE: A *kreeed* or *kreee-eed*. Various other high or scratchy calls given on breeding grounds. HABITAT: Similar to Western Grebe. DISTRIBUTION: W USA.

13 ALBATROSSES AND FULMAR

1 YELLOW-NOSED ALBATROSS (YELLOW-NOSED MOLLYMAWK)
Thalassarche chlororhynchos 71–81cm FIELD NOTES: Juvenile has a white head and an all black bill. Occurs around fishing boats and sometimes follows ships. VOICE: Usually silent. HABITAT: Maritime. DISTRIBUTION: Vagrant, recorded off the E coast and Gulf coast of USA.

2 SHY ALBATROSS (SHY MOLLYMAWK or WHITE-CAPPED ALBATROSS)
Thalassarche cauta 96–100cm FIELD NOTES: Juvenile pale headed with a dusky breast-band, bill greyish with a dark tip. Found around fishing boats and following ships. VOICE: Usually silent. HABITAT: Maritime. DISTRIBUTION: Vagrant, recorded off W coast of USA.

3 BLACK-BROWED ALBATROSS (BLACK-BROWED MOLLYMAWK)
Thalassarche melanophris 80–95cm FIELD NOTES: Juvenile pale headed with a greyish breast-band, underwing dark with a hint of a pale central stripe, bill grey with a dark tip. Occurs around fishing boats and follows ships. VOICE: Usually silent. HABITAT: Maritime. DISTRIBUTION: Vagrant, recorded off E coast of USA, Canada and Greenland.

4 WANDERING ALBATROSS (SNOWY or WHITE-WINGED ALBATROSS)
Diomedea exulans 107–135cm FIELD NOTES: Large. Many birds have upperwing mainly black, only very old birds attain plumage depicted. Juvenile chocolate-brown with a white face, underwing pattern similar to adult. Regularly follows ships. VOICE: Usually silent. HABITAT: Maritime. DISTRIBUTION: Vagrant, recorded off W coast of USA.

5 LAYSAN ALBATROSS *Phoebastria immutabilis* 79–81cm FIELD NOTES: The only albatross with a dark back, white head and underparts that occurs in the North Pacific. Occasionally follows ships. Juvenile as adult but with greyer bill. VOICE: Usually silent. HABITAT: Maritime. DISTRIBUTION: North Pacific.

6 BLACK-FOOTED ALBATROSS *Phoebastria nigripes* 68–74cm
FIELD NOTES: Some adults show pale greyish head and underparts. Juvenile sooty brown with a whitish area at base of bill. Often occurs around fishing boats or ships. VOICE: Usually silent, although groups may utter various moaning or squealing noises. HABITAT: Maritime. DISTRIBUTION: North Pacific.

7 LIGHT-MANTLED ALBATROSS (LIGHT-MANTLED SOOTY ALBATROSS) *Phoebetria palpebrata* 78–79cm FIELD NOTES: Juvenile very similar to adult, although may show pale feather tips on breast and mantle. Occasionally found around fishing boats or following ships. VOICE: Usually silent. HABITAT: Maritime. DISTRIBUTION: Vagrant, recorded off W coast of USA.

8 SHORT-TAILED ALBATROSS (STELLER'S ALBATROSS)
Phoebastria albatrus 79–81cm FIELD NOTES: Largest albatross in the North Pacific. Juvenile generally dark brown with pink bill. VOICE: Usually silent. HABITAT: Maritime. DISTRIBUTION: Off W coast, rare.

9 FULMAR (NORTHERN FULMAR) *Fulmarus glacialis* 45–50cm
FIELD NOTES: Flies with much stiffer wings than gulls. Intermediate forms also occur. VOICE: Guttural cackling, varying in speed. HABITAT: Breeds primarily on remote sea-cliffs, winters at sea. DISTRIBUTION: Breeds in the Canadian archipelago, south to Newfoundland and locally in Alaska and Greenland. Winters in North Pacific and North Atlantic.

1

2

3

4

5

6

7

8

9

dark form

light form

14 PETRELS

1 TRINIDADE PETREL *Pterodroma arminjoniana* 35–39cm FIELD NOTES: 'Gadfly' flight typical of the genus – beating wings to gain height followed by long glides and wide banking arcs. Much individual variation in the 3 main colour morphs. Occasionally follows ships. VOICE: Generally silent. HABITAT: Maritime. DISTRIBUTION: Rare off the E coast of USA.

2 MURPHY'S PETREL *Pterodroma ultima* 38–41cm FIELD NOTES: Typical 'gadfly' flight, *see* Herald Petrel. Not known to follow ships. VOICE: Usually silent. HABITAT: Maritime. DISTRIBUTION: Off W coast of USA.

3 GREAT-WINGED PETREL (GREY-FACED PETREL) *Pterodroma macroptera* 41cm FIELD NOTES: Often flies fast with twists and turns and high, towering arcs. Occasionally follows ships. VOICE: Silent at sea. HABITAT: Maritime. DISTRIBUTION: Vagrant, recorded off W coast of USA.

4 MOTTLED PETREL (SCALED or PEALE'S PETREL) *Pterodroma inexpectata* 33–35cm FIELD NOTES: Flight wild with high, bounding arcs. VOICE: Usually silent. HABITAT: Maritime. DISTRIBUTION: North Pacific, usually most frequent off S Alaska.

5 BLACK-CAPPED PETREL (DIABLOTIN, CAPPED PETREL)
Pterodroma hasitata 35–46cm FIELD NOTES: Some individuals show a much reduced white collar. Flight typical of the genus – *see* Herald Petrel. VOICE: Generally silent. HABITAT: Maritime. DISTRIBUTION: Atlantic coast of USA, scarce.

6 HAWAIIAN PETREL (DARK-RUMPED PETREL) *Pterodroma phaeopygia* 43cm FIELD NOTES: Occasionally soars to a great height, hanging in the wind. VOICE: Generally silent. HABITAT: Maritime. DISTRIBUTION: Vagrant, recorded off W coast.

7 BERMUDA PETREL (CAHOW) *Pterodroma cahow* 38cm FIELD NOTES: Typical 'gadfly' actions. VOICE: Generally silent. HABITAT: Maritime. DISTRIBUTION: Vagrant, recorded off E coast.

8 COOK'S PETREL (BLUE-FOOTED PETREL) *Pterodroma cookii* 25–30cm FIELD NOTES: Flight rapid and erratic, bat-like with jerky wing-beats. VOICE: Silent at sea. HABITAT: Maritime. DISTRIBUTION: Off California coast, scarce.

9 STEJNEGER'S PETREL *Pterodroma longirostris* 26cm FIELD NOTES: Flight rapid, weaving and banking with jerky, bat-like wing-beats. VOICE: Generally silent. HABITAT: Maritime. DISTRIBUTION: Vagrant, recorded off Pacific coast.

10 FEA'S PETREL (CAPE VERDE PETREL, GON-GON) *Pterodroma feae* 36–37cm FIELD NOTES: Note greyish, partial breast-band. Occasionally follows ships. VOICE: Generally silent. HABITAT: Maritime. DISTRIBUTION: Off the E coast, scarce.

11 WHITE-CHINNED PETREL *Procellaria aequinoctialis* 51–56cm FIELD NOTES: Variable white on face. Flight powerful with sustained glides. Often found around fishing boats or following ships. VOICE: A screaming *tititititititi* usually given when squabbling over food. HABITAT: Maritime. DISTRIBUTION: Vagrant from southern oceans. Recently recorded in N Atlantic off Maine.

12 PARKINSON'S PETREL (BLACK PETREL) *Procellaria parkinsoni* 46cm FIELD NOTES: Occasionally around fishing boats, does not follow ships. VOICE: Generally silent. HABITAT: Maritime. DISTRIBUTION: Vagrant, recorded off W coast.

light morph

1

dark morph

2

3

6

7

8

4

5

9

10

11

12

15 SHEARWATERS

1 CORY'S SHEARWATER *Calonectris diomedea* 46–53cm FIELD NOTES: Flight can appear lazy although is actually quite fast. Often occurs around fishing boats or ships. VOICE: Generally silent at sea. HABITAT: Maritime. DISTRIBUTION: Off E coast.

2 PINK-FOOTED SHEARWATER *Puffinus creatopus* 48cm FIELD NOTES: Flight unhurried, high rising wing-beats followed by long glides. Occurs alone or in small parties. VOICE: Usually silent at sea. HABITAT: Maritime. DISTRIBUTION: Off W coast of USA.

3 STREAKED SHEARWATER (WHITE-FACED SHEARWATER) *Calonectris leucomelas* 48cm FIELD NOTES: Pale headed. Flight very lazy, although often dynamic. Sometimes shows a pale crescent at base of tail. VOICE: Silent at sea. HABITAT: Maritime. DISTRIBUTION: Vagrant, recorded off W coast.

4 GREAT SHEARWATER (GREATER SHEARWATER) *Puffinus gravis* 43–51cm FIELD NOTES: Dark capped. Fast, strong wing-beats followed by long glides on stiff wings. Gregarious, often attracted to ships and fishing boats. VOICE: Noisy, sounds like fighting cats when feeding around trawlers, otherwise silent. HABITAT: Maritime. DISTRIBUTION: Off E coast, less common off Gulf coast.

5 FLESH-FOOTED SHEARWATER (PALE-FOOTED SHEARWATER) *Puffinus carneipes* 40–45cm FIELD NOTES: Pale bill and feet, dark underwing. Lazy wing-beats followed by long glides on stiff wings. Feeds alone or in small parties. VOICE: Generally silent at sea. HABITAT: Maritime. DISTRIBUTION: Off W coast.

6 SOOTY SHEARWATER *Puffinus griseus* 40–46cm FIELD NOTES: Quick wing-beats followed by a long glide. Gregarious, often found around fishing boats. VOICE: Usually silent at sea. HABITAT: Maritime. DISTRIBUTION: Off E and W coasts.

7 WEDGE-TAILED SHEARWATER *Puffinus pacificus* 41–46cm FIELD NOTES: Plumage variable, upperparts of light morph lack the dark cross bar of Buller's Shearwater and has dark secondaries. Wings held forward, slim rear end. VOICE: Usually silent. HABITAT: Maritime. DISTRIBUTION: Vagrant, recorded off W coast.

8 BULLER'S SHEARWATER (NEW ZEALAND or GREY-BACKED SHEARWATER) *Puffinus bulleri* 46cm FIELD NOTES: Distinctive upperpart pattern and striking white underparts. VOICE: Generally silent. HABITAT: Maritime. DISTRIBUTION: Off W coast.

9 SHORT-TAILED SHEARWATER (SLENDER-BILLED SHEARWATER) *Puffinus tenuirostris* 41–43cm FIELD NOTES: Similar habits to Sooty Shearwater, although said to be less graceful. Some birds show a paler underwing stripe. VOICE: Generally silent. HABITAT: Maritime. DISTRIBUTION: Off coasts of Alaska and W coast of USA and Canada.

dark morph

light morph

16 SHEARWATERS AND STORM-PETRELS

1 MANX SHEARWATER *Puffinus puffinus* 30–38cm FIELD NOTES: White under-tail coverts. Rapid wing-beats followed by a low swinging (side to side) glide. Often scavenges around fishing boats. Gregarious. VOICE: Generally silent while at sea. HABITAT: Maritime. DISTRIBUTION: Migrates off the E coast.

2 TOWNSEND'S SHEARWATER *Puffinus auricularis* 31–35cm FIELD NOTES: Low and fast flight with few glides. Note white flanks extending on to rump. VOICE: Usually silent. HABITAT: Maritime. DISTRIBUTION: Vagrant, recorded off W coast.

3 AUDUBON'S SHEARWATER *Puffinus lherminieri* 27–33cm FIELD NOTES: Dark under-tail coverts. Fluttering wing-beats followed by short, low glides. Often gregarious. VOICE: Generally silent while at sea. HABITAT: Maritime. DISTRIBUTION: Off E coast, less common off Gulf coast.

4 BLACK-VENTED SHEARWATER *Puffinus opisthomelas* 30–38cm
FIELD NOTES: Black under-tail coverts. Low flutter and glide flight. Often seen close to land. VOICE: Generally silent while at sea. HABITAT: Maritime. DISTRIBUTION: Off W coast, mainly California.

5 NORTH ATLANTIC LITTLE SHEARWATER *Puffinus baroli* 25–30cm
FIELD NOTES: Fast, shallow wing-beats followed by short, low glides; also fluttering flight close to the sea surface. VOICE: Generally silent while at sea. HABITAT: Maritime. DISTRIBUTION: Vagrant from Atlantic Ocean islands.

6 BULWER'S PETREL *Bulweria bulwerii* 26–28cm FIELD NOTES: Tail wedge-shaped when fanned. Usually flies low in an erratic, buoyant manner. VOICE: Generally silent at sea. HABITAT: Maritime. DISTRIBUTION: Vagrant from Atlantic Ocean islands.

7 FORK-TAILED STORM-PETREL (GREY STORM-PETREL)
Oceanodroma furcata 20–23cm FIELD NOTES: Feeds by snatching food from sea surface either when flying or swimming. Follows ships. VOICE: At breeding grounds utters a soft twittering, usually silent at sea. HABITAT: Breeds on isolated islands, otherwise maritime. DISTRIBUTION: W coast from Alaska south to California.

8 WHITE-FACED STORM-PETREL (FRIGATE PETREL)
Pelagodroma marina 20–21cm FIELD NOTES: Yellow webs between toes only noticeable at close range. Feeds in a series of swinging bounces, dangling feet at each bounce, often looks as though walking on water. VOICE: Generally silent at sea. HABITAT: Maritime. DISTRIBUTION: Off E coast of USA.

9 HORNBY'S STORM-PETREL (RINGED STORM-PETREL)
Oceanodroma hornbyi 21–23cm FIELD NOTES: Dark capped. Feeds by pattering, dipping to snatch food from sea surface. Often gregarious. VOICE: Silent. HABITAT: Maritime. DISTRIBUTION: Vagrant, recorded off W coast.

17 STORM-PETRELS

1 ASHY STORM-PETREL *Oceanodroma homochroa* 18–21cm FIELD NOTES: Fluttering flight with shallow wing-beats. Feeds by dipping and snatching food from sea surface. Often large numbers. VOICE: At breeding areas utters a variable purring with an inhaled gasp; generally silent at sea. HABITAT: Breeds on offshore islands, otherwise maritime. DISTRIBUTION: Summers and winters off California.

2 LEAST STORM-PETREL *Oceanodroma microsoma* 13–15cm FIELD NOTES: Note short, wedge-shaped tail. Flight swift and direct with deep wing-beats. VOICE: Silent. HABITAT: Maritime. DISTRIBUTION: Off California coast.

3 BLACK STORM-PETREL *Oceanodroma melania* 23cm FIELD NOTES: Large, long tailed. Flight Black Tern-like. Often in large numbers. VOICE: At breeding grounds utters a purring, silent at sea. HABITAT: Breeds on off shore islands. DISTRIBUTION: Summers off California coast.

4 TRISTRAM'S STORM-PETREL (SOOTY or STEJNEGER'S STORM-PETREL) *Oceanodroma tristrami* 24-25cm FIELD NOTES: Flight strong with steep-banked arcs. Feeds by foot pattering while snatching prey from sea surface. VOICE: Silent. HABITAT: Maritime. DISTRIBUTION: Vagrant, recorded off W coast.

5 LEACH'S PETREL *Oceanodroma leucorhoa* 19–22cm FIELD NOTES: Feeds erratically with bounding flight then hovers, with shallow wing-beats, often with foot pattering to seize food from sea surface. Darker-rumped forms generally occur off SW coast. VOICE: At breeding ground utters a slow purring interspersed with a high *whee-chaa*. Generally silent at sea. HABITAT: Breeds on remote islands, otherwise maritime. DISTRIBUTION: Breeds and summers off NE and W coasts.

6 MADEIRAN STORM-PETREL (HARCOURT'S or BAND-RUMPED STORM-PETREL) *Oceanodroma castro* 19-21cm FIELD NOTES: Flight petrel-like, even-flight with glides. Feeds by hovering to snatch prey from sea surface, usually without foot pattering. VOICE: Generally silent at sea. HABITAT: Maritime. DISTRIBUTION: Off E coast.

7 WEDGE-RUMPED STORM-PETREL (GALAPAGOS STORM-PETREL) *Oceanodroma tethys* 18-20cm FIELD NOTES: Note large white rump. Flies with deep wing-beats, fast, direct and often high above waves. VOICE: Silent. HABITAT: Maritime. DISTRIBUTION: Vagrant, recorded off California coast.

8 STORM-PETREL (EUROPEAN STORM-PETREL) *Hydrobates pelagicus* 14–17cm FIELD NOTES: Feeds excitedly, repeatedly hovering or fluttering before dipping to seize food. Follows ships and fishing boats. VOICE: Generally silent at sea. HABITAT: Maritime. DISTRIBUTION: Vagrant, recorded off E coast.

9 WILSON'S STORM-PETREL *Oceanites oceanicus* 15–19cm FIELD NOTES: Yellow webs between toes only noticeable at close range. Often dangles feet and dances on sea surface when feeding. Attracted to fishing boats. VOICE: Sometimes utters a rapid chattering. HABITAT: Maritime. DISTRIBUTION: Off E coast.

10 BLACK-BELLIED STORM-PETREL *Fregetta tropica* 20cm FIELD NOTES: Feeds by hugging waves, legs dangling, bouncing from trough to trough. VOICE: Silent. HABITAT: Maritime. DISTRIBUTION: Vagrant, recorded off W coast.

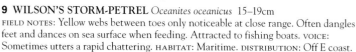

18 FRIGATEBIRDS, TROPICBIRDS, BOOBIES AND GANNET

All young frigatebirds undergo a complicated series of plumage changes before gaining adult plumage; see *Seabirds: an identification guide* (P. Harrison) for details.

1 GREAT FRIGATEBIRD *Fregata minor* 86–100cm FIELD NOTES: Pale brown upperwing bar on male. Scavenges around boats and aggressively pursues other seabirds to force regurgitation. VOICE: Generally silent. HABITAT: Maritime. DISTRIBUTION: Vagrant, recorded off W coast.

2 MAGNIFICENT FRIGATEBIRD *Fregata magnificens* 89–114cm FIELD NOTES: Scavenging actions similar to Great Frigatebird. Inflates pouch on breeding grounds. VOICE: On breeding grounds, rattling and drumming sounds made by snapping and vibrating bill. Generally silent at sea. HABITAT: Breeds on bushes on tropical islands, otherwise maritime. DISTRIBUTION: Florida and Gulf coast, scarce off E and W coasts.

3 LESSER FRIGATEBIRD *Fregata ariel* 71–81cm FIELD NOTES: Actions and habits as Great Frigatebird. Note white axillary area. VOICE: Generally silent. HABITAT: Maritime. DISTRIBUTION: Vagrant, recorded off NE coast of USA.

4 RED-TAILED TROPICBIRD *Phaethon rubricauda* 78–81cm FIELD NOTES: Flight pigeon-like, fluttering wing-beats followed by long glides. Catches fish by hovering then plunge-diving with half-closed wings. Juvenile has yellowish bill, no elongated tail streamers. Back and wing coverts barred black. VOICE: Generally silent. HABITAT: Maritime. DISTRIBUTION: Vagrant, recorded off California coast.

5 WHITE-TAILED TROPICBIRD *Phaethon lepturus* 70–82cm FIELD NOTES: Feeding and flight actions similar to Red-tailed Tropicbird. Juvenile has yellowish bill, black nape collar, dark primaries and no elongated tail streamers. Back and wing coverts with coarse black barring. VOICE: Generally silent. HABITAT: Maritime. DISTRIBUTION: Off Gulf and E coasts.

6 RED-BILLED TROPICBIRD *Phaethon aethereus* 90–105cm FIELD NOTES: Flight and feeding actions similar to Red-tailed Tropicbird. Juvenile has yellowish bill, dark primaries and primary coverts, lacks elongated tail streamers. Back and wing coverts with black barring. VOICE: Generally silent. HABITAT: Maritime. DISTRIBUTION: Off E and California coasts.

7 RED-FOOTED BOOBY *Sula sula* 66–77cm FIELD NOTES: Feeds by plunge-diving, usually at an angle. Juvenile has white parts tinged greyish brown. VOICE: Usually silent at sea. HABITAT: Mainly maritime. DISTRIBUTION: Scarce off E, Gulf and California coasts.

8 BROWN BOOBY *Sula leucogaster* 64–74cm FIELD NOTES: Pacific race *S. l. brewsteri* has greyish head. Feeding actions as Red-footed Booby. Juvenile has grey bill and greyish-white underparts. VOICE: Generally silent at sea. HABITAT: Mainly maritime. May be found roosting in coastal trees or on buoys. DISTRIBUTION: Off E, W and Gulf coasts.

9 BLUE-FOOTED BOOBY *Sula nebouxii* 79–84cm FIELD NOTES: Feeding actions similar to Red-footed Booby, often in small flocks. Juvenile head dark brown. VOICE: Generally silent. HABITAT: Mainly maritime. DISTRIBUTION: Off California coast, scarce.

10 MASKED BOOBY (WHITE or BLUE-FACED BOOBY) *Sula dactylatra* 81–92cm FIELD NOTES: Plunge-dive usually more vertical than other boobies. Juvenile very similar to adult Brown Booby but with a white collar on hindneck and white upper breast. VOICE: Generally silent. HABITAT: Maritime. DISTRIBUTION: SE coast, California and Gulf coasts.

11 GANNET (NORTHERN GANNET) *Moras bassanus* 87–100cm FIELD NOTES: Feeds by vertical plunge-dive. Immature plumage generally brown, sprinkled with white spots progressing to white with brown blotches on back and wings. VOICE: At breeding grounds utters a harsh, grating *urrah*. HABITAT: Summers on remote islands and stacks, winters at sea. DISTRIBUTION: Atlantic, from Greenland south to Florida, also off the Gulf coast.

46

1

2

3

♀

♂

♀

♂

♀

♂

4

5

6

dark
morph

white-tailed
morph

pale
morph

7

8

9

10

11

19 PELICANS, CORMORANTS AND ANHINGA

1 AMERICAN WHITE PELICAN *Pelecanus erythrorhynchos* 125–175cm
FIELD NOTES: Feeds by dipping bill into water while swimming, often in groups.
Juvenile has duller bill and brownish-grey mottled wing coverts. VOICE: On breeding
grounds utters a low grunting or croaking, otherwise silent. HABITAT: Marshes, lakes,
rivers and coastal areas. DISTRIBUTION: Summers mainly in CW Canada south through
prairies, winters primarily on California, Gulf and Florida coasts.

2 BROWN PELICAN *Pelecanus occidentalis* 105–150cm FIELD NOTES: Feeds by
plunge-diving, twists with open wings before entering the water; can look quite
dramatic. Gregarious. Pacific birds *P. o. califonicus* (fig 2b) have red pouch during
breeding season. Juvenile brownish grey above with a dingy brown neck and greyish-
white underparts. VOICE: Generally silent. HABITAT: Mainly coastal bays and lagoons.
DISTRIBUTION: S USA Atlantic and Pacific coasts, also along Gulf coast.

3 CORMORANT (GREAT CORMORANT) *Phalacrocorax carbo* 80–100cm
FIELD NOTES: Often perches holding wings 'out-to-dry'. In flight, outstretched neck
shows a distinct kink. Juvenile dark brown above, dirty white below, greyer on breast.
VOICE: At breeding sites utters various deep guttural calls, otherwise generally silent.
HABITAT: Coastal cliffs, estuaries and less so on inland waters. DISTRIBUTION: Summers
on E coast of Canada and W coast of Greenland, winters on E coast, south to Florida.

4 BRANDT'S CORMORANT *Phalacrocorax penicillatus* 84–89cm
FIELD NOTES: Gregarious. In flight, outstretched neck shows slight kink. Juvenile dull
brown with a buffish wash on breast and pale feathering at base of lower mandible.
VOICE: Croaks and grunts at breeding sites, otherwise generally silent. HABITAT:
Coastal, breeds on offshore rocks. DISTRIBUTION: W coast, from S British Columbia to
California.

5 DOUBLE-CRESTED CORMORANT *Phalacrocorax auritus* 74–91cm
FIELD NOTES: In breeding dress, NW birds show white plumes over eye. In flight,
outstretched neck shows a distinct kink. Gregarious. Juvenile dark brownish above,
dull brown below with paler greyish-white throat, foreneck and upper breast. VOICE:
Hoarse grunts at breeding sites, otherwise usually silent. HABITAT: Lakes, rivers and
coasts. DISTRIBUTION: Common breeder over much of USA and CS Canada, winters
on coasts and on rivers of Gulf coast states.

6 PELAGIC CORMORANT *Phalacrocorax pelagicus* 63–73cm FIELD NOTES: Thin
bill and neck, the latter straight and outstretched in flight. Juvenile dark brown. VOICE:
Grunts, groans and hisses at breeding sites, otherwise silent. HABITAT: Coasts and offshore
waters, breeds on cliffs. DISTRIBUTION: W coast, from Bering Straits south to California.

7 NEOTROPIC CORMORANT (OLIVACEOUS CORMORANT)
Phalacrocorax brasilianus 63–69cm FIELD NOTES: In flight, neck held outstretched with
a distinct kink. Juvenile dark brown above, slightly lighter below. VOICE: Utters grunts
and croaks at breeding sites, otherwise usually silent. HABITAT: Inland and coastal
waters. DISTRIBUTION: Mainly coasts of Texas and Louisiana.

8 RED-FACED CORMORANT *Phalacrocorax urile* 79–89cm FIELD NOTES: In
flight holds neck outstretched with a distinct kink. Juvenile dull dark brown. VOICE:
At breeding site utters a low, groaning croak, otherwise usually silent. HABITAT: Rocky
coasts and offshore islands and surrounding seas. DISTRIBUTION: S Alaska and the
Aleutian chain.

9 ANHINGA (AMERICAN DARTER, SNAKEBIRD) *Anhinga anhinga*
81–91cm FIELD NOTES: Regularly perches, cormorant-like, with wings held open to
dry feathers. Often swims with only head and neck protruding. Juvenile similar to female
but browner with less white on wing coverts. VOICE: A rapid series of clicking notes
and guttural grunts. HABITAT: Marshes, swamps, wooded lakes and sheltered coastal
waters. DISTRIBUTION: Primarily Gulf coast states and SE coast to North Carolina.

20 BITTERNS, NIGHT-HERONS AND HERONS

1 AMERICAN BITTERN *Botaurus lentiginosus* 60–85cm FIELD NOTES: Mainly terrestrial. Very secretive. Plumage tone variable, from warm cinnamon-brown to grey-brown. Juvenile lacks black neck patches. VOICE: A deep, far carrying *oonk-a-loonk*, when flushed may utter a rapid guttural *kok-kok-kok*. HABITAT: Marshes and bogs. DISTRIBUTION: Summers across S Canada and much of the USA, winters across S US states.

2 YELLOW BITTERN (CHINESE LITTLE or LONG-NOSED BITTERN) *Ixobrychus sinensis* 30–40cm FIELD NOTES: Skulking. Generally crepuscular or nocturnal. Juvenile browner with dark streaked upperparts. VOICE: In flight utters a sharp *kakak kakak*. HABITAT: Reed-beds, swamps and overgrown ditches. DISTRIBUTION: Vagrant from Manchuria and Japan.

3 LEAST BITTERN *Ixobrychus exilis* 28–36cm FIELD NOTES: Secretive. Clambers among reeds. A scarce dark morph, where buff areas are russet, occurs in the east. Juvenile like a dull female but with darker streaks on neck and pale feather edgings on upperparts. VOICE: General call is a quacking *rick-rick-rick-rick*. In flight utters a flat *kuk*. Breeding call is a low, descending *poopoopoopoo*. HABITAT: Reed-beds and marshes. DISTRIBUTION: Widely spread, away from mountain states, over the USA.

4 GREEN HERON *Butorides virescens* 40–48cm FIELD NOTES: Secretive, often encountered on well-vegetated stream sides searching for fish prey. Juvenile browner with pale streaks on neck and white spots on wing coverts. VOICE: When alarmed gives a piercing *skeow*, also a series of croaks. HABITAT: Mainly well-vegetated marshes, lakes, rivers and coastal areas. DISTRIBUTION: SE Canada, E and W USA, absent from the Rockies.

5 NIGHT HERON (BLACK-CROWNED NIGHT-HERON) *Nycticorax nycticorax* 58–65cm FIELD NOTES: Roosts during the day in trees or marshes. Juvenile has back and wings dark brown, spotted buff-white. Head, neck and underparts pale, streaked brown. VOICE: Various croaks uttered at breeding colonies. In flight gives a frog-like *kwawk*. HABITAT: Freshwater swamps, marshes, rivers and tidal marshes all with extensive border vegetation. DISTRIBUTION: Summers throughout much of the USA and CS and SE Canada. Winters along W, E and Gulf coasts of the USA.

6 YELLOW-CROWNED NIGHT-HERON *Nycticorax violaceus* 56–70cm FIELD NOTES: Nocturnal, although often feeds during daylight hours. Roosts in trees. Juvenile generally brown, with pale spotted wings and pale streaks on neck and underparts. VOICE: A squawking *kowk* or *kaow*, higher pitched than Night Heron. HABITAT: Marshes and thickets. DISTRIBUTION: Primarily Atlantic and Gulf coasts and inland in the Mississippi basin.

7 GREAT BLUE HERON *Ardea herodias* 110–125cm FIELD NOTES: Flies with large arched wings and retracted head. Often stands motionless, or walks stealthily in search of prey. Juvenile generally grey with dark crown and chestnut thighs. White morph (fig 7b) is regular in parts of Florida, and differs from the Great White Egret in having pale yellowish legs and a heavier bill. 'Würdemann's Heron', a morph with grey upperparts and a white head, occurs in S Florida. VOICE: In flight utters a deep, trumpeting *kraak*. HABITAT: Lakes, ponds, marshes and estuaries. DISTRIBUTION: Widespread over most of the USA and S Canada.

8 GREY HERON (HERON) *Ardea cinerea* 90–98cm FIELD NOTES: Actions and habits similar to Great Blue Heron. Note grey-white thighs. Juvenile has crown dull black. VOICE: In flight utters a harsh *frank*. HABITAT: Various wetlands including marshes, lakes, rivers and estuaries. DISTRIBUTION: Vagrant from Europe, recorded on Greenland.

21 EGRETS AND HERONS

1 CATTLE EGRET *Bubulcus ibis* 48–53cm FIELD NOTES: Sociable. Often feeds on insects disturbed by grazing animals or farm machinery. VOICE: Short croaks at breeding sites, otherwise generally silent. HABITAT: Grassland, arable fields and marshes. DISTRIBUTION: Much of S, E and W USA.

2 GREAT WHITE EGRET (GREAT EGRET) *Ardea alba* 85–102cm FIELD NOTES: Walks stealthily, with neck erect, when foraging. Juvenile and non-breeding adults lack long back plumes. White morph of Great Blue Heron has pale legs and a heavy bill. VOICE: A guttural *kroow*, also a grating *karrrr*. HABITAT: Marshes, ponds and estuaries. DISTRIBUTION: Much of USA away from the grassland and mountain interior.

3 CHINESE EGRET (SWINHOE'S EGRET) *Egretta eulophotes* 65–68cm FIELD NOTES: Often feeds by dashing to and fro with wings flapping and held half open. Non-breeding birds have legs and facial skin yellowish-green and no plumes on head and back. VOICE: Generally silent. HABITAT: Coastal bays and tidal mudflats. DISTRIBUTION: Vagrant from E China and Korea.

4 LITTLE EGRET *Egretta garzetta* 55–65cm FIELD NOTES: Often feeds by dashing to and fro, sometimes with wings held open. Breeding adults have, for a short while, yellowish lores. Juveniles and non-breeding adults lack head and back plumes. Juvenile has bill and feet greenish yellow. VOICE: Gives a hoarse *aaah* when disturbed. HABITAT: Coastal ponds and lagoons, also inland in marshes, river and lake edges. DISTRIBUTION: Vagrant, increasingly recorded in E coastal areas.

5 SNOWY EGRET *Egretta thula* 55–65cm FIELD NOTES: Foraging actions much as Little Egret. Adults show more yellow on rear of tarsus compared to Little and Chinese Egret. Juveniles and non-breeding adults lack head and back plumes. Juveniles have greenish legs with darker front to legs. VOICE: A rasping *graarr* or a nasal *hraaa*. In flight may utter a hoarse *charf*. HABITAT: Freshwater swamps, rivers and saltwater lagoons. DISTRIBUTION: Summers W, E and S USA. Resident along E and Gulf coasts, otherwise migrates south in winter.

6 WESTERN REEF EGRET (WESTERN REEF HERON) *Egretta gularis* 55–67cm FIELD NOTES: Habits much as Little Egret. Intermediates, with varying amounts of darkish feathers, also occur. Loses head, back and breast plumes in non-breeding plumage. VOICE: Utters a guttural croak when feeding or alarmed, otherwise generally silent. HABITAT: Rocky and sandy coasts, tidal mudflats and coastal lagoons. DISTRIBUTION: Vagrant to NE North America.

7 TRICOLOURED HERON (LOUISIANA HERON) *Egretta tricolor* 63–68cm FIELD NOTES: Forages in an active, dashing fashion. In flight shows white underwing coverts and abdomen. Juvenile has rufous neck with a white foreneck stripe, back and wings also tinged rufous. VOICE: A nasal croak, usually given when disturbed. HABITAT: Primarily coastal areas including marshes, mangrove swamps and estuaries. DISTRIBUTION: Mainly along Gulf coast and E coast north to New England.

8 LITTLE BLUE HERON *Egretta caerulea* 61–64cm FIELD NOTES: Stealthy forager. Juvenile white, very similar to 'white egrets' but usually has dusky tips to primaries and yellowish-green legs and feet. One year old birds have wings and back blotched with dusky feathers. VOICE: Various croaks at breeding sites. A harsh *gerr* usually given in flight. HABITAT: Lakes, marshes, coastal pools, estuaries and inlets. DISTRIBUTION: Summers over much of E USA, winters along coasts of the Gulf and Atlantic as far north as New England.

9 REDDISH EGRET *Egretta rufescens* 69–81cm FIELD NOTES: Animated foraging action, often with wings held open. Non-breeding white morph has greyish bill and dark lores. Juvenile of dark morph has neck and back tinged 'chalky', bill grey. VOICE: A short grunt or soft groan. HABITAT: Mainly sheltered, shallow coastal waters. DISTRIBUTION: Texas and Florida coasts.

1

n-br

br

2

3

4

5

6

dark morph

light morph

8

n-br

br

7

n-br

br

9

br

9

n-br

9

white morph

22 IBISES, SPOONBILLS, STORKS AND FLAMINGO

1 WHITE-FACED IBIS *Plegadis chihi* 56–63cm FIELD NOTES: Flies with neck outstretched, often in loose flocks or in undulating lines. Iris and legs red. Juvenile duller than adult with white flecks on head and neck. VOICE: Generally silent although may utter a grunting sheep-like *grru* or *graa*. HABITAT: Mainly freshwater marshes and ponds. DISTRIBUTION: Summers in California, inland to Montana. Winters on coasts of S California and Texas.

2 GLOSSY IBIS *Plegadis falcinellus* 55–65cm FIELD NOTES: Gregarious, usually in small groups. Flight actions and habits similar to White-faced Ibis. Iris dark. Juvenile duller than adult with white flecks on head and neck. VOICE: Similar to White-faced Ibis. HABITAT: Shallow marshes, mudflats and coastal lagoons. DISTRIBUTION: Atlantic and Gulf coasts, scattered records from much of E USA.

3 WHITE IBIS (AMERICAN WHITE IBIS) *Eudocimus albus* 56–71cm FIELD NOTES: Gregarious. In flight, with neck outstretched, shows black tips to outer primaries. Juvenile has brown back and wings, as bird ages these areas become increasingly blotched with white; white rump and tail, the latter with black tip, head and neck buff-white finely streaked darker, underparts white, bill orange. VOICE: In flight, or when disturbed, gives a nasal honking. Feeding groups utter a murmuring *huu-huu-huu*. HABITAT: Freshwater and saltwater areas. DISTRIBUTION: Gulf coast and Atlantic coast, north to Carolina.

4 SCARLET IBIS *Eudocimus ruber* 56–61cm FIELD NOTES: Breeding adult has a black bill. In flight, with neck outstretched, shows black tips to outer primaries. Juvenile similar to White Ibis, but rump tinged pink-buff. VOICE: Similar to White Ibis. HABITAT: Freshwater and saltwater areas. DISTRIBUTION: Vagrant, recorded from S Florida.

5 SPOONBILL (EURASIAN or WHITE SPOONBILL) *Platalea leucorodia* 80–90cm FIELD NOTES: Flies with neck outstretched. In non-breeding plumage, loses yellow tinge to crest and breast. Juvenile similar to adult but bill and legs pinkish and primaries dark tipped. VOICE: Usually silent. HABITAT: Brackish and freshwater lakes, reed swamps, coastal mudflats and estuaries. DISTRIBUTION: Vagrant, recorded from Greenland.

6 ROSEATE SPOONBILL *Ajaia ajaja* 76–81cm FIELD NOTES: Flies with neck outstretched. Juvenile has head and neck white, back and wings pale pink and primaries tipped dusky. VOICE: A low grunting *huh-huh-huh-huh* and a low, rasping *rrek-ek-ek-ek-ek*. HABITAT: Coastal wetlands. DISTRIBUTION: S Florida and Gulf coasts with scattered records along Atlantic and California coasts.

7 JABIRU *Jabiru mycteria* 122–140cm FIELD NOTES: Juvenile has head and neck dusky, upperparts grey with pale feather edges, underparts whitish. VOICE: Generally silent. HABITAT: Shallow marshes, ponds, wet pastures and coastal estuaries. DISTRIBUTION: Vagrant from Mexico, recorded from Texas and Oklahoma.

8 WOOD STORK *Mycteria americana* 85–100cm FIELD NOTES: In flight, with neck and legs outstretched, shows black primaries, secondaries and tail. Juvenile has yellowish bill, dark face and a brownish feathered neck. VOICE: At breeding sites utters hissing noises along with bill clattering, otherwise generally silent. HABITAT: Swamps and marshes with trees, also coastal lagoons and mudflats. DISTRIBUTION: Along Gulf and Atlantic coasts north to South Carolina.

9 GREATER FLAMINGO *Phoenicopterus ruber* 107–122cm FIELD NOTES: Unmistakeable. Often feeds with head submerged while walking steadily forward. In flight, with neck and legs outstretched, shows black primaries and secondaries. Juvenile mainly dirty grey-brown. Immature white with a pale pink flush. VOICE: Utters a low babbling when feeding and a honking *ka-ha* in flight. HABITAT: Coastal estuaries and lagoons. DISTRIBUTION: Vagrant to Gulf, Florida and Atlantic coasts, north to Carolina.

23 VULTURES, CONDOR AND EAGLES

1 BLACK VULTURE (AMERICAN BLACK VULTURE) *Coragyps atratus*
56–68cm FIELD NOTES: Shorter tailed than Turkey Vulture, with silvery primaries. Soars with wings virtually level. Gregarious. VOICE: Soft hisses and barks, usually silent. HABITAT: Open country, human settlement rubbish dumps and shorelines. DISTRIBUTION: SE USA and extreme S Arizona.

2 TURKEY VULTURE *Cathartes aura* 64–81cm FIELD NOTES: From below, all flight feathers silvery grey. Soars with wings in a shallow V. Juvenile has grey head. VOICE: Usually silent but may utter soft hissing, clucking or whining. HABITAT: Open country, woodlands and farmland. DISTRIBUTION: Summers throughout the USA and in the Canadian prairies. During the winter leaves most N and C states.

3 CALIFORNIA CONDOR *Gymnogyps californianus* 117–134cm
FIELD NOTES: Soars with wings held level or slightly raised. Juvenile has grey head and greyish-white underwing coverts. VOICE: Generally silent although may utter grunts and hisses. HABITAT: Arid and sparsely wooded foothills and mountains. DISTRIBUTION: Very local in C California and C Arizona. Endangered. Captive birds are used to help reintroductions into former breeding areas.

4 BALD EAGLE *Haliaeetus leucocephalus* 31–37cm FIELD NOTES: Soars with wings almost level. Juvenile all brown, underwing brown with white axillaries and coverts, tail white with dark tip. Second-year birds have belly, mantle and underwing white with odd darker feathers. In third year head becomes whitish with dark eye-stripe, breast brownish. VOICE: A cackling *kweek-kik-ik-ik-ik-ikik* and a lower *kak-kak-kak-kak*. HABITAT: Coasts, rivers and lakes, in winter may occur well away from water. DISTRIBUTION: Summers over much of Alaska, Canada south of the Arctic, Great Lakes region and parts of W and SE USA. Winters along Pacific coast and over much of the USA.

5 WHITE-TAILED EAGLE (WHITE-TAILED SEA-EAGLE) *Haliaeetus albicilla*
69–92cm FIELD NOTES: Soars with wings held level. Juvenile generally brown mixed with silvery grey feathers on breast, axillaries and underwing greater coverts. Tail whitish with dark tip. Bill grey. VOICE: A shrill *klee klee klee klee*, when alarmed utters a lower *klek klek klek*. HABITAT: Rocky coasts. DISTRIBUTION: SW Greenland. Vagrant to outer Aleutians.

6 STELLER'S SEA-EAGLE (WHITE-SHOULDERED SEA-EAGLE)
Haliaeetus pelagicus 85–94cm FIELD NOTES: Juveniles lack white shoulders, underwing shows whitish patch at base of primaries, white bands on median coverts and whitish axillaries, tail white with darker tip. VOICE: A barking *kyow-kyow-kyow* and a stronger *kra kra kra kra*. HABITAT: Rocky coasts. DISTRIBUTION: Vagrant, recorded on the Aleutians, Pribilofs and Kodiak Island.

7 GOLDEN EAGLE *Aquila chrysaetos* 76–93cm FIELD NOTES: Soars with wings slightly raised. In flight, juveniles show white patches at base of primaries and a white tail with a broad, black terminal band. VOICE: Generally silent, but sometimes gives a weak mewing or yelping. HABITAT: Mountains or hilly terrain, tundra and open country. DISTRIBUTION: Alaska, W Canada and W USA. Northern birds move south over much of the USA.

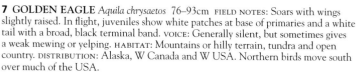

24 CARACARA, OSPREY, KITES AND HARRIER

1 CRESTED CARACARA *Caracara cheriway* 50–63cm FIELD NOTES: Soars with wings slightly bowed. Juvenile browner with dark streaking on breast and upper breast, bare parts duller. VOICE: A harsh, cackling *ca-ca-ca-ca*. HABITAT: Open country. DISTRIBUTION: Extreme S Arizona, SE Texas and C Florida.

2 OSPREY *Pandion haliaetus* 56–61cm FIELD NOTES: Head-on flight gull-like, with wings bowed. Feeds on fish, soaring over water before plunging feet first on to prey. Juvenile similar to adult but feathers of mantle and upperwing with pale edgings. VOICE: A series of mournful whistles, also a shrill, whistled *teeeeaa*. HABITAT: Lakes, rivers, coastal lagoons and estuaries. DISTRIBUTION: Occurs in summer over much of Canada, Great Lakes region, NE USA, NW USA and Florida, migrates southward to winter in Florida, Gulf coast and coastal California.

3 HOOK-BILLED KITE *Chondrohierax uncinatus* 38–43cm FIELD NOTES: Loose, buoyant flight. Clambers in trees in a parrot-like fashion searching for tree snails. Juvenile brown above, white below barred light russet, white cheeks and collar. VOICE: A rattling *kekekekekeke* and a quiet *huey*. HABITAT: Dense, brushy woods. DISTRIBUTION: Rare in extreme S Texas.

4 SNAIL KITE (EVERGLADE KITE) *Rostrhamus sociabilis* 43–48cm FIELD NOTES: Flight slow and buoyant. Juvenile much like dull adult female, mottled brown above, buff below streaked brown. Legs yellow to orange. VOICE: A cackling *ka-ka-ka-ka-ka*, a grating *krrkrrkrrkrr* and a harsh *kerwuck*. HABITAT: Marshes. DISTRIBUTION: Rare resident in S Florida.

5 AMERICAN SWALLOW-TAILED KITE (SWALLOW-TAILED KITE) *Elanoides forficatus* 51–66cm FIELD NOTES: Agile, graceful flier. Juvenile very similar to adult but buff-streaked on head and breast. VOICE: A whistled *ke-wee-wee heweewe* or *peat-peat klee-klee-klee*. HABITAT: Damp woodlands, thickets and marshland. DISTRIBUTION: Summers in coastal SE USA.

6 MISSISSIPPI KITE *Ictinia mississippiensis* 35–38cm FIELD NOTES: Captures insects in midair. Gregarious feeding in groups and often nesting in loose colonies. In flight shows white secondaries on upperwing. Juvenile has russet underwing coverts, underparts buff with russet blotches, tail grey with dark bands. VOICE: A high-pitched whistle *pe-teew*, also an excited *pee-tititi*. HABITAT: Woodland, usually close to water. DISTRIBUTION: Summers in SE USA west to the Great Plains and Arizona.

7 WHITE-TAILED KITE *Elanus leucurus* 38–43cm FIELD NOTES: Hunts by hovering then dropping to catch prey, usually small rodents. Juvenile has a buffy wash on breast, crown and nape. VOICE: A high, rising whistle followed by a dry note *sweeekrrkrr*. When angry a low, grating *karrrr*. HABITAT: Parkland, fields and grasslands with trees. DISTRIBUTION: Resident in Oregon, California, S Texas and S Florida. Scattered records over much of USA.

8 NORTHERN HARRIER (HEN HARRIER) *Circus cyaneus* 44–52cm FIELD NOTES: Soars with wings held slightly raised. Juvenile similar to adult female but underparts and underwing coverts plain rufous tinged. VOICE: A piercing *eeeya*, also a rapid *chek-ek-ek-ek-ek-ek*. HABITAT: Marshes and rough grassland. DISTRIBUTION: Summers over most of North America south of the Arctic, winters throughout most of the USA and W coast of Canada.

1 SHARP-SHINNED HAWK *Accipiter striatus* 23–35cm FIELD NOTES: Flight dashing and agile when tracking prey, soars (note square-ended tail) and glides with occasional flaps while exploring territory. Juvenile brown above, buff-white below with coarse tawny streaking. *A. s. suttoni* (fig 1b) has orange thighs, and occurs in S New Mexico. VOICE: A high-pitched *kew kew kew kew*. HABITAT: Forests, more open woodland in winter. DISTRIBUTION: Alaska, most of Canada south of the Arctic and mountainous areas in the USA. Winters throughout the USA.

2 COOPER'S HAWK *Accipiter cooperii* 35–51cm FIELD NOTES: Hunting flight agile and dashing; when soaring, note the rounded tail. Juvenile brown above, buff-white below with thin dark streaks. VOICE: A nasal *cac cac cac* also a long *keeee*, female gives a drawn out *whaaaaaa*. HABITAT: Mainly deciduous woodland with clearings, in winter uses other habitats, including urban areas. DISTRIBUTION: Throughout most of the USA and S Canada; in winter, northern birds move south.

3 GOSHAWK (NORTHERN GOSHAWK) *Accipiter gentilis* 48–62cm FIELD NOTES: White eyebrow. Agile hunting flight through trees in search of small- to medium-sized birds. Juvenile brown above, buff-white below with dense streaking. VOICE: A loud *kyee kyee kyee*, during display a gull-like *KREE-ah*. HABITAT: Mixed or deciduous forest, preferring forest edge and clearings. DISTRIBUTION: Alaska, Canada south of the Arctic, NE USA and much of W USA. In winter, some northern birds move to C USA.

4 CRANE HAWK *Geranospiza caerulescens* 43–51cm FIELD NOTES: Juvenile greyish brown above with a pale forehead, throat and short eye-brow, below greyish with pale mottling. Often feeds by clinging to tree trunks to insert double-jointed legs into hollows in search of prey. VOICE: A clear, whistled *wheeoo*. HABITAT: Variable, including wooded grassland and dry or wet forests. DISTRIBUTION: Very rare vagrant from Mexico.

5 GREY HAWK *Asturina nitida* 41–43cm FIELD NOTES: Swoops on to ground-dwelling prey from tree perch. Juvenile brown above with pale mottling, buff-white below with dark streaks on breast and dark spots on belly, tail grey, finely barred darker with wide, dark grey subterminal bar. VOICE: A series of long, plaintive whistles. HABITAT: Streamside woods with nearby open land. DISTRIBUTION: Summer in SE Arizona and S New Mexico, a rare resident in the Rio Grande Valley, Texas.

6 COMMON BLACK HAWK *Buteogallus anthracinus* 51–58cm FIELD NOTES: Single white tail-bar. Juvenile dark above, pale below with dark streaking on breast and dark barring on thighs and undertail coverts, tail pale with 4 or 5 dark bars. VOICE: A series of sharp whistles or screams, also a harsh *haaaah*. HABITAT: River and stream sides. DISTRIBUTION: Summer in S Arizona and SW New Mexico.

7 HARRIS HAWK *Parabuteo unicinctus* 46–56cm FIELD NOTES: Juvenile upperparts similar but duller than adult, pale below with coarse dark streaks and spots on breast and belly; in flight, underwing shows pale bases to primaries. VOICE: A harsh *raaaaaak* also a grating *keh keh keh keh....* HABITAT: Semiarid woodland, brushland and semi-desert. DISTRIBUTION: SE California, S Arizona, SE New Mexico and S Texas.

8 ROADSIDE HAWK *Buteo magnirostris* 33–41cm FIELD NOTES: Juvenile pale buff-white below, streaked dark on throat and breast, belly and thighs barred light rufous-brown, upper parts brownish-grey with pale streaking on neck and back. VOICE: A drawn-out *rreeeaew*. HABITAT: Open and semi-open country. DISTRIBUTION: Vagrant from Mexico, recorded in Texas.

9 ZONE-TAILED HAWK *Buteo albonotatus* 45–56cm FIELD NOTES: Tail with 2 or 3 pale grey bars. Juvenile browner, sparsely spotted below with small white spots, tail finely barred grey and black. VOICE: A screaming *meeeeeahhr*. HABITAT: Wooded gorges, riparian woodland and scrubland. DISTRIBUTION: Summer in Arizona, New Mexico and W Texas.

26 HAWKS

1 RED-SHOULDERED HAWK *Buteo lineatus* 40–61cm FIELD NOTES: Flies with wings slightly bowed. Variable, Florida race *B. l. extimus* (fig 1b) paler below and paler grey above, California race *B. l. elegans* (fig 1c) much more solid orange below. Juvenile of nominate race brown above mottled pale, buff-white below with dark streaks. Florida juvenile paler, California juvenile more orange. VOICE: A squealing, repeated *keeyuur*. Also a high *kilt* or *kilt kilt kilt*. HABITAT: Wet woodland. DISTRIBUTION: California, most of E USA and SE Canada. Northern, and the more western birds move south in winter.

2 BROAD-WINGED HAWK *Buteo platypterus* 35–41cm FIELD NOTES: Shy. Flies with wings held level or slightly angled down. Dark morph rare. Juvenile brown above, pale buff below with brown streaks. VOICE: A piercing high-pitched whistle *teeteeeee*. HABITAT: Deciduous and mixed woodland. DISTRIBUTION: Summer in E USA north into S Canada, west to Alberta. Some birds winter in S Florida.

3 SHORT-TAILED HAWK *Buteo brachyurus* 37–46cm FIELD NOTES: Soars with wing-tips upswept. Dark morph more common than light. Juveniles of light morph lack the chestnut on neck. VOICE: A long, high-pitched *keeeea* or *clee-u clee-u*, also a high *klee*. HABITAT: Mixed woodland. DISTRIBUTION: Florida.

4 SWAINSON'S HAWK *Buteo swainsoni* 48–56cm FIELD NOTES: Soars with wings slightly raised, glides with wings bowed. Light morph more common. Juvenile has dark upperparts, fringed buff, underparts pale heavily blotched dark brown. VOICE: A long, high scream, also a whistled *pi-tip pi-tip pi-tip*. HABITAT: Woodlands, plains and open grassland. DISTRIBUTION: Summers in much of W and C USA and Canada.

5 WHITE-TAILED HAWK *Buteo albicaudatus* 51–61cm FIELD NOTES: Flies with wings held in shallow V. Juvenile very dark above, throat black, breast white, belly blotched and barred blackish, tail pale grey. VOICE: A high-pitched *ke ke ke ke*, also a harsh *kareeeev*. HABITAT: Coastal grassland, semiarid bush. DISTRIBUTION: S Texas.

6 RED-TAILED HAWK *Buteo jamaicensis* 48–64cm FIELD NOTES: Often perches on roadside poles. Flies with wings level or slightly raised. Very variable, depicted are the Eastern race *B. j. borealis*, Alaskan race *B. j. harlani* (fig 6b) and the western race, light and dark morphs *B. j. calurus* (fig 6c); there is an intermediate morph, which has a russet breast. The rare pale race, *B. j. kriderii*, is found in the prairies. Juveniles have dark streaked belly and pale finely barred tail. VOICE: A rasping scream, *keeeeer*. HABITAT: Open areas with nearby woods. DISTRIBUTION: Throughout North America south of the Arctic. Northernmost birds move south for the winter.

7 FERRUGINOUS HAWK *Buteo regalis* 56–64cm FIELD NOTES: Soars with wings slightly raised. Dark morph less common than light morph. Juvenile has dark brown upperparts, pale head streaked dark, underparts white with dark markings on flanks. VOICE: A low, gull-like *kree-a*, also a whistled *k-hiiiiiiiiw*. HABITAT: Open arid grasslands. DISTRIBUTION: Widespread over much of W USA, avoids mountainous areas. Northern birds move to SW USA in winter.

8 ROUGH-LEGGED BUZZARD (ROUGH-LEGGED HAWK) *Buteo lagopus* 50–60cm FIELD NOTES: Dark morph more common in the east. Soars with wings slightly raised. Female usually has more solid, dark belly. Juvenile paler below, tail with single, wide grey subterminal bar. VOICE: A squealing *keeeeer*. HABITAT: Open areas, including fields, tundra, light woodland and marshes. DISTRIBUTION: Alaska and N Canada. Migrates to winter in SW Canada and over most of USA, much rarer in the southern states.

1   1b

1c

2   dark morph

dark morph

3   dark morph

dark morph

light morph

4   dark morph

intermediate morph

5

5

6c   dark morph

6c

6   dark morph

6b

6

6b

7

7   dark morph

dark morph

8   8

dark morph

dark morph   dark morph

27 FALCONS

1 COLLARED FOREST FALCON *Micrastur semitorquatus* 46–56cm
FIELD NOTES: Clambers around in trees, also runs on forest floor. Juvenile dark brown above with pale feather edging, buff below barred brown, nuchal collar greyish white. VOICE: A far-carrying *cowh*. HABITAT: Evergreen and deciduous forest. DISTRIBUTION: Very rare vagrant from Mexico.

2 KESTREL (COMMON or EUROPEAN KESTREL) *Falco tinnunculus* 31–37cm
FIELD NOTES: Frequently hovers or uses a prominent perch when seeking prey. VOICE: A shrill *kee-kee-kee-kee* and a trilling *vriii*. HABITAT: Almost any type of country, from sea-cliffs to towns. DISTRIBUTION: Vagrant, recorded from Greenland, Alaska and the E coast.

3 APLOMADO FALCON *Falco femoralis* 37–38cm FIELD NOTES: Agile flier when pursuing birds or insects. Juvenile has breast buff, streaked blackish, belly and vent cinnamon-buff. VOICE: A harsh *kek kek kek*, also a sharp *chip*. HABITAT: Grassland. DISTRIBUTION: S Texas (reintroduced), rare in Arizona and New Mexico.

4 AMERICAN KESTREL *Falco sparverius* 21–31cm FIELD NOTES: Hovers or uses an exposed perch to seek prey. VOICE: A shrill *killy-killy-killy* or *kee kee kee*.... HABITAT: Cosmopolitan, from open country, forest edge to towns. DISTRIBUTION: Widespread over much of North America south of the Arctic. Northern birds move south in winter.

5 RED-FOOTED FALCON (WESTERN RED-FOOTED FALCON)
Falco vespertinus 28–31cm FIELD NOTES: Agile flier when chasing flying insects. Juvenile dark brown above with paler fringes, dark moustachial stripe, brown crown, pale forehead and collar, white throat, breast to belly white, streaked dark brown, under-tail coverts buff-white. VOICE: A chattering *kekekeke...*; female gives a lower, slower *kwee-kwee-kwee*.... HABITAT: Open country with patches of trees. DISTRIBUTION: Very rare vagrant from Europe.

6 HOBBY (EURASIAN or NORTHERN HOBBY) *Falco subbuteo* 30–36cm
FIELD NOTES: Fast acrobatic flier, catches insects and small birds in flight. Juvenile has buff under-tail coverts. VOICE: A rapid *kew-kew-kew-kew*.... HABITAT: Open areas with stands of trees. DISTRIBUTION: Rare vagrant from Europe.

7 MERLIN *Falco columbarius* 25–30cm FIELD NOTES: Hunting flight fast, with glides and sudden stoops. Depicted are nominate, *F. c. richardsoni* (fig 7b) from the Great Plains and *F. c. suckleyi* (fig 7c) coastal from Alaska to N Washington. VOICE: A chattering *kikikikiki*.... HABITAT: Open areas including open woods. DISTRIBUTION: Summers from Alaska across Canada and south into the Rockies. Migrates to C and coastal USA.

8 PEREGRINE (PEREGRINE FALCON) *Falco peregrinus* 41–51cm FIELD NOTES: Prey usually killed in midair following high-speed pursuit and stoop. Juvenile brown above, whitish below with dark streaking, head pattern as adult but browner. Two other races, not depicted, *F. p. pealei* of NW North America, buffy underparts with heavy dark markings, and *F. p. tundrius* of Arctic North America and Greenland, generally paler. VOICE: A loud *ka-yak ka-yak ka-yak* or when alarmed a shrill *kek-kek-kek*. HABITAT: Sea-cliffs, mountainous regions and open areas, especially on migration. DISTRIBUTION: Arctic North America and SW and SE Greenland, W and E coasts of USA. Northern birds migrate through Canada and USA to winter on all USA coasts.

9 GYRFALCON *Falco rusticolus* 48–60cm FIELD NOTES: Tends to hunt at low level, prey often taken on the ground. Grey morph predominates. Juveniles browner and heavily streaked below. VOICE: A harsh *kak-kak-kak*. HABITAT: Tundra. DISTRIBUTION: Alaska, Arctic Canada and coastal Greenland. Some northern birds move south to the coasts of Alaska, Labrador and Hudson Bay.

10 PRAIRIE FALCON *Falco mexicanus* 43–51cm FIELD NOTES: Hunts ground squirrels and other small mammals. Juvenile streaked below with dark patch on flanks. VOICE: A shrill *kree-kree-kree*. HABITAT: Mountains areas with nearby arid open country. DISTRIBUTION: Widespread in W USA, north into SW Canada.

1

2

3

4

♀

♂

♀

♂

5

♀

6

4

3

5

♂

7b

7

♀

♂

7

♀

♂

7c

8

♂

8

9

light morph

10

grey morph

dark morph

dark morph

9

grey morph

9

light morph

10

28 RAILS AND CRAKES

1 BLACK RAIL *Laterallus jamaicensis* 14cm FIELD NOTES: Usually stays hidden in marsh plants. VOICE: A high-pitched *kic-kic-kerr*, when alarmed gives a growling *kr-kr-kr*. HABITAT: Saline and freshwater marshes. DISTRIBUTION: Atlantic coast of USA, from New England to Florida, locally on Gulf and California coasts and scattered inland localities.

2 YELLOW RAIL *Coturnicops noveboracensis* 16–19cm FIELD NOTES: Secretive. In flight shows white secondaries. VOICE: A repeated *tic-tic tictictic*, likened to tapping 2 stones together. HABITAT: Wet meadows, freshwater and saltwater marshes. DISTRIBUTION: Summers in C and E Canada and adjacent areas over the US border. Winters on California, Gulf and Atlantic coasts.

3 CORNCRAKE *Crex crex* 27–30cm FIELD NOTES: More often heard than seen. VOICE: A monotonous, dry *krek-krek krek-krek*. HABITAT: Grasslands. DISTRIBUTION: Vagrant, recorded from Greenland and E coast of North America.

4 CLAPPER RAIL *Rallus longirostris* 31–40cm FIELD NOTES: Mainly crepuscular. Generally back markings less contrasting and neat than those of King Rail. Variable, Atlantic coast race *R. l. crepitans* (fig 4b) being the greyest, and similar to juveniles of the brighter races. VOICE: A series of 'clapping' notes, accelerating then slowing. HABITAT: Salt marsh. DISTRIBUTION: Gulf, Atlantic and California coasts of the USA.

5 KING RAIL *Rallus elegans* 38–48cm FIELD NOTES: Secretive. Generally brighter and clearly marked. VOICE: A clapping *kek kek kek kek...*, usually deeper than that of Clapper Rail. HABITAT: Mainly freshwater marshes. DISTRIBUTION: Summers in scattered localities throughout E USA and SE Canada, resident on Atlantic and Gulf coasts, Florida and in the Mississippi basin.

6 VIRGINIA RAIL *Rallus limicola* 20–25cm FIELD NOTES: Secretive. Juvenile lacks orange tones. VOICE: A rapid *kickit-kickit-kickit*, also a descending pig-like grunting. HABITAT: Marshes, mainly freshwater, with dense vegetation. DISTRIBUTION: In summer, widespread across the USA and S Canada apart from SE USA where it occurs during the winter; also winters on Pacific coast of the USA.

7 WATER RAIL *Rallus aquaticus* 25–28cm FIELD NOTES: Secretive. More often heard than seen. Usually seen walking along edge of waterside plants. VOICE: Various grunts and squeals. HABITAT: Dense reed-beds, marshes and overgrown ditches. DISTRIBUTION: Very rare vagrant, recorded on Greenland.

8 SORA (SORA RAIL or CRAKE) *Porzana carolina* 20–23cm
FIELD NOTES: Secretive, but will often feed in the open. Black throat is more obscure during winter. Juvenile lacks black face and has a buff breast. VOICE: A high-pitched, descending whinny, also a sharp *kooEE*. HABITAT: Marshes. DISTRIBUTION: Summers throughout USA and S Canada, winters in S USA.

9 LITTLE CRAKE *Porzana parva* 18–20cm FIELD NOTES: Long primary projection. Often feeds in the open by walking, wading or swimming. VOICE: A far-carrying, accelerating chatter. HABITAT: Marshes and lakes with extensive aquatic vegetation. DISTRIBUTION: Vagrant, recorded on Greenland.

10 SPOTTED CRAKE *Porzana porzana* 22–24cm FIELD NOTES: Generally secretive although often feeds on patches of mud near cover. VOICE: A whiplash-like *whit*, a ticking *tik-tak* and a croaking *qwe-qwe- qwe*. HABITAT: Marshes, bogs and wet meadows. DISTRIBUTION: Rare vagrant, recorded from Greenland.

11 PAINT-BILLED CRAKE *Neocrex erythrops* 18–20cm FIELD NOTES: Secretive, apparently attracted to lighted windows. VOICE: A loud, guttural *qur-r-r-rk* or *qurrrk auuk qurrrk auk*. HABITAT: Marshes, wet pastures and overgrown grassy thickets. DISTRIBUTION: Very rare vagrant, recorded from Texas and Virginia.

12 SPOTTED RAIL *Pardirallus maculatus* 28cm FIELD NOTES: Very secretive, more often heard then seen. VOICE: A grunt followed by a rasping screech, also an accelerating *tuk-tuk-tuk-tuk*. HABITAT: Freshwater swamps with emergent vegetation. DISTRIBUTION: Very rare vagrant, recorded from Texas and Pennsylvania.

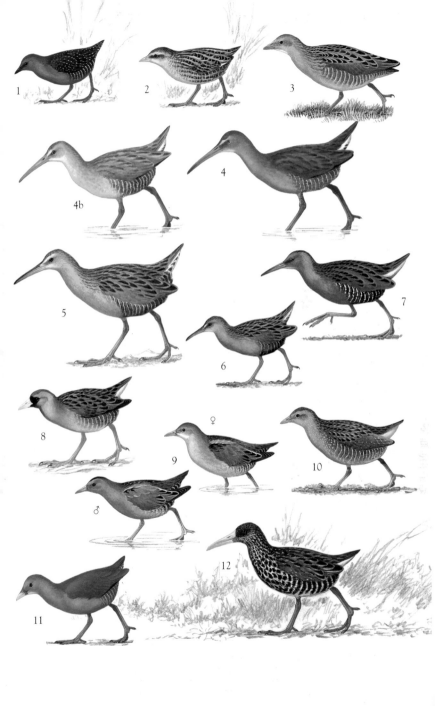

29 GALLINULES, COOTS, LIMPKIN AND CRANES

1 AMERICAN PURPLE GALLINULE (PURPLE GALLINULE) *Porphyrio martinica* 30–36cm FIELD NOTES: Often feeds in the open, although typically stays close to cover. Walks on floating vegetation and clambers among reeds and bushes. Juvenile has head, neck and flanks ochre-brown, underparts whitish. VOICE: A honking *pep-pep-pep pePApePA*, a wailing *ka-ka-ka* and a high-pitched *kyik*. HABITAT: Well vegetated lakes, pools and marshes. DISTRIBUTION: Summers in Gulf coast region, Florida and Atlantic coast of USA. Winters on Gulf coast and Florida.

2 AZURE GALLINULE *Porphyrio flavirostris* 23–26cm FIELD NOTES: Skulking, sometimes seen perching on floating vegetation. VOICE: May utter a short trill. HABITAT: Marshes. DISTRIBUTION: Very rare vagrant from South America. There is a disputed record from New York.

3 MOORHEN (COMMON MOORHEN) *Gallinula chloropus* 31–35cm FIELD NOTES: Often relatively tame, swims with a jerky action. Juvenile dark grey above, paler grey below with whitish flank strike. VOICE: A bubbling *currick* and a cackling *kik-kik-kik-kik*. HABITAT: Margins of ponds, lakes and rivers. DISTRIBUTION: Summer in E USA and SE Canada, resident in south from California to Florida (apart from W Texas) and on Atlantic coast north to Virginia.

4 COOT (EURASIAN or COMMON COOT) *Fulica atra* 36–38cm FIELD NOTES: Under-tail coverts black. Often grazes on waterside grass. VOICE: Various metallic, explosive notes, including a short *kow* and a sharp *kick*. HABITAT: Lakes, ponds and rivers; in winter may use sheltered coastal waters. DISTRIBUTION: Rare vagrant from Europe.

5 AMERICAN COOT *Fulica americana* 34–43cm FIELD NOTES: White under-tail coverts. Gregarious. Actions and habits as Coot. Juvenile dull brownish-grey above, paler grey below. VOICE: A sharp *kuk-kuk-kuk*, also a short *prik* or *priKI priKI....* HABITAT: Lakes, ponds, rivers and coastal bays and estuaries. DISTRIBUTION: Widespread in summer in North America (not SE US states, apart from Florida), north to SE Alaska across to Nova Scotia; interior birds move to the E and SE in winter.

6 LIMPKIN *Aramus guarauna* 66cm FIELD NOTES: Secretive, generally crepuscular. Best located by call. Flight floppy, with neck and legs outstretched. VOICE: A loud wailing *kwEEEeeer* or *krr-oww*, also a short *kwaouk*. HABITAT: Marshes, swamps and wet wooded areas. DISTRIBUTION: Florida and SE Georgia.

7 SANDHILL CRANE *Grus canadensis* 86–102cm FIELD NOTES: Often stained russet. Usually in flocks. Flies with neck and legs outstretched. Juvenile browner above, lacks the red crown. Race *G. c. tabida* from mid North America much larger. VOICE: A loud bugle-like rattle *gar-oo-oo*. HABITAT: Marshes, bogs, wet meadows and fields. DISTRIBUTION: Summers in much of Alaska, across Canada to the Great Lakes, the prairies and in Florida. Winters in SE California, SE New Mexico, W and SE Texas and Florida.

8 COMMON CRANE (EURASIAN CRANE) *Grus grus* 110–120cm FIELD NOTES: May associate with migrating Sandhill Cranes. In flight, with neck and legs outstretched, shows black primaries and secondaries. Juvenile generally brownish-grey, without the distinct head and neck markings. VOICE: A far-carrying *krooh* and a repeated harsh *kraah*. HABITAT: Winters in open country with or without nearby lakes or marshes. DISTRIBUTION: Vagrant, recorded from Alaska, W Canada and the Great Plains.

9 WHOOPING CRANE *Grus americana* 114–127cm FIELD NOTES: Flies with neck and legs outstretched, showing black primaries. Juvenile brownish-ochre on head, neck and back. VOICE: A loud, rolling trumpeting. HABITAT: Breeds in bogs, winters in marshes. DISTRIBUTION: Breeds in Wood Buffalo NP in WC Canada, winters in coastal Texas at the Aransas National Wildlife Refuge. Experimental populations introduced in Idaho, New Mexico and Florida.

30 JACANA, AVOCET, STILTS, OYSTERCATCHERS AND THICK-KNEE

1 NORTHER JACANA *Jacana spinosa* 19–23cm FIELD NOTES: Forages principally by walking on floating vegetation. Frequently raises wings, when bright yellow primaries and secondaries become apparent. Juvenile brown above, white below, rear neck, crown and ear coverts dark brown, white eyebrow. VOICE: A noisy cackling, usually given in flight. HABITAT: Ponds, swamps and rivers with emergent vegetation. DISTRIBUTION: Rare vagrant to S Texas and S Arizona.

2 AMERICAN AVOCET *Recurvirostra americana* 40–50cm
FIELD NOTES: Unmistakeable. Usually feeds by sweeping bill from side to side in water, also readily swims, up-ending to feed, much like a dabbling duck. Juvenile a dull version of adult. VOICE: A high-pitched *kleet* or *kluit*. HABITAT: Shallows of lakes, lagoons and tidal mudflats. DISTRIBUTION: Widespread in summer in W USA, SC Canada and mid- Atlantic coast of USA. Winters on or near the coasts of Florida, Gulf of Mexico and California.

3 BLACK-NECKED STILT *Himantopus mexicanus* 34–39cm FIELD NOTES: In flight, black wings, a white tail and rump that extends as a V on the back. In juvenile, black replaced by grey with pale fringes on back and wings. VOICE: A loud, repeated *kik-kik-kik-kik....* HABITAT: Various water bodies, including freshwater pools, salt marshes and coastal mudflats. DISTRIBUTION: California, Florida, Gulf coast, Atlantic coast north to Virginia and locally in interior of W USA. Leaves interior areas in winter.

4 BLACK-WINGED STILT *Himantopus himantopus* 35–40cm FIELD NOTES: Some birds may show a greyish crown and hind-neck, but never as dark as Black-necked Stilt. Black wings, white tail and rump that extends as a V on the back. VOICE: Similar to Black-necked Stilt. HABITAT: Similar to Black-necked Stilt. DISTRIBUTION: Rare vagrant from Europe.

5 AMERICAN BLACK OYSTERCATCHER *Haematopus bachmani* 43–45cm
FIELD NOTES: Unmistakeable. All black in flight. Juvenile dark brown with pale fringes mainly on wings and back. VOICE: A rapid *peep-peep-peep* or *pee-up*. HABITAT: Rocky coasts, occasionally on adjacent shingle and sandy beaches. DISTRIBUTION: Pacific coast from Alaska to California.

6 AMERICAN OYSTERCATCHER *Haematopus palliatus* 40–44cm
FIELD NOTES: Usually in pairs or small flocks. In flight, upperwing shows wide, white wing bar extending to inner primaries and a white lower rump. Juvenile has pale fringes to feathers on wings and back. VOICE: A shrill, piping *kleep kleep kleep....* HABITAT: Coasts with rocky, shingle or sandy shores. DISTRIBUTION: Atlantic coast south from New England, Gulf coast and in winter in Florida.

7 OYSTERCATCHER (EURASIAN OYSTERCATCHER) *Haematopus ostralegus* 40–46cm FIELD NOTES: In flight shows a wide, long white wing bar and a white rump that extends in a V on the back. VOICE: A sharp *kleep* or *kle-eap*; when alarmed gives a sharp *kip*. HABITAT: Beaches, salt marshes and inland on farmland or by lakes and rivers. DISTRIBUTION: Very rare vagrant from Europe.

8 DOUBLE-STRIPED THICK-KNEE *Burhinus bistriatus* 43–48cm
FIELD NOTES: Mainly crepuscular or nocturnal. In flight, upperwing shows white patch on inner primaries. VOICE: A strident *ca-ca-ca-ca-ca-ca...* descending in pitch, often given at night. HABITAT: Open grassland and agricultural land. DISTRIBUTION: Very rare vagrant, recorded from Texas.

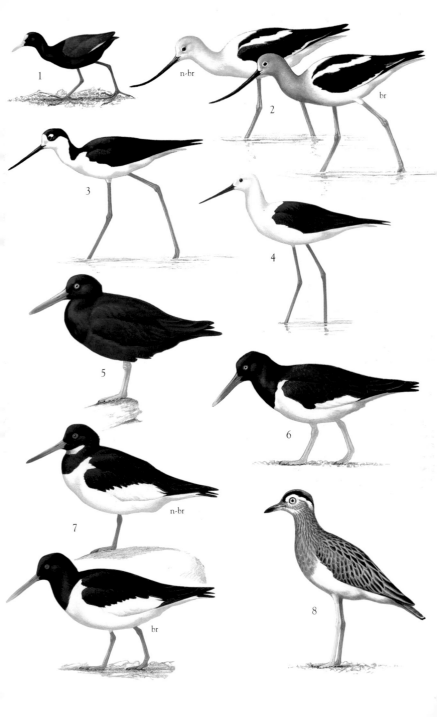

31 PLOVERS

1 LAPWING (NORTHERN LAPWING, GREEN PLOVER, PEEWIT)
Vanellus vanellus 28–31cm FIELD NOTES: In flight looks black and white, from above shows mainly white tail with a black tip and dark wings with white tips on outer primaries. VOICE: A plaintive *pee-wit*. HABITAT: Grassland, less often on coastal marshes and estuaries. DISTRIBUTION: Vagrant from Europe.

2 GREY PLOVER (BLACK-BELLIED PLOVER) *Pluvialis squatarola* 27–30cm
FIELD NOTES: In flight shows white rump and upperwing bar, underwing is white with black axillary patches, the latter stand out more in non-breeding plumage. VOICE: A mournful *tlee-oo-ee*. During display utters a melodious *kudiloo....* HABITAT: Breeds in tundra, winters primarily on coasts. DISTRIBUTION: Summer in Arctic Canada and W coast of Alaska, winters on all US coasts.

3 PACIFIC GOLDEN PLOVER (ASIAN or EASTERN GOLDEN PLOVER)
Pluvialis fulva 23–26cm FIELD NOTES: Wing-tips project beyond tail. Longer tertials and longer legged than Golden and American Golden Plover. Underwing dusky grey. VOICE: A rapid *chu-wit* and a drawn-out *klu-ee*. HABITAT: Breeds on tundra, winters on shores, coastal lagoons and sometimes on short grassland. DISTRIBUTION: Summers in extreme W Alaska, migrants occur on Pacific coast post breeding.

4 AMERICAN GOLDEN PLOVER (LESSER GOLDEN PLOVER)
Pluvialis dominica 24–28cm FIELD NOTES: Wings project beyond tail, tertials shorter than those of Pacific Golden Plover. Longer legged than Golden Plover, slightly shorter legged than Pacific Golden Plover. Underwing dusky grey. Non-breeding birds tend to be greyer than Golden or Pacific Golden Plover. VOICE: A sharp *klu-eet*, *kleep* or *klu-ee-uh*. Display call a repeated *wit wit weee wit weee...* or *koweedl koweedl....* HABITAT: Breeds in tundra, migrants occur on inland grassland and coastal mudflats. DISTRIBUTION: Summers in Alaska and Canadian tundra, migrates over much of North America, avoiding the W mountain ranges.

5 GOLDEN PLOVER (EURASIAN GOLDEN PLOVER) *Pluvialis apricaria* 26–29cm FIELD NOTES: Wing-tips slightly projecting or level with tail. Underwing coverts white. Legs shorter than American and Pacific Golden Plover. VOICE: A mellow *too-ee* or *tloo*. HABITAT: Breeds in tundra, winters on fields, salt marsh and coastal mudflats. DISTRIBUTION: Vagrant to extreme NE North America and Greenland.

6 DOTTEREL (EURASIAN or MOUNTAIN DOTTEREL) *Charadrius morinellus* 20–24cm FIELD NOTES: In flight has plain wings. VOICE: In flight gives a high *pweet-pweet-pweet* or *kwip-kwip*, also utters a trilling *skeer*. HABITAT: Breeds on rocky tundra or open mountain tops; on passage occurs on mountains, hills and farmland. DISTRIBUTION: Vagrant to NW Alaska (where it may breed) and the Pacific coast.

7 ORIENTAL PLOVER (ORIENTAL DOTTEREL, EASTERN SAND PLOVER) *Charadrius veredus* 22–25cm FIELD NOTES: Wary. Inconspicuous white bar on upperwing. VOICE: A piping *klink*. In flight utters a sharp, whistled *chip-chip-chip*. HABITAT: Margins of lakes and rivers, also arid inland areas. DISTRIBUTION: Very rare vagrant from Mongolia and S Siberia.

8 MOUNTAIN PLOVER *Charadrius montanus* 23cm FIELD NOTES: In flight has small white bar on inner primaries, black patch at tip of tail. Often in large flocks post breeding. VOICE: In flight gives a harsh *grrrt*. During display gives a clear *wee-wee-wee*. HABITAT: Breeds on dry upland grassland, winters on bare fields or in semi-desert. DISTRIBUTION: Summers in E Rockies from Montana south to N New Mexico. Winters in S California, S Arizona and S Texas.

9 KILLDEER *Charadrius vociferus* 23–26cm FIELD NOTES: In flight, upperwing shows a prominent white wing bar and a chestnut-orange rump. VOICE: A shrill *kill-dee kill-deeah* or variations such as *twill-wee-wee-wee*. HABITAT: Fields and grasslands, in winter may occur on beaches and mudflats. DISTRIBUTION: Widespread in the USA and temperate Canada, locally in Alaska. Northern and central birds move south in winter.

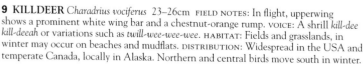

1 COLLARED PLOVER *Charadrius collaris* 14–15cm FIELD NOTES: In flight, upperwing shows a very narrow white wing bar and white sides to the tail. Juvenile lacks the black frontal crown and black breast-band, the latter replaced by a dark pectoral smudge. VOICE: A sharp *peck*, also a short *kip*. HABITAT: Coastal mudflats, beaches, coastal lagoons and river banks. DISTRIBUTION: Very rare vagrant from Mexico.

2 SNOWY PLOVER *Charadrius alexandrinus* 14–15cm FIELD NOTES: Forages by running interspersed with short stops to pick up food. In flight, upperwing shows a white wing bar and white sides to the tail. VOICE: A low *ku-wweet*, a hard *quip* and a low *krut*. HABITAT: Sandy beaches, barren saltpans and dry mudflats. DISTRIBUTION: Breeds in the USA on the Pacific and Gulf coasts and locally inland in the west. Winters on Pacific and Gulf coasts.

3 LITTLE RINGED PLOVER *Charadrius dubius* 14–17cm FIELD NOTES: Obvious yellow eye ring. Upperwing shows noticeable white wing bar. VOICE: A far-carrying *pee-oo* that descends in pitch. When alarmed gives a *pip-pip-pip*. HABITAT: Margins of lakes, rivers and reservoirs. DISTRIBUTION: Very rare vagrant, recorded from the Aleutians.

4 RINGED PLOVER (GREATER or COMMON RINGED PLOVER) *Charadrius hiaticula* 18–20cm FIELD NOTES: Upperwing shows a prominent white wing bar. In breeding plumage, usually shows longer, white rear eye-brow than the very similar Semipalmated Plover, best distinguished by voice. VOICE: A *too-lee*, rising in pitch, with an emphasis on the 1st syllable. When alarmed utters a soft *too-weep*. HABITAT: Tundra, lakesides and coastal beaches. DISTRIBUTION: Summers in NE Canada, Greenland.

5 SEMIPALMATED PLOVER *Charadrius semipalmatus* 17–19cm FIELD NOTES: Slightly more obvious yellow eye ring than Ringed Plover, but not as noticeable as on Little-ringed Plover, best distinguished from the former by voice. Upperwing shows white bar. VOICE: A clear, thin *tu-wee* or *che-wee*, increasing in pitch with the emphasis on the 2nd syllable. In alarm utters a sharp *chip* or *kwiip*. During display gives a repeated, *kerrwee-kerrwee....* HABITAT: Breeds on tundra, coasts and the margins of rivers, lakes and ponds, winters mainly on coastal mudflats. DISTRIBUTION: Summers from Alaska and W Canada (N states), around the shores of Hudson Bay and along the coast of NE Canada. Migrates across North America to winter on US coasts of California, the Gulf and Atlantic.

6 PIPING PLOVER *Charadrius melodus* 17–19cm FIELD NOTES: In flight appears very pale, upperwing shows prominent white bar and white upper tail coverts. Typical plover feeding actions, *see* Snowy Plover, but rather more deliberate. VOICE: A mellow, whistled *peep*, *peep-lo* or *peep peep peep-lo*. When alarmed utters a series of soft whistles. HABITAT: Sandy shores of coasts or lakes. DISTRIBUTION: Summers on the Great Plains, Great Lakes and on the Atlantic coast from Newfoundland south to North Carolina. Winters in the USA on the coasts of the Atlantic, south from North Carolina, and Gulf of Mexico.

7 LESSER SAND PLOVER (MONGOLIAN PLOVER) *Charadrius mongolus* 19–21cm FIELD NOTES: In non-breeding plumage similar to Little Ringed, Ringed and Semipalmated Plovers, but longer-legged. Shows a narrow white bar on upperwing. VOICE: A short *drrit*; also a sharp *chitik*. HABITAT: Mountain steppe, tundra, coastal beaches and mudflats. DISTRIBUTION: Vagrant to the Aleutians and Alaska, where it may breed.

8 WILSON'S PLOVER (THICK-BILLED PLOVER) *Charadrius wilsonia* 18–20cm FIELD NOTES: In flight shows white patch on either side of tail, upperwing has a white wing bar. VOICE: A musical, whistled *quit* or *queet*. When alarmed gives a sharp *dik* or *dik-ik*. HABITAT: Sandy beaches, edges of coastal lagoons in winter, also on mudflats. DISTRIBUTION: From Gulf to Atlantic coast north to Virginia, winters in Florida and on the Gulf coast.

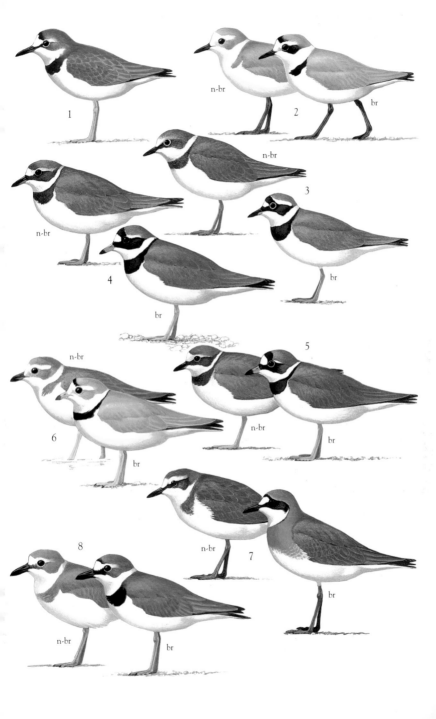

33 SHANKS AND SANDPIPERS

1 REDSHANK *Tringa totanus* 27–29cm FIELD NOTES: Noisy and timid. In flight shows white oval in centre of back and striking white secondaries and inner primaries. VOICE: A piping *teu-hu* or *teu-hu-hu* or similar. When alarmed utters a loud *tli-tli-tli-tli*. HABITAT: Wide variety of coastal and inland wetlands. DISTRIBUTION: Vagrant, recorded from Greenland.

2 SPOTTED REDSHANK (DUSKY REDSHANK) *Tringa erythropus* 29–32cm FIELD NOTES: Moulting birds much as non-breeding but blotched with black. In flight shows white oval in centre of back. Often wades up to belly. VOICE: In flight gives a distinctive *chu-it*. When alarmed utters a short *chip*. HABITAT: Lakes, marshes, coastal lagoons and estuaries. DISTRIBUTION: Rare vagrant recorded on Atlantic and Pacific coasts and the Aleutians and Pribilofs.

3 GREENSHANK (COMMON GREENSHANK) *Tringa nebularia* 30–35cm FIELD NOTES: In flight shows a white rump and back, toes project slightly beyond tail. VOICE: A ringing *chew-chew-chew* and a *kiu kiu kiu* given in alarm. HABITAT: On migration and during winter occurs on a large variety of coastal and inland wetlands. DISTRIBUTION: Migrant on Aleutians and Pribilofs, vagrant elsewhere.

4 LESSER YELLOWLEGS *Tringa flavipes* 23–25cm FIELD NOTES: Active feeder, often runs through water. Appears more delicate than larger Greater Yellowlegs. In flight shows plain wings and square white rump, toes project well beyond tail. VOICE: A flat, harsh *tew-tew* or *tew*. HABITAT: Breeds among forest bogs and grassy clearings, thereafter occurs on a wide variety of coastal and inland wetlands. DISTRIBUTION: Summers in most of Alaska and Canada, west of Hudson Bay, migrates throughout USA to winter on the coasts of California, Gulf of Mexico and the Atlantic, south of Delaware.

5 GREATER YELLOWLEGS *Tringa melanoleuca* 29–33cm FIELD NOTES: Very similar to smaller Lesser Yellowlegs. In flight shows square white rump and plain wings, toes project well beyond tail. VOICE: A clear, slightly descending *teu-teu-teu*. HABITAT: Breeds among forest bogs; during non-breeding season occurs on a wide variety of freshwater and brackish wetlands. DISTRIBUTION: Summers in a band from S Alaska through C Canada to Newfoundland, winters in the USA, in the S states and on the Pacific, Gulf and Atlantic coasts.

6 MARSH SANDPIPER *Tringa stagnatilis* 22–26cm FIELD NOTES: Very delicate wader. In flight looks like a small Greenshank, but toes project well beyond tail. VOICE: A plaintive *keeuw* or *kyu-kyu-kyu*. When flushed utters a loud *yip*. HABITAT: Post breeding frequents marshes, ponds, salt marshes and estuaries. DISTRIBUTION: Rare vagrant from Europe.

7 WOOD SANDPIPER *Tringa glareola* 19–21cm FIELD NOTES: In flight shows white rump and narrow barring on tail. VOICE: A high-pitched *chiff-iff-iff* and a *chip-chip-chip* when alarmed. HABITAT: On migration occurs on inland lakes, pools, flooded grasslands and marshes. DISTRIBUTION: Migrant, mainly in spring, on the Aleutians, Pribilofs and St Lawrence Island.

8 GREEN SANDPIPER *Tringa ochropus* 21–24cm FIELD NOTES: In flight shows white rump and broad barred tail. Actions similar to Solitary Sandpiper. VOICE: A musical *kLU-Ueet-wit-wit* and a sharp *wit-wit-wit* when alarmed. HABITAT: On migration occurs on pools, lake edges, stream sides and ditches. DISTRIBUTION: Rare spring migrant on the Aleutians.

9 SOLITARY SANDPIPER *Tringa solitaria* 18–21cm FIELD NOTES: Walks slowly and deliberately, picking food delicately off the surface of water or ground. In flight shows dark rump, outer tail feathers white with broad dark bars. VOICE: An excited *peet*, *peet-weet-weet* or *tewit-weet*. Display call similar but more bell-like. HABITAT: In breeding season on pools and marshes in woodland, post breeding occurs on ponds, stream sides and ditches. DISTRIBUTION: Summers in the boreal zone, from Alaska across Canada. Migrates across USA to winter in South America; some winter in S Texas.

34 WILLET, TATTLERS AND SANDPIPERS

1 WILLET *Tringa semipalmatus* 33–41cm FIELD NOTES: Often the first from mixed groups to fly off in alarm. In flight, wings look distinctly black and white. Breeding birds of W race *T. s. inornatus* generally less boldly marked. VOICE: In flight utters a ringing *kyaah yah* or a harsh *wee-wee-wee*. In alarm gives a loud *wik wik wik wik*. Territorial call is a rolling *pill-will-willet*. HABITAT: E birds occur on salt marsh and coastal areas, W birds occur mainly on inland ponds and lakes; post breeding most birds are usually found on coasts. DISTRIBUTION: E birds are resident on Gulf and Atlantic coasts, from Nova Scotia southward. Western birds summer in C Rockies and N Prairies into Canada, winters on Pacific coast south from British Columbia.

2 WANDERING TATTLER *Tringa incana* 26–29cm FIELD NOTES: In flight appears plain grey with a white belly. When foraging, constantly bobs and teeters. Very similar to Grey-tailed Tattler, best distinguished by voice. VOICE: In flight utters a ringing *pew-tu-tu-tu-tu-tu*, a rapid *lidididid* and a sharp *klee-ik*. Display call is a whistled *deedle-deedle-deedle-dee*. HABITAT: Breeds by mountain streams, post breeding primarily on rocky coasts. DISTRIBUTION: Summers in Alaska and adjacent Canada, winters on California coast.

3 GREY-TAILED TATTLER (POLYNESIAN or SIBERIAN TATTLER, GREY RUMPED SANDPIPER) *Tringa brevipes* 24–27cm FIELD NOTES: Breeding birds less strongly barred below than Wandering Tattler, non-breeding birds very similar, best distinguished by voice. Actions as Wandering Tattler. VOICE: In flight utters an upslurred *tu-whip*, and when alarmed a *klee, klee-klee*. HABITAT: Sandy, muddy or rocky coasts. DISTRIBUTION: Migrant on the Aleutians, Pribilofs and St Lawrence Island.

4 COMMON SANDPIPER *Actitis hypoleucos* 19–21cm FIELD NOTES: Flies low with flicking wings. Bobs tail while walking. Non-breeding birds similar to Spotted Sandpiper, differs in having a longer white wing bar on upperwing and a slightly longer tail. VOICE: In flight gives a piping *tswee-wee-wee* and a *sweet-eet* when alarmed. HABITAT: Upland streams and various freshwater and saltwater wetlands. DISTRIBUTION: Migrant mainly in spring on the Aleutians, Pribilofs and St Lawrence Island.

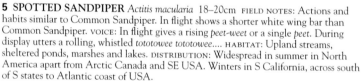

5 SPOTTED SANDPIPER *Actitis macularia* 18–20cm FIELD NOTES: Actions and habits similar to Common Sandpiper. In flight shows a shorter white wing bar than Common Sandpiper. VOICE: In flight gives a rising *peet-weet* or a single *peet*. During display utters a rolling, whistled *tototowee tototowee....* HABITAT: Upland streams, sheltered ponds, marshes and lakes. DISTRIBUTION: Widespread in summer in North America apart from Arctic Canada and SE USA. Winters in S California, across south of S states to Atlantic coast of USA.

6 BUFF-BREASTED SANDPIPER *Tryngites subruficollis* 18–20cm FIELD NOTES: In flight shows white underwing with dark grey tips to primaries and primary coverts, the latter forming dark crescent. VOICE: In flight gives a quiet *greet* or *pr-r-r-reet*. In display utters rapid clicking notes. HABITAT: Breeds on Arctic tundra, on migration short-grass areas or dry mud by lakes and rivers. DISTRIBUTION: Summers in the Canadian Arctic, west of Hudson Bay and in NE Alaska, migrates mainly through C North America.

7 UPLAND SANDPIPER *Bartramia longicauda* 28–32cm FIELD NOTES: Usually single or in small groups. Regularly perches on posts or poles. Sometimes forages plover-like with short runs and sudden stops. VOICE: In flight utters a piping *quip-ip-ip-ip*. In display gives a strange bubbling *bububuLEEillayoooooooo*. HABITAT: Grasslands. DISTRIBUTION: Summers from Alaska through the Prairies across to NE USA.

8 TEREK SANDPIPER *Xenus cinereus* 22–25cm FIELD NOTES: In flight shows a wide white trailing edge to secondaries. VOICE: In flight gives a rippling *du-du-du-du-du*. HABITAT: Lakes, marshes, saltpans and estuaries. DISTRIBUTION: Migrant on the Aleutians, St Lawrence Island and W Alaskan coast.

35 CURLEWS

1 LITTLE CURLEW (LITTLE WHIMBREL) *Numenius minutus* 29–32cm
FIELD NOTES: In flight, underwing buff with dark barring. At rest, wing-tips level with tail. VOICE: Flight call is a whistled *te-te-te* or a harsher *tchew-tchew-tchew*. When alarmed, a hard *kweek-ek.* HABITAT: Various types of short grassland. DISTRIBUTION: Very rare vagrant, recorded from California.

2 ESKIMO CURLEW *Numenius borealis* 29–34cm FIELD NOTES: Critically endangered, possibly extinct. Underwing coverts cinnamon, closely barred dark brown. At rest, wing-tips project beyond tail. VOICE: Not well documented, some calls said to be similar to Little Curlew or Upland Sandpiper. Those noted are a rippling *tr-tr-tr* and a soft, whistled *bee-bee.* HABITAT: Breeds on Arctic tundra, on migration on various types of short grassland. DISTRIBUTION: Summers in NW Northwest Territories in Canada and perhaps Alaska, migrates down E North America, returns on a more westerly route.

3 WHIMBREL *Numenius phaeopus* 40–46cm FIELD NOTES: 3 races occur: American *N. p. hudsonicus*, with a dark rump and buffy brown, barred dark brown underwing; European *N. p. phaeopus* (fig 3b), rare vagrant on Atlantic coast, has a white rump, back and underwing coverts; Siberian *N. p. variegatus*, rare vagrant to Alaska and Pacific coast, has a white upper rump and back lightly barred brown, white underwing barred dark brown. VOICE: In flight utters a liquid *quiquiquiquiqui.* HABITAT: Breeds in tundra, winters on beaches and marshes. DISTRIBUTION: Summers in Alaska, Arctic NW Canada and coastal areas of SW Hudson Bay. Winters on coasts of California, Gulf and Atlantic, south of Virginia.

4 SLENDER-BILLED CURLEW *Numenius tenuirostris* 36–41cm
FIELD NOTES: Critically endangered. In flight shows a white rump and lower back. Juvenile has streaks on flanks in place of spots. VOICE: A short *cour-lee* and a sharp *cu-wee* given when disturbed. HABITAT: Migrants occur on fresh or brackish waters with nearby grassland. DISTRIBUTION: Probably extirpated from the region, old record from Lake Erie.

5 BRISTLE-THIGHED CURLEW *Numenius tahitiensis* 40–44cm FIELD NOTES: In flight shows a buffy cinnamon rump and upper tail. Underwing coverts bright cinnamon barred black. VOICE: In flight gives a whistled *chi-u-it* or *teeoip.* During display gives a *wiiteew wiiteew...* followed by a *pidl WHIDyooooo.* HABITAT: Barren tundra in mountains. DISTRIBUTION: Summers in W Alaska.

6 LONG-BILLED CURLEW *Numenius americanus* 51–66cm FIELD NOTES: In flight, upperwing shows much cinnamon on inner primaries and secondaries. Underwing coverts distinctly cinnamon. VOICE: A loud, rising *cur-lee* or *coooLI.* Display song is a prolonged, rolling *cur-leeeeeeeu* or similar. HABITAT: Prairie, damp meadows and short grassland, winters on coasts. DISTRIBUTION: Summers in higher areas of W USA and adjacent areas in W Canada. Winters on California and Gulf coasts, less common on Atlantic coast.

7 CURLEW (EURASIAN, WESTERN or COMMON CURLEW)
Numenius arquata 50–60cm FIELD NOTES: In flight shows a white rump and lower back, underwing coverts mainly white. Females slightly larger and longer billed than males. VOICE: A far-carrying *cour-lee* and when disturbed a stammering *tutututu.* HABITAT: On migration mainly coastal, although may occur on pastures. DISTRIBUTION: Vagrant, recorded from the E coast.

8 FAR-EASTERN CURLEW (EASTERN or AUSTRALIAN CURLEW)
Numenius madagascariensis 60–66cm FIELD NOTES: Long bill, the longest of any wader. Like a warm-coloured Curlew, but lacks white on rump, back and underwing. VOICE: A flat *cour-lee;* when disturbed utters a strident *ker ker-ee-ker- ee* or similar. HABITAT: Migrants mainly on estuaries and beaches. DISTRIBUTION: Vagrant recorded from the Aleutians.

36 DOWITCHERS, GODWITS AND RUFF

1 SHORT-BILLED DOWITCHER (COMMON DOWITCHER)
Limnodromus griseus 25–29cm FIELD NOTES: Difficult to separate from Long-billed
Dowitcher, especially in non-breeding plumage, best distinguished by call. In flight
shows a white oval from upper rump to mid-back and pale secondaries. Inland race
L. g. hendersoni (fig 1b) breeds in C Canada. VOICE: In flight utters a mellow, rapid
tutututu. HABITAT: Breeds in open marshes; on migration occurs on a wide variety
of inland and coastal wetlands; winters mainly on coastal mudflats. DISTRIBUTION:
Summers in S coastal Alaska, C Canada and C NE Canada.

2 LONG-BILLED DOWITCHER *Limnodromus scolopaceus* 27–30cm
FIELD NOTES: Difficult to separate from Short-billed Dowitcher in non-breeding
plumage, although breast tends to be slightly darker grey, ending abruptly on lower
breast. Flight pattern similar to Short-billed Dowitcher. White bars on tail usually
narrower than black bars, making tail appear dark. VOICE: In flight utters a thin, high
keek or *kik-kik-kik-kik*. HABITAT: Breeds on tundra bogs; on migration and in winter
usually on fresh or brackish marshes, less common on coastal mudflats. DISTRIBUTION:
Summers in coastal N Alaska and adjacent coastal NW Canada, migrates across North
America to winter in extreme S of USA and Pacific coast south of Washington and on
Atlantic coast south of North Carolina.

3 BLACK-TAILED GODWIT *Limosa limosa* 40–44cm FIELD NOTES: In flight, from
above appears black and white, due to bold white wing bar, white rump and black tail.
Underwing mainly white. VOICE: In flight gives a yelping *kip* or *kip-kip-kip*. HABITAT:
Estuaries, mudflats, lakeshores and grassland. DISTRIBUTION: Spring migrant on
W Aleutians, rare winter vagrant on Atlantic coast.

4 MARBLED GODWIT *Limosa fedoa* 40–51cm FIELD NOTES: In flight superficially
resembles Long-billed Curlew, but bill shorter and straight. VOICE: In flight utters a
harsh *cor-ack* or *kaaWEK*. HABITAT: Breeds on grassy meadows near lakes and ponds,
winters on coasts and on salt marshes and coastal pools. DISTRIBUTION: Summers on
the Prairies of USA and Canada, winters on the coasts of USA, mainly south from
Oregon and North Carolina.

5 HUDSONIAN GODWIT *Limosa haemastica* 36–42cm FIELD NOTES: In flight,
above similar to Black-tailed Godwit, although white wing bar narrower and confined
to primaries and outer secondaries. Underwing grey with black wing coverts. VOICE:
A soft *chow-chow*, a nasal *toe-wit, wit* or *kweh-weh*. HABITAT: Breeds in sedgey
marshland close to coast or river; on migration and winter, muddy estuaries, coastal
lagoons and flooded grassland. DISTRIBUTION: Summers locally from NW and S Alaska
to Hudson Bay. Migrates mainly over E USA to South America.

6 BAR-TAILED GODWIT *Limosa lapponica* 37–41cm FIELD NOTES: In flight,
upperwing plain with dark primary coverts, underwing white, barred dark grey, rump
white, barred dark grey. Rare European race *L. l. lapponica* has a white rump and
underwing coverts. VOICE: A high-pitched *kik, kiv-ik* or *kak-kak-kak-kak*, with variation
on these. HABITAT: Breeds on lowland tundra, post breeding favours coastal beaches
and mudflats. DISTRIBUTION: Summers in W Alaska, vagrants occur along Pacific coast.
European race is rare vagrant on Atlantic coast.

7 RUFF (REEVE: female) *Philomachus pugnax* 26–32cm FIELD NOTES: Breeding
males are unmistakeable but very variable, moulting males resemble breeding females
but have breast and flanks splattered with dark blotches. In flight, shows a narrow
white bar on upperwing and prominent white U on upper tail coverts. Recorded
swimming, feeding phalarope-like. VOICE: Generally silent; in flight may utter a
grunted *kurr, kook* or a shrill *hoo-ee*. HABITAT: Breeds on coastal tundra, marsh
fringes and damp meadows, post breeding frequents lake, pool and river margins, wet
grasslands and marshes. DISTRIBUTION: Regular vagrant over much of North America,
especially coastal areas, rare in Greenland.

n-br

1b   br

n-br

1

br

2

br

n-br

3

br

n-br   4   br

n-br

5

♀ br

6

br

♂ br

♂ n-br

7

7   ♂ n-br   ♀ br

♂ br

♂ breeding varieties

37 TURNSTONES, SURFBIRD AND *CALIDRIS* SANDPIPERS

1 TURNSTONE (RUDDY TURNSTONE) *Arenaria interpres* 21–26cm
FIELD NOTES: In flight, upperwing shows prominent white bar and white stripe on inner coverts, centre of back and lower rump white split by a black band on upper rump. VOICE: A rapid, staccato *trik-tuk-tuk-tuk* or *chit-uk*. In alarm gives a sharp *chick-ik* or *teu*. During display gives a long rolling rattle. HABITAT: Tundra islands, rocky and sandy shores, mudflats and estuaries. DISTRIBUTION: Summers in Arctic Alaska, Canada and Greenland, winters on all coasts of the USA.

2 BLACK TURNSTONE *Arenaria melanocephala* 22–25cm FIELD NOTES: In flight very similar to Turnstone, but lacking any rufous. May roost alongside Turnstones. VOICE: In flight utters a trilling *keerrt*. When disturbed gives a rattling *krkrkrkrkrkr....* HABITAT: Breeds on coastal plains, winters mainly on rocky coasts. DISTRIBUTION: Summers in coastal W Alaska, winters along Pacific coast.

3 SURFBIRD *Aphriza virgata* 23–26cm FIELD NOTES: In flight, upperwing shows a white wing bar and a white tail with a black tip. VOICE: In flight gives a soft *iif iif iif*; feeding flocks utter chattering nasal squeaks. HABITAT: Breeds on rocky mountain ridges, winters mainly on rocky coasts. DISTRIBUTION: Summers on Alaskan mountains and the Yukon Mountains in Canada, winters along Pacific coast.

4 GREAT KNOT (EASTERN or GREATER KNOT, GREAT SANDPIPER)
Calidris tenuirostris 26–28cm FIELD NOTES: In flight, upperwing shows a narrow white wing bar, lower rump is white sparsely marked with black, appears white, tail dark grey. VOICE: A low *nyut-nyut*, also a low *chuker-chuker-chuker* and a soft *prrt*. HABITAT: After breeding occurs on sandy or muddy shores. DISTRIBUTION: Rare vagrant, recorded from W Alaska.

5 KNOT (RED or LESSER KNOT) *Calidris canutus* 23–25cm FIELD NOTES: In flight, upperwing shows a narrow white wing bar, rump white narrowly barred with black, appears greyish, tail grey. VOICE: A soft nasal *knut*, *wutt* or *whet*. During display gives a melancholy *poor-me*. HABITAT: Breeds on open, stony tundra near water. Post breeding favours sandy or muddy coasts. DISTRIBUTION: Arctic Canada, Greenland and W coast of Alaska. Winters in USA on Atlantic, Gulf and California coasts.

6 SANDERLING *Calidris alba* 20–21cm FIELD NOTES: Feeds along water's edge, typically with rapid runs interspersed with quick dips to pick up food. In flight, upperwing shows a broad white wing bar and a dark leading edge, the latter most noticeable in non-breeding plumage. VOICE: In flight gives a hard *twick* or *kip*, often repeated or forming a quick trill. During display utters various trills, purrs and churring notes. HABITAT: Breeds on barren stony tundra near water, winters mainly on sandy or muddy coasts. DISTRIBUTION: Summers in the Canadian Arctic and Greenland, winters on Atlantic, Pacific and Gulf coasts.

7 PECTORAL SANDPIPER *Calidris melanotos* 19–23cm FIELD NOTES: In flight, upperwing shows a narrow white wing bar and clear, white sides to lower rump and upper tail coverts. VOICE: In flight gives a reedy *churk* or *trrt*. During display gives a hooting *oo-ah oo-ah....* HABITAT: Breeds in Arctic tundra, post breeding frequents coastal and inland wetlands. DISTRIBUTION: Summers in N Alaska and Arctic Canada, west to Hudson Bay, migrates across North America to winter in South America.

8 SHARP-TAILED SANDPIPER (SIBERIAN PECTORAL SANDPIPER)
Calidris acuminata 17–21cm FIELD NOTES: In flight has a narrow white bar on upperwing and white sides to upper tail coverts and lower rump. Juvenile has a buffy breast with a few streaks and a white eyebrow that is broad behind eye. VOICE: A soft *wheep*, *pleep* or *trrt*, also a twittering *prrt-wheep-wheep*. HABITAT: On migration and during winter occurs on lakes, lagoons, wet grasslands and coastal mudflats. DISTRIBUTION: Regular in autumn in Alaska, vagrant elsewhere.

38 *CALIDRIS* SANDPIPERS

1 SEMIPALMATED SANDPIPER *Calidris pusilla* 13–15cm FIELD NOTES: Short straight bill. Forages by running head down with frequents stops to probe for food. VOICE: In flight gives a harsh *chrup*, *chirk* or *kreet*. Feeding flocks utter a rapid *tweed-do-do-do-do*. HABITAT: Breeds on damp grassy tundra; on migration occurs on coasts, lake and pool sides. DISTRIBUTION: Summers in N Alaska across N Canada to Labrador. Migrates across North America, mainly E of the Rockies.

2 WESTERN SANDPIPER *Calidris mauri* 14–17cm FIELD NOTES: Compared to Semipalmated Sandpiper bill is slightly more down-turned, longer and thicker based. Tends to forage more often in water. VOICE: A thin, high-pitched *jeet*. HABITAT: Breeds on dry tundra, post breeding occurs on coasts and on inland wetlands. DISTRIBUTION: Summers in N and W Alaska, winters on all US coasts.

3 RED-NECKED STINT (RUFOUS-NECKED STINT) *Calidris ruficollis* 13–16cm FIELD NOTES: In non-breeding plumage very similar to Little Stint, rear end appears more attenuated and bill slightly blunter and shorter. Some breeding adults have paler rufous throat and breast, so can also look like Little Stint. Feeding action similar to Little Stint. VOICE: A coarse *chit*, *kreep*, *creek* or *chritt*. HABITAT: Breeds on dry tundra, post breeding frequents coastal or pool shores. DISTRIBUTION: Probably breeds in W Alaska, otherwise a rare migrant on the Aleutians, vagrant elsewhere.

4 LITTLE STINT *Calidris minuta* 12–14cm FIELD NOTES: Thin short bill. Has a quick running around foraging action. Juveniles show a distinct pale V on mantle. VOICE: A short *stit-tit*. HABITAT: On migration and winter occurs on a wide variety of fresh- and saltwater wetlands. DISTRIBUTION: Uncommon vagrant, recorded from Alaska, the Aleutians, and Pacific and Atlantic coasts of USA and Canada.

5 TEMMINCK'S STINT *Calidris temminckii* 13–15cm FIELD NOTES: Greenish-yellow legs. At rest, white-sided tail projects beyond wing-tips. Has a slow, deliberate foraging action. VOICE: A rapid *tiririririr* or trilled *trirr*. HABITAT: On migration occurs on marshes, lakes, ponds and estuaries. DISTRIBUTION: Rare vagrant mainly to W Alaska and the Aleutians.

6 LONG-TOED STINT *Calidris subminuta* 13–16cm FIELD NOTES: Pale yellow legs. When alarmed, often stands upright with neck extended. Usually feeds among waterside vegetation. VOICE: A short, rippling *prrt*, *chrrup* or *chulip* and a sharp *tik-tik-tik*. HABITAT: On migration favours edges of pools and lakes, also marshes and tidal mudflats. DISTRIBUTION: Regular migrant on the Aleutians, vagrant elsewhere.

7 LEAST SANDPIPER *Calidris minutilla* 13–15cm FIELD NOTES: Very similar to Long-toed Stint, although usually looks more compact or crouched, bill finer and slightly decurved. VOICE: A shrill *trreee* or *prreep*, also a lower, purring *prrrt* and a high *dididi*. HABITAT: Breeds in sub-Arctic tundra and marsh areas in spruce forests; on migration occurs on open coasts and on inland wetlands. DISTRIBUTION: Summers in Alaska and east across sub-Arctic N Canada to Newfoundland. Migrates across North America to winter in S USA.

8 WHITE-RUMPED SANDPIPER *Calidris fuscicollis* 15–18cm FIELD NOTES: At rest, wings project beyond tail. In flight shows white upper tail coverts. VOICE: A high-pitched *jeet*, a short *tit* or *teet*. HABITAT: Breeds on tundra, on migration occurs on a variety of inland and coastal wetlands. DISTRIBUTION: Summers in NE Alaska and Arctic Canada. Migrates across E North America.

9 BAIRD'S SANDPIPER *Calidris bairdii* 14–17cm FIELD NOTES: At rest, wings project beyond tail. Less gregarious than others of the genus. VOICE: A low *preeet*, also a grating *krrt* and a sharp *tsick*. HABITAT: Breeds on dry upland tundra; post breeding on lakes and pools bordered by short grassland, less often on coasts. DISTRIBUTION: Summers in N Alaska, Arctic Canada and NW Greenland.

39 *CALIDRIS* SANDPIPERS

1 SPOON-BILLED SANDPIPER (SPOONBILL SANDPIPER)
Eurynorhynchus pygmeus 14–16cm FIELD NOTES: In flight, upperwing shows prominent white wing bar, sides of rump white. Sweeps bill from side to side while feeding in shallow water. VOICE: A rolling *preep* and a shrill *wheet*. HABITAT: Coastal tundra and, on passage, muddy coasts and coastal lagoons. DISTRIBUTION: Rare vagrant from Kamchatka.

2 BROAD-BILLED SANDPIPER *Limicola falcinellus* 16–18cm FIELD NOTES: In flight, upperwing shows a narrow white bar, in non-breeding plumage shows a dark leading edge, much like a non-breeding Sanderling. VOICE: A buzzing *chrrreet* or *trrreet*. HABITAT: On migration occurs on soft muddy areas at the edges of ponds and lakes, also tidal mudflats. DISTRIBUTION: Rare vagrant from Scandinavia and N Russia.

3 STILT SANDPIPER *Calidris himantopus* 18–23cm FIELD NOTES: In flight shows a white rump and plain upperwing, feet project well beyond tail. Often wades up to belly. VOICE: A soft *kirrr* or *drrr*, also a low *djew* or *toof*. During display utters a series of nasal, buzzy trills. HABITAT: Breeds in tundra; post breeding favours inland and coastal wetlands. DISTRIBUTION: Summers on C Canadian and Alaskan tundra and the SW area of Hudson Bay. Migrates across E North America; some birds winter in SW Texas and S Florida.

4 CURLEW SANDPIPER *Calidris ferruginea* 18–23cm FIELD NOTES: In flight shows a white rump and prominent white wing bar on upperwing. Regularly wades, often up to belly, in shallow water. VOICE: A rippling *chirrup*. HABITAT: Coastal lagoons, marshes and mudflats. DISTRIBUTION: Vagrant in North America, mainly on Atlantic coast.

5 DUNLIN (RED-BACKED SANDPIPER) *Calidris alpina* 16–22cm
FIELD NOTES: In flight shows prominent white wing bar on upperwing and white sides to rump. When feeding walks quickly, often with short runs, probing and pecking vigorously. Breeding plumage and size varies according to race: *C. a. pacifica* (SW Alaska) and *C. a. hudsonia* (C Canada) bright with long bills; *C. a. schinzii* (SE Greenland) smaller with short bill; *C. a. arctica* (NE Greenland) also small, mantle colour more yellowish. VOICE: A rasping *kreep* or *pjeev*. During display utters a descending, reedy trill. HABITAT: Breeds on Arctic tundra, winters mainly on coasts and coastal marshes. DISTRIBUTION: Summers E Greenland, Arctic Alaska and Canada east to Hudson Bay. Winters on all coasts of USA and Pacific coast of Canada.

6 ROCK SANDPIPER *Calidris ptilocnemis* 20–23cm FIELD NOTES: In flight shows prominent white wing bar on upperwing and white sides to rump. Very variable, race on the Aleutians *C. p. couesi* darker on mantle, head and breast. VOICE: Similar to those of Purple Sandpiper. HABITAT: Breeds on upland tundra in coastal areas; post breeding occurs on rocky and stony shores. DISTRIBUTION: Summers in W Alaska, winters along Pacific coast.

7 PURPLE SANDPIPER *Calidris maritima* 20–22cm FIELD NOTES: Very similar to dark race of Rock Sandpiper but lacks dark belly. In flight shows narrow white wing bar on upperwing and white sides to rump. VOICE: A short *whit* or *kut*. During display utters various buzzing and wheezing trills along with low moans. HABITAT: Breeds on upland tundra, winters on rocky shores and man-made jetties or breakwaters etc. DISTRIBUTION: Summers in NE Canada and W and E Greenland. Winters on Atlantic coast, from Newfoundland south to Carolina.

40 SNIPE, WOODCOCK, PHALAROPES AND PRATINCOLE

1 JACK SNIPE *Lymnocryptes minimus* 17–19cm FIELD NOTES: Secretive, tends to wait until nearly trodden on before being flushed, flies away with less erratic movements than Snipe. VOICE: Generally silent, although may utter a weak *gah* when flushed. HABITAT: Wet grassy places surrounding lakes, pools, rivers etc. DISTRIBUTION: Very rare vagrant from Europe.

2 SNIPE (COMMON or WILSON'S SNIPE) *Gallinago gallinago* 25–27cm
FIELD NOTES: When flushed flies of in an erratic, zigzag manner. In flight, upperwing shows a white trailing edge, underwing looks dark, actually tightly barred black and white. European birds G. *g. gallinago*, which is a rare vagrant, have white bars on underwing. The American race G. *g. deicata* (Wilson's Snipe) is often considered a full species. VOICE: When flushed gives a harsh *scarp* or *scresh*. In display utters a *tika tika tika*, and in flight display, outer tail feathers produce a hollow, buzzing 'drumming'. HABITAT: Breeds in boggy or marshy places, post breeding also spreads to flooded pastures, edges of ponds and rivers. DISTRIBUTION: Summers in Alaska, Canada, apart from northernmost tundra, and N states of the USA; winters across S USA.

3 PIN-TAILED SNIPE *Gallinago stenura* 25–27cm FIELD NOTES: In flight similar to Wilson's Snipe, but lacks white trailing edge, also eye-brow wider at base of bill and at rest tertials overlap primaries. VOICE: A short *scaap* when flushed. HABITAT: Similar to Snipe, may favour dryer areas. DISTRIBUTION: Very rare vagrant from Russia.

4 WOODCOCK (EURASIAN WOODCOCK) *Scolopax rusticola* 33–35cm
FIELD NOTES: Usually only encountered when flushed. VOICE: Occasionally utters a snipe-like *schaap*. HABITAT: Mixed, conifer or deciduous forest with glades and damp areas. DISTRIBUTION: Very rare vagrant from Europe.

5 AMERICAN WOODCOCK *Scolopax minor* 25–31cm FIELD NOTES: Flies with fluttering wing-beats. Wings produce a whistling on takeoff. VOICE: In ground display gives a nasal *beent* and a cooing *chako*. HABITAT: Rich, moist woodland with open glades. DISTRIBUTION: Summers over most of E USA and adjacent Canada. Northern birds move south to SE USA in winter.

6 WILSON'S PHALAROPE *Phalaropus tricolor* 22–24cm FIELD NOTES: In flight shows a white rump. Tends to swim less than others of the genus. When feeding on land has a hurried walk with a feverish pecking action. VOICE: A soft, muffled *wemf* or *vimp*. HABITAT: Breeds on pools and small lakes in prairie and taiga, on passage uses various types of inland waters. DISTRIBUTION: Summers over much of W and C North America.

7 GREY PHALAROPE (RED PHALAROPE) *Phalaropus fulicaria* 20–22cm
FIELD NOTES: In flight, upperwing shows wide white wing bar. Regularly swims, spinning on water to stir up food particles. VOICE: In flight utters a sharp *pik*. At breeding grounds gives a buzzing *prrrt* and various chirpings and twitterings. HABITAT: Breeds in coastal tundra marshes; on migration sometimes on coastal pools or lagoons, otherwise strictly pelagic. DISTRIBUTION: Summers on the tundra coasts of Alaska, Canada and E and W Greenland, migrates coastally.

8 RED-NECKED PHALAROPE (NORTHERN PHALAROPE)
Phalaropus lobatus 18–19cm FIELD NOTES: In flight, upperwing shows a white wing bar. Feeding actions similar to Grey Phalarope. VOICE: In flight utters a harsh *twick*. HABITAT: Breeds on tundra bogs; on migration often occurs on lakes, pools and coastal waters. DISTRIBUTION: Summers on Alaskan and Canadian tundra and on SE tip of Greenland; migrates mainly down coasts.

9 ORIENTAL PRATINCOLE (EASTERN or LARGE INDIAN PRATINCOLE)
Glareola maldivarum 23–24cm FIELD NOTES: In flight has a deeply forked tail, white rump and chestnut underwing coverts. VOICE: A sharp *kyik*, or *chik-chik*. HABITAT: Flat open areas, usually near water. DISTRIBUTION: Very rare vagrant from Asia.

41 GULLS

Due to the complex plumages of young gulls (often a 4-year process to get from the brown of juveniles to the grey of adults) it is difficult to cover all of these adequately within such a limited text. It would therefore be advisable for the reader to refer to books that cover this area more fully (*see* Further Reading).

1 IVORY GULL *Pagophila eburnea* 40–43cm FIELD NOTES: Aggressive scavenger, especially around animal carcasses. Juvenile white with black mask and black spots at tips of mantle and wing feathers. VOICE: A shrill tern-like *kree-ar* or *preeo*. HABITAT: Cliffs, rock or flat shores. Winters around pack ice. DISTRIBUTION: Arctic N Canada and Greenland, disperses to winter on seas around breeding area.

2 SABINE'S GULL *Xema sabini* 27–33cm FIELD NOTES: In flight has distinctive tricoloured upperwing pattern, grey coverts, black outer primaries and coverts, white inner primaries and secondaries. Tail forked. VOICE: A grating *krr*. HABITAT: Near marshes and pools in Arctic tundra; post breeding mainly pelagic. DISTRIBUTION: Summers on N and W coasts of Alaska, N Canada and W and E Greenland. Migrates off E and W coasts.

3 SWALLOW-TAILED GULL *Creagrus furcatus* 51–57cm FIELD NOTES: Forked tail, upperwing pattern similar to Sabine's Gull. VOICE: A harsh scream and a rattle. HABITAT: Post breeding mainly pelagic. DISTRIBUTION: Very rare vagrant from the Galapagos.

4 ROSS'S GULL *Rhodostethia rosea* 30–32cm FIELD NOTES: In flight shows a wedge-shaped tail and a mid-grey underwing with white secondaries and inner primaries. VOICE: A melodic *a-wo a-wo a-wo*, a soft *kew* and a tern-like *kik-kik-kik....* HABITAT: Tundra marshes, winters at sea. DISTRIBUTION: Summers locally in Arctic Canada and Greenland.

5 LITTLE GULL *Hydrocoloeus minutus* 25–30cm FIELD NOTES: Buoyant tern-like flight. Dark underwing. Upperwing grey with white tips to primaries and secondaries. VOICE: A tern-like *kek-kek-kek*. HABITAT: Vegetated, freshwater lakes and marshes. Winters on coasts and nearby lakes. DISTRIBUTION: Locally on the Great Lakes, winters mainly on Atlantic coast of NE USA.

6 LAUGHING GULL *Leucophaeus atricilla* 36–41cm FIELD NOTES: Upperwing has a white trailing edge and black outer primaries. VOICE: A high-pitched, laughing *ka-ka-ka-ka-ka-kaa-kaa-kaaa-kaaa*; also a shorter *kahwi*. HABITAT: Coastal areas. DISTRIBUTION: Atlantic coast south from Maine, northern breeders move south in winter.

7 FRANKLIN'S GULL *Leucophaeus pipixcan* 32–38cm FIELD NOTES: In flight shows grey centre to tail, upperwing has a white trailing edge and broad white tips on outer primaries broken by a black subterminal band. VOICE: A short, soft *kruk*, *queel* or *kowii*. HABITAT: Lakes and marshes. DISTRIBUTION: Summers on prairies and grasslands of C North America.

8 BONAPARTE'S GULL *Chroicephalus philadelphia* 28–30cm FIELD NOTES: Underwing mainly pale grey with black tips to primaries. Upperwing shows a white wedge on outer primaries and primary coverts. VOICE: A grating tern-like *gerr* or *reek*. HABITAT: Tree-lined marshes, ponds and lakes. Winters on lakes and coastal waters. DISTRIBUTION: Alaska, east across C Canada to Quebec. Winters on the Great Lakes and on all US coasts.

9 BLACK-HEADED GULL (COMMON BLACK-HEADED GULL)
Chroicephalus ridibundus 37–43cm FIELD NOTES: Upperwing shows a white wedge on outer primaries and primary coverts. Underwing shows dark grey inner primaries, outer pair white with black tips. VOICE: A high-pitched *kreeay* or *karr*. HABITAT: Coastal and inland wetlands. DISTRIBUTION: Winter visitor to E coast, vagrant to Greenland.

10 GREY-HEADED GULL (GREY-HOODED GULL)
Chroicephalus cirrocephalus 38–43cm FIELD NOTES: Upperwing shows a white wedge on primary coverts and base of outer primaries, otherwise primaries black with small white subterminal spots on outer pair. VOICE: A harsh *gurr* and a drawn-out *caw-caw*. HABITAT: Coasts, lakes and rivers. DISTRIBUTION: Very rare vagrant from South America.

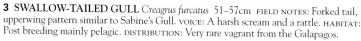

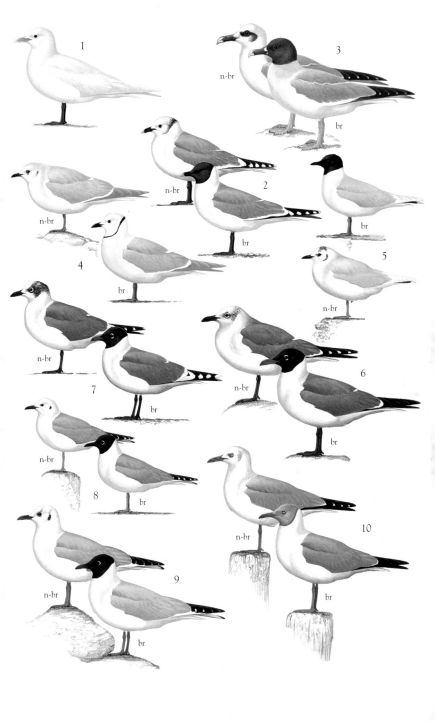

42 GULLS

See note on plate 41 referring to young gulls.

1 LESSER BLACK-BACKED GULL *Larus fuscus* 51–61cm FIELD NOTES: Mantle variable, paler race from Britain and W Europe *L. f. graellsii* (fig 1b) more common than darker form. Upperwing shows a white trailing edge. Black primaries, outer 1 or 2 with a small white subterminal spot. Third-winter birds have black spot near tip of bill, legs yellowish. VOICE: Similar to, but lower-pitched than, American Herring Gull. HABITAT: Coastal areas. DISTRIBUTION: Winter visitor, mainly on Atlantic coast.

2 SLATY-BACKED GULL *Larus schistisagus* 55–67cm FIELD NOTES: Some show paler grey mantle. In flight shows a broad white trailing edge and often has an indistinct white band dividing the slaty upperwing from the black outer primaries, the latter with white subterminal spot on outer feather. Third-winter birds have black spot near tip of bill, legs pinkish. VOICE: Similar to Glaucous-winged Gull (p.96). HABITAT: Cliffs and coastal shores. DISTRIBUTION: Rare vagrant to Alaska (possibly summers), the Aleutians and North Pacific.

3 WESTERN GULL *Larus occidentalis* 54–66cm FIELD NOTES: Dark-mantled race *L. o. wymani* (fig 3b) occurs in California. In flight shows white trailing edge, primaries black with white subterminal spot on outermost feather. Third-winter birds have black spot near bill tip, legs pale pink. VOICE: Similar to, but lower than American Herring Gull. HABITAT: Coasts. DISTRIBUTION: Pacific coast south of Vancouver.

4 YELLOW-FOOTED GULL *Larus livens* 60–67cm FIELD NOTES: Very similar to dark race of Western Gull but heavier bill and yellow legs. Second-winter (reaches adult plumage by third year) birds have black-tipped yellow bill. VOICE: A low *quock kuck kuck kuck*. HABITAT: Mainly coasts. DISTRIBUTION: Regular in S California.

5 GREAT BLACK-BACKED GULL *Larus marinus* 64–78cm FIELD NOTES: Aggressive and predatory. Flight heavy and powerful. In flight, black upperwing shows white trailing edge and large white subterminal spots on outer pair of primaries. Third-year birds have black spot near bill tip, legs very pale pink-grey. VOICE: A hoarse *oow-oow-oow* and a deep *owk*. All notes gruffer than other large gulls. HABITAT: Rocky and sandy coasts and locally on inland lakes. DISTRIBUTION: S Greenland, NE Canada south to NE USA, far northern birds move south to winter along Atlantic coasts and on the Great Lakes.

6 KELP GULL *Larus dominicanus* 54–65cm FIELD NOTES: Legs pale greenish-yellow. In flight, very similar to dark race of Western Gull. VOICE: A strident *ki-och*. HABITAT: Coastal. DISTRIBUTION: Rare vagrant from South America.

7 BELCHER'S GULL (BAND-TAILED or SIMEON'S GULL) *Larus belcheri* 48–52cm FIELD NOTES: In flight shows black wings with white trailing edge and black subterminal band on tail. VOICE: High-pitched laughing call, reminiscent of a child's bugle. HABITAT: Rocky shores. DISTRIBUTION: Very rare vagrant from South America.

8 BLACK-TAILED GULL (JAPANESE or TEMMINCK'S GULL)
Larus crassirostris 44–47cm FIELD NOTES: Upperwing primaries are black with small white tips. Outermost feather may have a small, white subterminal spot. VOICE: A plaintive mewing. HABITAT: Coastal areas. DISTRIBUTION: Rare vagrant from Russia and Japan.

9 HEERMANN'S GULL *Larus heermanni* 43–49cm FIELD NOTES: Flight buoyant on long wings. In flight, upperwing shows large white patch on primary coverts, tail black with white terminal band. VOICE: A low trumpeting nasal *yoww*; also a short *yek* and a *ye ye ye ye....* HABITAT: Coastal areas. DISTRIBUTION: Winter resident on Pacific coast, north to British Columbia.

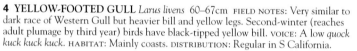

43 GULLS

See note on plate 41 referring to young gulls.

1 COMMON GULL (MEW GULL) *Larus canus* 40–46cm FIELD NOTES: *L. c. kamtschatschensis* from NE Siberia (fig 1b) occurs in Alaska and the Aleutians. VOICE: A laughing *gleeoo* and a yelping *keeea*. HABITAT: Cliffs, marshes and beaches, winters mainly on coasts. DISTRIBUTION: Alaska and E Canada, winters on Pacific coast; E records are vagrant European birds.

2 RING-BILLED GULL *Larus delawarensis* 43–47cm FIELD NOTES: Black primaries have a small subterminal white spot on outermost feather. VOICE: A mellow *kowk*. Laughing call higher than Common Gull. HABITAT: Marshes, lakes and coasts. DISTRIBUTION: Summers in a band E from N California and adjacent British Columbia to the Great Lakes and NE Canada. Winters in the USA in S states and on all coasts.

3 CALIFORNIA GULL *Larus californicus* 47–67cm FIELD NOTES: Bill with black and red spot. Wing pattern similar to American Herring Gull. VOICE: A scratchy *aow* and a high-pitched laughing call. HABITAT: Inland lakes and marshes, winters on coasts. DISTRIBUTION: C Canada and NW USA, winters on Pacific coast south of British Columbia.

4 HERRING GULL *Larus argentatus* 55–67cm FIELD NOTES: Less bulky than American Herring Gull. VOICE: Very similar to American Herring Gull. HABITAT: Coasts. DISTRIBUTION: Rare vagrant to Atlantic coast and Greenland. Siberian race *L. a. vegae* (Vega Gull) (fig 4b) occurs in Alaska.

5 AMERICAN HERRING GULL *Larus smithsonianus* 55–67cm FIELD NOTES: Most widespread gull of North America. Black primaries with distinct white subterminal spot on outer pair of feathers. VOICE: A loud, laughing *keeah-keeah-keeah-keah-kau-kau...* and a short *keeow*. HABITAT: Coasts, inland lakes and rivers. DISTRIBUTION: Much of Canada and Alaska, winters in E USA and on Pacific and Atlantic coasts.

6 YELLOW-LEGGED GULL *Larus michahellis* 52–58cm FIELD NOTES: Wing pattern similar to American Herring Gull. VOICE: Similar to American Herring Gull. HABITAT: Coasts. DISTRIBUTION: Rare vagrant from Europe.

7 GLAUCOUS-WINGED GULL *Larus glaucescens* 61–68cm FIELD NOTES: Primaries grey with white subterminal spots. VOICE: A low *klook-klook-klook* and a screamed *ka-ka-ako*. HABITAT: Primarily coastal. DISTRIBUTION: W Alaska south to Vancouver, further south in winter.

8 THAYER'S GULL *Larus thayeri* 56–63cm FIELD NOTES: Primaries dark grey with white subterminal spots. VOICE: Like a muffled American Herring Gull. HABITAT: Coastal cliffs, winters mainly on coasts. DISTRIBUTION: Arctic Canada and W Greenland, winters mainly on Pacific coast.

9 ICELAND GULL *Larus glaucoides* 55–64cm FIELD NOTES: Canadian race *L. g. kumlieni* (Kumlien's Gull) (fig 9b) has variable coloured primaries from dark grey, with white subterminal spots to white. At rest, wings project beyond tail. VOICE: Similar to American Herring Gull. HABITAT: Primarily on cliffs, winters on coasts, inland lakes and rivers. DISTRIBUTION: S and W Greenland, NE Canada (Baffin Island). Winters on the E coast from Newfoundland to Virginia.

10 GLAUCOUS GULL *Larus hyperboreus* 64–77cm FIELD NOTES: At rest, wings reach end of tail. VOICE: Similar to American Herring Gull, but hoarser. HABITAT: Coastal cliffs, winters on coasts and on inland lakes. DISTRIBUTION: Greenland, Arctic Canada and Alaska, winters on E and W coasts of Canada, Hudson Bay and the Great Lakes.

11 KITTIWAKE (BLACK-LEGGED KITTIWAKE) *Rissa tridactyla* 38–40cm FIELD NOTES: Slightly forked tail. Plain black primaries. VOICE: A nasal, wailing *kitt-i-waak....* HABITAT: Coastal cliffs, winters at sea. DISTRIBUTION: Alaska, NE Canada and Greenland, winters off E and W coasts.

12 RED-LEGGED KITTIWAKE *Rissa brevirostris* 36–38cm FIELD NOTES: Underwing grey, otherwise flight pattern similar to Kittiwake. VOICE: Similar to Kittiwake, but higher pitched. HABITAT: Coastal cliffs, winters at sea. DISTRIBUTION: Breeds on the Aleutians and Pribilofs. Winters in North Pacific.

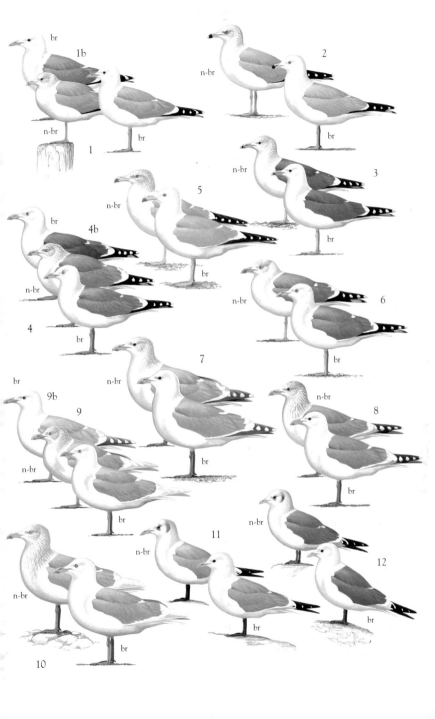

44 TERNS

1 CASPIAN TERN *Hyrdroprogne caspia* 47–54cm FIELD NOTES: Feeds mainly by hovering then plunge-diving. Short forked tail. VOICE: A loud croaking *kraah*, *krah-krah* or *kree-ahk*. HABITAT: Coasts, lakes and rivers. Winters on coasts. DISTRIBUTION: Disjointed breeding range, C Canada, W USA, NE USA and Gulf coast. Winters on Gulf coast, Florida and SE Atlantic coast.

2 ROYAL TERN *Sterna maxima* 45–50cm FIELD NOTES: Feeds mainly by plunge-diving. Tail deeply forked. VOICE: A low-pitched, grating *kerriup*, *kree-it* or *kirruck*. HABITAT: Coastal beaches. DISTRIBUTION: Resident on Atlantic coast, south of New England, Gulf coast, and winter on Californian coast.

3 ELEGANT TERN *Sterna elegans* 39–43cm FIELD NOTES: Feeds by plunge-diving. Bill colour varies from deep yellow to orange-red. Tail deeply forked. VOICE: A nasal, rasping *karreek* or *ka-zeek*. HABITAT: Sandy beaches and islands; after breeding, on coastal shores, lagoons and estuaries. DISTRIBUTION: Summers in S California, disperses north to N California after breeding.

4 ROSEATE TERN *Sterna dougallii* 33–38cm FIELD NOTES: Feeds mainly by plunge-diving, hovers less and tends to 'fly into water'. Tail deeply forked with very long streamers. VOICE: A rasping *kraak* or *zraaach* and a short, soft *cher-vik*. HABITAT: Islands, beaches. DISTRIBUTION: Summers on Atlantic coast from Nova Scotia to New York and S Florida. Migrates down Atlantic.

5 COMMON TERN *Sterna hirundo* 32–39cm FIELD NOTES: Feeds mainly by plunge-diving. Tail deeply forked with long streamers. Inner primaries on underwing appear translucent. Siberian race *S. h. longipennis* (fig 5b) occurs as a vagrant to Alaska. VOICE: A rapid *kye-kye-kye-kye...*; also a *kirri-kirri-kirri* or similar. When alarmed gives a screeching *kreeeearh*, *kreee-er* and a sharp *kik*. HABITAT: Marshes, lakes and sandy beaches, at sea on migration. DISTRIBUTION: Summers across S Canada east of the Rockies. Migrates south down both coasts and inland in E USA.

6 FORSTER'S TERN *Sterna forsteri* 33–36cm FIELD NOTES: Feeds by plunge-diving, after a short hover. Usually looks bulkier than Common or Arctic tern. Tail deeply forked, grey centred with long streamers. VOICE: A rolling, nasal *kyarr*, *kwarr* or *kreerr*; also a rapid *kek-ke-kek....* HABITAT: Sheltered ponds, lakes, marshes and coastal waters. DISTRIBUTION: Summers in a disjointed band across C North America and on the Gulf coast, winters on the Atlantic, north to the Carolinas, Gulf and S California coasts.

7 ARCTIC TERN *Sterna paradisaea* 33–38 FIELD NOTES: Feeding habits similar to Forster's Tern. On underwing, all primaries appear translucent. Tail deeply forked with long streamers. VOICE: A piping *pee-pee-pee*, a rattling *kt-kt-kt-krr-kt* and when alarmed a high *kree-ah*. HABITAT: Tundra marshes and shores; after breeding, mainly pelagic. DISTRIBUTION: Greenland, N Canada and Alaska, migrates south along E and W coasts.

8 SANDWICH TERN *Sterna sandvicensis* 36–41cm FIELD NOTES: Feeds mainly by plunge-diving, often from a considerable height. Tail deeply forked. VOICE: A grating *kirruck* or *kerRICK*; also a short *krik* or *krik-krik*. HABITAT: Coastal marshes and shores. DISTRIBUTION: Resident on Gulf and Atlantic coasts, mainly north to Delaware.

9 GULL-BILLED TERN *Gelochelidon nilotica* 33–43cm FIELD NOTES: Feeds by hawking or dipping to pick food from water or ground. Shallow forked tail. VOICE: A nasal *kayWEK kayWEK* and rattling when alarmed. HABITAT: Coastal marshes. DISTRIBUTION: Atlantic coast, south of New York, Gulf coast and S California. Winters on Gulf coast and Florida.

10 LEAST TERN (AMERICAN LITTLE TERN) *Sternula antillarum* 22–25cm FIELD NOTES: Feeds by plunge-diving, with much hovering. Tail and rump grey, tail deeply forked. VOICE: A rapid *kid-ick kid-ick...* and a rasping *zr-e-e-e-p*. HABITAT: Beaches, lakes and rivers. DISTRIBUTION: Summers on the coasts of California, Gulf and Atlantic, north to Maine, also inland on the Mississippi river system.

45 TERNS

1 ALEUTIAN TERN (KAMCHATKA TERN) *Onychoprion aleutica* 32–34cm
FIELD NOTES: Feeds by dipping to pick food from water. White rump and tail, the latter deeply forked. Crown white in non-breeding plumage. VOICE: A soft wader-like *twee-ee-ee*. HABITAT: Coastal plains, marshes, bogs on rocky islands; after breeding, mainly at sea. DISTRIBUTION: Summers on the Aleutians and on E and S Alaskan coasts.

2 BRIDLED TERN (BROWN-WINGED TERN) *Onychoprion anaethetus* 34–36cm FIELD NOTES: Feeds by plunge-diving and by dipping to pick food from water. Rump and tail dark grey, the latter deeply forked and broadly white edged. VOICE: A yapping *wep-wep* or *wup-wup*. HABITAT: Pelagic. DISTRIBUTION: Summer visitor off the Gulf and Atlantic coasts of USA.

3 SOOTY TERN (WIDEAWAKE TERN) *Onychoprion fuscata* 36–45cm
FIELD NOTES: Feeds mainly by dipping to pick food from water, occasionally plunge-dives. Tail black, deeply forked and narrowly white edged. VOICE: A distinctive *ker-wacki-wah* or *wide-a-wake*. HABITAT: Rocky, stony or sandy islands; after breeding, pelagic. DISTRIBUTION: Breeds on islands in the Gulf, winters at sea mainly off the Gulf coast.

4 LARGE-BILLED TERN *Phaetusa simplex* 38cm FIELD NOTES: Feeds mainly by plunge-diving. Tail deeply forked. In flight, upperwing pattern distinctive, lesser coverts grey, primaries black and a diagonal white bar from primary coverts to tertials. VOICE: A raucous *sqe-ee* and a nasal *ink-oink*. HABITAT: Inland water bodies, beaches and estuaries. DISTRIBUTION: Very rare vagrant from South America.

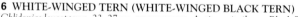

5 WHISKERED TERN *Chlidonias hybrida* 23–29cm FIELD NOTES: Actions similar to Black Tern. Non-breeding birds have rump and tail grey, the latter shallowly forked. VOICE: A short *kek* or *kek-kek*. HABITAT: Lakes, marshes and sheltered coastal areas. DISTRIBUTION: Very rare vagrant from Europe.

6 WHITE-WINGED TERN (WHITE-WINGED BLACK TERN)
Chlidonias leucopterus 23–27cm FIELD NOTES: Actions similar to Black Tern. Non-breeding birds have a white rump and a pale grey tail; the latter shallowly forked, often appearing square. VOICE: A short *kek* and a rasping *kesch*. HABITAT: Lakes, marshes and estuaries. DISTRIBUTION: Vagrant from Europe, mainly to Atlantic coast.

7 BLACK TERN *Chlidonias niger* 22–24cm FIELD NOTES: Buoyant flight, regularly dipping to pick insects from water. Non-breeding birds have a grey rump and tail, the latter shallowly forked. VOICE: A weak *kik* or *kik-kik*; also a shrill, nasal *kyeh* or *kreek* when alarmed. HABITAT: Lakes and marshes, also coastal lagoons and at sea during migration. DISTRIBUTION: Summers across much of C North America, migrates south.

8 BROWN NODDY (COMMON NODDY) *Anous stolidus* 38–45cm
FIELD NOTES: Feeds mainly by hovering and dipping to pick prey from water. Underwing coverts generally paler than Black Noddy. VOICE: A crow-like *kwok-kwok*, *karruuk* or *krao*. HABITAT: Breeds on isolated islets; post breeding, primarily pelagic. DISTRIBUTION: Summers on the Dry Tortugas (Florida), otherwise off Gulf and Atlantic coasts of the USA.

9 BLACK NODDY (WHITE-CAPPED NODDY) *Anous minutus* 35–39cm
FIELD NOTES: Feeding actions similar to Brown Noddy. Underwing coverts generally darker than Brown Noddy. VOICE: A distinctive *tik-tikoree* and a staccato rattle. HABITAT: Breeds on isolated islets; after breeding, mainly pelagic. DISTRIBUTION: Some summer among Brown Noddies on the Dry Tortugas.

10 BLACK SKIMMER (AMERICAN SKIMMER) *Rynchops niger* 40–51cm
FIELD NOTES: Unmistakeable. Feeds by 'ploughing' water with lower mandible whilst in skimming flight. Often nocturnal. VOICE: A soft, nasal *yep* or *yip*. HABITAT: Sheltered coastal waters, lagoons and salt marshes. DISTRIBUTION: Resident in the USA on Atlantic, Gulf and S California coasts.

46 SKUAS

1 POMARINE SKUA (POMARINE JAEGER) *Stercorarius pomarinus* 46–51cm
FIELD NOTES: The bulkiest of all the 'smaller' skuas. Pursues other seabirds in a bid to
steal food, has been known to go as far as killing the victim of these chases. Juveniles
show white flashes at base of primaries, they lack the elongated central tail feathers and
have variable coloured upperparts, from mid to dark brown with pale bars, underparts
paler barred dark, head uniform from grey-brown to dark brown. VOICE: On breeding
grounds gives various yelping and barking notes as well as a wavering *ehwewewewe*.
Generally silent away from breeding sites. HABITAT: Breeds on coastal tundra; after
breeding, mainly pelagic. DISTRIBUTION: Summers in tundra areas of N Alaska and
N Canada. Winters off the coasts of S USA.

2 ARCTIC SKUA (PARASITIC JAEGER) *Stercorarius parasiticus* 41–46cm
FIELD NOTES: Performs aerial acrobatics while chasing and harrying seabirds in an attempt
to make them disgorge food. Juveniles lack the elongated central tail feathers, colours
very variable, many similar to juvenile Pomarine Skuas, especially dark individuals, pale
forms usually show buff or grey-buff head; in flight shows distinct white flashes at base of
primaries. VOICE: On breeding grounds utters a loud, nasal mewing, also a harsh *kek* or
kook and a crowing *feee-leerrr*. HABITAT: Breeds on tundra, post breeding mainly pelagic.
DISTRIBUTION: Summers on coastal Alaska, Arctic Canada, W and S Greenland. Winters
off coasts of S USA.

3 LONG-TAILED SKUA (LONG-TAILED JAEGER) *Stercorarius longicaudus*
48–53cm FIELD NOTES: In flight often gives the impression of being heavy-chested.
Less piratical than other skuas, usually chooses terns if indulging in pursuits. The 'dark'
morph shown is very rare and said to only occur on Greenland, some experts seem to
doubt the validity of this 'form'. Juveniles lack the long central tail feathers, although
they do have a slight extension, and are very variable in colour, generally dark above,
barred paler, paler below barred dark; there is a very dark morph that appears almost
totally black; all forms show less white on the primaries than other 'small' skuas. VOICE:
On breeding grounds gives a rattling *krr-krr-krr-kri-kri-kri* followed by a repeated,
mournful *pheeeu*. HABITAT: Breeds on coastal and inland tundra; after breeding, mainly
pelagic. DISTRIBUTION: Summers in W and N Alaska, N Canada and Greenland.
Migrates off Pacific and Atlantic coasts.

4 SOUTH POLAR SKUA (MacCORMICK'S SKUA) *Stercorarius maccormicki*
50–55cm FIELD NOTES: Various intermediate morphs between the two depicted, all
tend to lack any rufous in plumage. Juveniles of pale and dark morphs are similar to
respective adults, but with some pale feathers on upperparts and a black-tipped blue
bill. VOICE: Generally silent. HABITAT: Pelagic. DISTRIBUTION: Migrants occur off both
Pacific and Atlantic coasts.

5 GREAT SKUA (BONXIE) *Stercorarius skua* 53–58cm FIELD NOTES: Some birds
paler than that shown. Very aggressive to other seabirds, recorded killing victims when
attempting to rob them of food. Juvenile has underparts uniform rufous, upperparts
grey-brown with paler rufous spots and fringes, head grey-brown. VOICE: Generally
silent. HABITAT: Mainly pelagic. DISTRIBUTION: Winters off North Atlantic coast.

1 dark morph

pale morph

1 dark morph

light morph

1 dark morph

2

dark morph

2 dark morph

light morph

3 dark morph

dark morph

3

pale morph

3 light morph

dark morph

intermediate morph

4

4

dark morph

light morph

4

5

5

5

47 AUKS

1 GUILLEMOT (COMMON MURRE) *Uria aalge* 38–43cm FIELD NOTES: Rapid whirring flight. Underwing has white wing coverts and a dark axillary area with a small dark 'arm-pit' bar. VOICE: A *ha-ha-ha* leading into a guttural *ha-rrh*. At sea, juveniles give a plaintive *peeeooee*. HABITAT: Coastal cliffs, winters at sea. DISTRIBUTION: Summers in the west from Alaska to California and in the east from S Greenland to NE North America; winters at sea, mainly near breeding areas but also south as far as North Carolina in the east.

2 BRÜNNICH'S GUILLEMOT (THICK-BILLED MURRE) *Uria lomvia* 39–43cm FIELD NOTES: Underwing has white wing coverts and a dark axillary area, no dark bar on 'arm-pit'. VOICE: A groaning *aoorrr*. HABITAT: Coastal cliffs, winters at sea. DISTRIBUTION: Alaska and the Aleutians, NE Canada and Greenland, winters at sea, mainly near breeding sites but also south to British Columbia and New Jersey.

3 RAZORBILL *Alca torda* 37–39cm FIELD NOTES: Rapid, whirring flight. Underwing pattern similar to Brünnich's Guillemot. VOICE: A guttural *goarrr*. At sea, juveniles give a piping whistle. HABITAT: Coastal cliffs or rocky areas below; winters at sea. DISTRIBUTION: SW Greenland and NE North America, south to Maine. Winters at sea off breeding areas, spreading south to North Carolina.

4 BLACK GUILLEMOT (TYSTIE) *Cepphus grylle* 30–36cm FIELD NOTES: Rapid, whirring flight. In flight shows white underwing coverts and a large white patch on upperwing. VOICE: A high *peeeeeh* or *seeeeeuu*; also a *sip-sipp-sipp....* HABITAT: Rocky coasts, winters at sea. DISTRIBUTION: N Alaska, N and E Canada and W and E Greenland. Winters at sea, mainly near breeding sites.

5 PIGEON GUILLEMOT (SEA PIGEON) *Cepphus columba* 30–37cm FIELD NOTES: Underwing coverts are dark grey VOICE: A wheezy *peeeeee*. HABITAT: Rocky coasts, winters at sea. DISTRIBUTION: W Alaska, Aleutians south to California, winters at sea near breeding sites.

6 LONG-BILLED MURRELET *Brachyramphus perdix* 26cm FIELD NOTES: Pale throat. In flight, underwing has pale grey coverts. Flight is rapid and whirring. VOICE: Undescribed. HABITAT: Winters at sea. DISTRIBUTION: Rare vagrant from Siberia.

7 MARBLED MURRELET *Brachyramphus marmoratus* 24cm FIELD NOTES: Underwing is dark grey. Non-breeding birds have a white collar. VOICE: A high-pitched *peeeaah-peeeaah*. HABITAT: Coastal forests, feeds at sea. Winters along coasts. DISTRIBUTION: Resident from W Alaska and the Aleutians south to California.

8 KITTLITZ'S MURRELET (SHORT-BILLED MURRELET)
Brachyramphus brevirostris 22–23cm FIELD NOTES: Underwing pattern similar to Marbled Murrelet. Flight swift and wilder than others of the genus. VOICE: A low, groaning *urrrhhn*. HABITAT: Coastal mountain slopes, feeds at sea. DISTRIBUTION: The Aleutians, S and W Alaska, winters in seas near breeding areas.

9 ANCIENT MURRELET *Synthliboramphus antiquus* 24–27cm FIELD NOTES: Underwing coverts white, contrasting with grey flanks. Flight rapid and whirring. VOICE: Low whistles and chirping or clinking notes. HABITAT: Islands, often with dense vegetation. Winters off coasts. DISTRIBUTION: Resident from the Aleutians and S Alaska south to Queen Charlotte Islands, winters as far south as California.

10 CRAVERI'S MURRELET *Synthliboramphus craveri* 21cm FIELD NOTES: Black chin. In flight, underwing plain mid-grey. VOICE: A high-pitched trill. HABITAT: Offshore waters. DISTRIBUTION: Post breeding, disperses north to California from breeding islands off Mexico.

11 XANTUS'S MURRELET (SCRIPP'S MURRELET)
Synthliboramphus hypoleucus 23–25cm FIELD NOTES: White chin. In flight, underwing-coverts white. Northern birds *S. h. scrippsi* (fig 11b) lack white crescents in front of eye. VOICE: Northern birds utter a high-pitched *seep seep seep....* Southern birds give a rattling trill. HABITAT: Rocky islands, winters at sea near breeding grounds. DISTRIBUTION: S California, disperses in winter as far north as British Columbia.

48 AUKS

1 LITTLE AUK (DOVEKIE) *Alle alle* 17–19cm FIELD NOTES: Rapid, whirring flight. Underwing dark. VOICE: A chattering *krii-ek ak ak ak ak*. HABITAT: Rock scree on coastal slopes. Winters at sea. DISTRIBUTION: NW Alaska (St Lawrence Island), Canadian archipelago (Baffin Island) and Greenland. Winters in low Arctic waters on E coast as far south as the Carolinas.

2 CASSIN'S AUKLET *Ptychoramphus aleuticus* 20–23cm FIELD NOTES: No marked difference in non-breeding plumage. Rapid flight. Underwing shows a pale wing bar. VOICE: A hoarse *RREP-nerreer* or similar. HABITAT: Coastal islands, winters at sea. DISTRIBUTION: Aleutians, south to California; northern birds move south.

3 CRESTED AUKLET *Aethia cristatella* 23–27cm FIELD NOTES: Typical rapid, whirring flight. Gregarious, often in large flocks mixed with other auks. Juvenile lacks white face plumes and has a much reduced crest. VOICE: Honking and grunting sounds. HABITAT: Scree slopes and cliffs on islands, winters at sea. DISTRIBUTION: Islands off W Alaska, winters in the Bering Sea and the North Pacific.

4 WHISKERED AUKLET (PYGMY AUKLET) *Aethia pygmaea* 17–18cm FIELD NOTES: Juvenile lacks crest, but may show 'ghost' head plumes. VOICE: A high-pitched *eeaah ah ah ah...* or *eeaah ik eah*. HABITAT: Rocky islands, winters at sea usually near coasts. DISTRIBUTION: W Aleutians, winter at sea near breeding sites.

5 LEAST AUKLET (KNOB-BILLED AUKLET) *Aethia pusilla* 12–14cm FIELD NOTES: Gregarious, often very large flocks. Juveniles lack head plumes and knob on bill. VOICE: At breeding sites utters various chattering, twittering and squealing calls. HABITAT: Rocky islands, winters at sea usually near coasts. DISTRIBUTION: Islands in the Bering Sea, winters in the Bering Sea and North Pacific.

6 PARAKEET AUKLET *Cyclorrhynchus psittacula* 23–25cm FIELD NOTES: Usually in pairs or small groups. Juvenile similar to non-breeding adult, but bill black and eye grey. VOICE: At breeding colonies gives a whistle or trill, rising in pitch. HABITAT: Rocky islands, winters at sea. DISTRIBUTION: W Alaskan coast, Aleutians and islands in the Bering Sea. Winters in the North Pacific and Bering Sea.

7 RHINOCEROS AUKLET *Cerorhinca monocerata* 35–38cm FIELD NOTES: In winter often occurs in large groups close inshore. Juvenile lacks head plumes, otherwise similar to non-breeding adult. VOICE: At breeding sites utters growling and shrieking cries. HABITAT: Grassy slopes on islands or coasts. Winters at sea near coasts. DISTRIBUTION: Aleutians south to California, northern birds move south in winter.

8 PUFFIN (COMMON or ATLANTIC PUFFIN) *Fratercula arctica* 26–36cm FIELD NOTES: Orange feet often conspicuous in flight. Juvenile has small dark bill with an orange tip, otherwise very similar to non-breeding adult. VOICE: At breeding sites utters a growling *arr* or *arr-uh*. HABITAT: Rocky and grassy slopes on coasts and islands. Winters offshore of breeding areas. DISTRIBUTION: Greenland and NE North America, south to Maine. Winters in the North Atlantic, Baffin Bay and Labrador Sea.

9 HORNED PUFFIN *Fratercula corniculata* 36–41cm FIELD NOTES: Orange feet often conspicuous in flight. Juvenile similar to non-breeding adult, but bill small and dull. VOICE: At breeding sites utters harsh grunting and growling calls. HABITAT: Rocky coastal cliffs and offshore islands. Winters offshore of breeding areas. DISTRIBUTION: Coasts of Alaska and NW Canada. Winters in the North Pacific and Bering Sea.

10 TUFTED PUFFIN *Fratercula cirrhata* 36–41cm FIELD NOTES: Juvenile similar to non-breeding adult but bill smaller and duller, underparts sometimes pale greyish white. VOICE: At breeding grounds utters soft grunts and growls. HABITAT: Rocky coasts and islands. Winters offshore of breeding sites. DISTRIBUTION: Coasts of Alaska and the Pacific, south to California. Winters in the Pacific and Bering Sea.

49 PIGEONS AND DOVES

1 ROCK DOVE *Columba livia* 31–34cm FIELD NOTES: Known throughout the world, these very variable 'town pigeons' all originate from the true Rock Dove of Europe (main figure). VOICE: A moaning *oorh*, or *oh-oo-oor*, also a hurried *oo-roo-coo t coo* given during display. HABITAT: Cliffs, cities, towns and villages. DISTRIBUTION: The whole of temperate North America.

2 SCALY-NAPED PIGEON (RED-NECKED PIGEON) *Patagioenas squamosa* 36–40cm FIELD NOTES: Mainly arboreal, feeding on fruits, buds and succulent leaves. VOICE: A strongly accentuated *who who hoo-oo-hoo*, the last 3 syllables sounding like *who-are-you*. HABITAT: Mainly forests, but may occur in towns or villages. DISTRIBUTION: Very rare vagrant from the Antilles.

3 WHITE-CROWNED PIGEON *Patagioenas leucocephala* 33–36cm FIELD NOTES: Feeds primarily in treetops, often in flocks. Juvenile has a greyish crown and no glossy neck feathers. VOICE: A loud, clear *Cruu cru cu-cruuu*, sounding like *who-took-two*. HABITAT: Coastal mangroves and inland fruiting trees. DISTRIBUTION: Florida.

4 RED-BILLED PIGEON *Patagioenas flavirostris* 32–37cm FIELD NOTES: Mainly arboreal. In display flight, climbs with exaggerated wing-beats before gliding down, in circles, with wings held in a shallow V. Juvenile generally plain grey. VOICE: A hoarse *Hhooo hwooo hwooooo hup hupA hwoooo hup hupA hwooooo....* HABITAT: Forest and woodland with thick undergrowth. DISTRIBUTION: S Texas.

5 BAND-TAILED PIGEON *Patagioenas fasciata* 34–40cm FIELD NOTES: In display flies horizontally with tail and wings spread and neck extended, then glides in a circle, calling before beating wings with rapid, shallow beats. Feeds on the ground or in trees. Juvenile generally pale grey, lacking white collar and glossy neck feathers. VOICE: A low *coo-cooo...* and a grating *raaaaan*. HABITAT: Coniferous and mixed woodland, parks and gardens. DISTRIBUTION: Summers on Pacific coast north to British Columbia and in SW US states, winters in California.

6 ORIENTAL TURTLE DOVE (RUFOUS TURTLE DOVE)
Streptopelia orientalis 30–35cm FIELD NOTES: Usually appears scalier on wings and mantle than Turtle Dove and rump generally clean blue-grey. VOICE: A mournful *coo-cooroo-cooroo* or *gur-grugroo*. HABITAT: Open wooded areas near cultivation, open areas with scattered trees and bushes, parks and gardens. DISTRIBUTION: Very rare vagrant from Asia.

7 TURTLE DOVE (EUROPEAN or COMMON TURTLE DOVE)
Streptopelia turtur 26–28cm FIELD NOTES: Arboreal, but finds most food on the ground. Looks less scaly than Oriental Turtle Dove, rump blue-grey tinged brown. VOICE: A purring *turrrr turrrrr turrrrr*. HABITAT: Open woodland, forest edge, copses and hedgerows. DISTRIBUTION: Very rare vagrant from Europe.

8 COLLARED DOVE (EUROPEAN COLLARED DOVE) *Streptopelia decaocto* 31–33cm FIELD NOTES: Feeds mainly on the ground. In flight, all outer tail feathers show a broad white terminal band. Buff-grey under-tail coverts, the domesticated Ringed Turtle Dove *S. d. risoria* is paler with white under-tail coverts. Juveniles of both races lack the black and white neck collar. VOICE: A loud, low-pitched *koo-KOOO-kook* or *koo-KOOO-koo* or similar. On landing gives a harsh *kreair* or *whaaa*. HABITAT: Towns, cities, parks and gardens. DISTRIBUTION: Stronghold in SE USA, spreading (Introduced).

9 SPOTTED DOVE (NECKLACE DOVE) *Streptopelia chinensis* 30cm
FIELD NOTES: Feeds mainly on the ground. In flight, dark tail with large white tips to all outer tail feathers. Juvenile lacks the spotted neck pattern. VOICE: A melodious *coo croo-oo croo-oo* or *coocoo croor-croor*. HABITAT: Cultivated areas and around human habitations. DISTRIBUTION: S California (Introduced).

feral varieties

50 DOVES

1 WHITE-WINGED DOVE *Zenaida asiatica* 28–30cm FIELD NOTES: In flight, upperwings show a broad white central patch, tail dark with white tips to all outer tail feathers. Feeds in trees and on the ground, usually gregarious. VOICE: A rhythmic *who hoo who hoo-oo* or *who hoo who hoo hoo-ah-hoo-hoo-ah who oo*. HABITAT: Dry woodland, orchards, arid scrub and semi-desert. DISTRIBUTION: US–Mexican border. Winters along Gulf coast and Florida.

2 ZENAIDA DOVE *Zenaida aurita* 25–28cm FIELD NOTES: Primarily a ground feeder, but will feed in fruiting trees. In flight, secondaries have a white trailing edge and the outer tail feathers have greyish-white tips. VOICE: A mournful *coo-oo coo coo coo*, similar, but shorter and faster than Mourning Dove. HABITAT: Open coastal areas, urban gardens, open woodland and thickets. DISTRIBUTION: Very rare vagrant from the West Indies, recorded in Florida.

3 MOURNING DOVE (AMERICAN MOURNING DOVE) *Zenaida macroura* 30–31cm FIELD NOTES: Feeds mainly on the ground. Female paler with less iridescence on neck and less grey on the head. Juvenile has pale ear coverts and eye-brow, body feathers with pale fringes. VOICE: A mournful *oo-woo woo woo woo* or *ooAH cooo coo coo*. HABITAT: Open country, agricultural land and suburban areas. DISTRIBUTION: Widespread in S Canada and the USA, northern birds move south in winter.

4 INCA DOVE *Columbina inca* 19–22cm FIELD NOTES: Ground feeder. In flight, from above shows rufous primaries and white-sided tail. Underwing rufous with dark markings on coverts. Female slightly more drab than male. VOICE: A strong, high COO-*pup* COO-*pup* COO-*pup*.... HABITAT: Parks and gardens in suburban areas, farms and semi-desert. DISTRIBUTION: SW and SC USA.

5 COMMON GROUND-DOVE *Columbina passerina* 15–18cm
FIELD NOTES: Mainly a ground feeder. In flight, from above shows rufous primaries and a black tail with white corners. Underwing rufous with a dark trailing edge. VOICE: A repetitive *coo coo coo coo coo....*, *co-coo co-coo co-coo...* or *hoooip hoooip hoooip....* HABITAT: Dry brush country and open ground. DISTRIBUTION: Mexican–US border, Gulf coast states, Florida and SW Georgia.

6 RUDDY GROUND-DOVE *Columbina talpacoti* 15–18cm FIELD NOTES: Ground feeder. In flight, very similar to Common Ground-Dove, but underwing shows blackish coverts. Western birds slightly duller. VOICE: A repeated *puwoh-puwoh-puwoh....* HABITAT: Lightly wooded open areas, cultivations and suburbs. DISTRIBUTION: Rare visitor to SW USA and S Texas.

7 WHITE-TIPPED DOVE (WHITE-FRONTED DOVE) *Leptotila verreauxi* 28–30cm FIELD NOTES: Secretive. Ground feeder. In flight, underwing shows grey flight feathers and rufous coverts. VOICE: A strong, low *poo pooorr* or *coo CRRRRRoo cup*, said to resemble the sound made by blowing across the top of a bottle. HABITAT: Dense, shady woodland. DISTRIBUTION: S Texas (lower Rio Grande).

8 RUDDY QUAIL-DOVE *Geotrygon montana* 21–28cm FIELD NOTES: Forages on the ground, usually under cover. In flight shows much rufous on wings. VOICE: A low, fading *cooo*, *whoooo* or *oooooooh*. HABITAT: Dense woodland. DISTRIBUTION: Very rare vagrant in Florida.

9 KEY WEST QUAIL-DOVE *Geotrygon chrysia* 27–31cm FIELD NOTES: Secretive. Forages on the ground, usually under the cover of bushes and trees. In flight shows much rufous on the wings. Juvenile a dull version of adult. VOICE: A low, slightly descending *ooooo*; also an *ooooowoo*, with the 2nd syllable accentuated and slightly higher. HABITAT: Dense woodland and thickets. DISTRIBUTION: Rare vagrant to Florida Keys.

51 HOOPOE, ANIS, CUCKOOS AND ROADRUNNER

1 HOOPOE (EURASIAN HOOPOE) *Upupa epops* 26–28cm
FIELD NOTES: Unmistakeable. Fans crest on landing or when agitated. In flight gives the appearance of a giant butterfly. VOICE: A low *hoop-hoop-hoop*. HABITAT: Grassland and farmland with scattered trees, parkland, groves and orchards. DISTRIBUTION: Very rare vagrant from Europe.

2 CUCKOO (COMMON or EURASIAN CUCKOO) *Cuculus canorus* 32–34cm
FIELD NOTES: Often perches horizontally with tail cocked and wings drooped. Female has a brownish tinge to breast. VOICE: A far-carrying *ku-koo* or variants such as *kuk-kuk-kuk-oo*. Female utters a rapid bubbling. HABITAT: Wide ranging, including woodland, farmland with trees and bushes, scrub and coastal areas. DISTRIBUTION: Rare vagrant from Europe mainly to the Aleutians and Pribilofs.

3 ORIENTAL CUCKOO *Cuculus saturatus* 30–32cm FIELD NOTES: Only safely separated from Cuckoo by voice. Barring on flanks slightly broader and upperparts darker. VOICE: A resonant *poo-poo-poo-poo*. HABITAT: Open woodland, forests, forest edge and clearings. DISTRIBUTION: Very rare vagrant from E Europe, recorded mainly from the Aleutians and Pribilofs.

4 BLACK-BILLED CUCKOO *Coccyzus erythropthalmus* 27–31cm
FIELD NOTES: Skulking. In flight, upperwing shows a dull rufous-brown on base of primaries. Undertail of adult is grey, each feather with a narrow white tip and a narrow black subterminal bar; juvenile tail has smaller white tips and no black. VOICE: A hollow *cu cu cu* or *cu cu cu cu*; also a descending *k-k-k-k* or *kru-dru*. HABITAT: Forests, woodlands and thickets, often along streams. DISTRIBUTION: Summers in E and C USA and S Canada, east of the Rockies.

5 YELLOW-BILLED CUCKOO *Coccyzus americanus* 28–32cm FIELD NOTES: Skulking. In flight, upperwing shows distinct rufous bases to primaries. Undertail of adults blackish with wide white tips, juvenile similar but tips a little smaller. VOICE: A hollow *kuk-kuk-kuk-kuk-kuk-kuk...kow-kow-kow-kowlp-kowlp*; also a dove-like *cloom...cloom...cloom*. HABITAT: Woodland, forest edge, thickets and open country with bushes and trees. DISTRIBUTION: Widespread in summer in the USA, east of the Rockies.

6 MANGROVE CUCKOO *Coccyzus minor* 28–30cm FIELD NOTES: Skulking. In flight, upperwing uniform brown. Undertail black with wide white tips. Pale morph resident, darker morph a rare vagrant. VOICE: A low *gawk gawk gawk gawk...*; also a single *whit*. HABITAT: Mangroves. DISTRIBUTION: Resident in Florida, vagrant to Gulf coast from Mexico.

7 SMOOTH-BILLED ANI *Crotophaga ani* 30–33cm FIELD NOTES: Usually occurs in small noisy flocks, walking on the ground, on branches or clambering through vegetation in search of insects. Flight is direct, with quick choppy wing-beats interspersed with short glides. Juvenile browner with smaller bill. VOICE: An ascending, whistled *queee-ik*; also a thin, descending *teeew*. HABITAT: Scrubland and farmland. DISTRIBUTION: S Florida.

8 GROOVE-BILLED ANI *Crotophaga sulcirostris* 33–35cm FIELD NOTES: Smaller billed. Actions as Smooth-billed Ani. Juvenile browner and smaller billed. VOICE: A liquid *TEE-ho, TEET-way* or *TEEt*; also a sharp *pep pep....* HABITAT: Farmland. DISTRIBUTION: Summers in S Texas (Rio Grande Valley), winter from S Texas along Gulf Coast to Louisiana.

9 GREATER ROADRUNNER *Geococcyx californianus* 56–59cm
FIELD NOTES: Unmistakeable. Often perches on rocks or posts. Runs after prey such as insects, lizards and snakes. VOICE: A dove-like, descending *cooo cooo cooo cooo coo coo*; also a rattle produced by the bill. HABITAT: Dry open country with scattered brush. DISTRIBUTION: SW USA.

1

3   rufous
     morph

♂   ♀

♂   2

                          ♀
              rufous morph

4

                5

light
morph   6

                dark morph   7   8

9

52 OWLS

1 BARN OWL *Tyto alba* 32–38cm FIELD NOTES: Nocturnal, although often hunts by day. VOICE: A hissing screech. HABITAT: Farmland, woodland, parks and suburbs. DISTRIBUTION: Most of the USA, apart from CN states.

2 STYGIAN OWL *Asio stygius* 41–46cm FIELD NOTES: Nocturnal. Pale forehead. VOICE: A loud *woof*, *wupf* or *whu*. HABITAT: Dense forests. DISTRIBUTION: Very rare vagrant.

3 SHORT-EARED OWL *Asio flammeus* 35cm FIELD NOTES: Active at dusk and dawn. In flight, primaries look dark tipped. VOICE: A short *hoo hoo hoo...*; also barking and wheezy calls. HABITAT: Open country, including grassland, marshes and tundra. DISTRIBUTION: Much of North America from N Canada to C USA, leaves northern areas to winter mostly in the USA.

4 LONG-EARED OWL *Asio otus* 35–37cm FIELD NOTES: Mainly nocturnal. In flight, primary tips show 4 or 5 bars. VOICE: A soft, hooting *wooip*; when alarmed, gives a barking *bwah bwah bwah*. HABITAT: Forests and woodlands. DISTRIBUTION: Across most of North America, south of the tree line, apart from SE USA; northern birds move south in winter.

5 GREAT HORNED OWL *Bubo virginianus* 53–58cm FIELD NOTES: Mainly nocturnal. Very variable, depicted are the eastern form, the pale *B. v. subarcticus* (fig 5b) from the western taiga and the dark *B. v. saturatus* (fig 5c) from SE Alaska to California. VOICE: A deep, muffled *hooo hoo hoo*; during courtship, female answers with a barking call. HABITAT: Varied, including mountains, forests, parks and suburbs. DISTRIBUTION: All of North America south of the Arctic.

6 SNOWY OWL *Bubo scandiacus* 53–65cm FIELD NOTES: Usually hunts at dusk or dawn, although throughout the day during summer. VOICE: A booming *goo goo*; when alarmed, male utters a cackling *kre-kre-kre* and female a loud whistling or mewing. HABITAT: Open tundra. DISTRIBUTION: Arctic Alaska, Canada and N and E Greenland; often erupts to winter in Canada and N USA.

7 GREAT GREY OWL *Strix nebulosa* 65–70cm FIELD NOTES: Mainly crepuscular. Feeds on rodents. VOICE: A soft, deep *hoo-hoo-hoo-hoo-hoo...*, female replies with a mellow whistle. HABITAT: Dense boreal and mountain conifer forests with clearings and bogs. DISTRIBUTION: Boreal forests of Canada east to the Great Lakes, south to NE Minnesota, N Idaho and N California.

8 BARRED OWL *Strix varia* 48–51cm FIELD NOTES: Mainly nocturnal. Barred breast and streaked belly and flanks. VOICE: A clear *hoo hoo ho-ho, hoo hoo ho-hoooooaw* often transcribed as *who cooks for you, who cooks for you all*. HABITAT: Conifer and mixed woodland with nearby open country. DISTRIBUTION: E USA and E S Canada, westward across C Canada to British Columbia, south to N California.

9 SPOTTED OWL *Strix occidentalis* 41–48cm FIELD NOTES: Nocturnal. Belly and flanks spotted and barred. VOICE: A barking *whoop-hu-hu-hooo*. HABITAT: Wooded canyons and damp forests. DISTRIBUTION: Pacific coast and inland in the SW USA.

10 MOTTLED OWL *Strix virgata* 29–38cm FIELD NOTES: Nocturnal. Streaked on breast. VOICE: A frog-like *gwho gwho gwho...* that increases in pitch and volume. HABITAT: Various forests and woodlands with open areas. DISTRIBUTION: Very rare vagrant from Mexico.

11 BROWN HAWK-OWL (ORIENTAL HAWK-OWL) *Ninox scutulata* 27–33cm FIELD NOTES: Mainly nocturnal, although often hunts, nightjar-like, at dusk. VOICE: A mellow, rising *coo-coo...*, repeated monotonously. HABITAT: Woodland, parks and gardens with large trees. DISTRIBUTION: Very rare vagrant from E Asia.

12 HAWK OWL (NORTHERN HAWK OWL) *Surnia ulula* 36–39cm FIELD NOTES: Mainly diurnal. Searches for prey from treetops or by hovering, also chases prey like a Sharp-shinned Hawk. VOICE: A long, burbling *prullul-lullu...*; also a chattering *ke-ke-ke-ki*. HABITAT: Open woods, burned areas and forest edge. DISTRIBUTION: Boreal Alaska and Canada, from W to E coast.

53 OWLS

1 FLAMMULATED OWL *Otus flammeolus* 15–17cm FIELD NOTES: Nocturnal. Dark eyes. Variable, with intermediates between the 2 morphs depicted. VOICE: A hollow, low *hoop* singly or repeated at 2–3 second intervals. HABITAT: Mountain pine, or pine mixed with oak or aspen. DISTRIBUTION: W mountain areas.

2 ORIENTAL SCOPS-OWL (EASTERN or ASIAN SCOPS-OWL)
Otus sunia 18–21cm FIELD NOTES: Nocturnal. Roosts high, in dense foliage. VOICE: A toad-like *oot-to-ta* or *oot-ta*. HABITAT: Deciduous or mixed forest, orchards, parks and gardens. DISTRIBUTION: Very rare vagrant from E Asia.

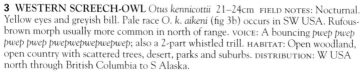

3 WESTERN SCREECH-OWL *Otus kennicottii* 21–24cm FIELD NOTES: Nocturnal. Yellow eyes and greyish bill. Pale race O. *k. aikeni* (fig 3b) occurs in SW USA. Rufous-brown morph usually more common in north of range. VOICE: A bouncing *pwep pwep pwep pwep pwepwepwepwepwep*; also a 2-part whistled trill. HABITAT: Open woodland, open country with scattered trees, desert, parks and suburbs. DISTRIBUTION: W USA north through British Columbia to S Alaska.

4 EASTERN SCREECH-OWL (COMMON SCREECH-OWL) *Otus asio* 16–25cm FIELD NOTES: Nocturnal. Yellow eyes and yellowish bill. Variable, the rufous morph most common in the mid-eastern states. VOICE: A low-pitched, descending whinny; also long whistled trill. HABITAT: Woodland, with clearings, orchards, parks and suburban gardens. DISTRIBUTION: Throughout E USA.

5 WHISKERED SCREECH-OWL (SPOTTED SCREECH-OWL) *Otus trichopsis* 16–18cm FIELD NOTES: Nocturnal. Yellow eyes. Underparts appear spotted. VOICE: A steady *boo boo boo boo boo boo...*; also a soft, descending *oooo*. HABITAT: Dense oak and oak–pine forests. DISTRIBUTION: SE Arizona.

6 NORTHERN PYGMY-OWL (CALIFORNIAN PYGMY-OWL)
Glaucidium californicum 16–18cm FIELD NOTES: Most active at dawn and dusk. Back of head shows 'false eyes', a black patch surrounded by white. VOICE: A monotonous *hoo* or *hoo-hoo*. HABITAT: Coniferous and deciduous forest and forest edge. DISTRIBUTION: W North America from British Columbia southward.

7 FERRUGINOUS PYGMY-OWL *Glaucidium brasilianum* 15–19cm FIELD NOTES: Mostly active at dawn and dusk. Shows same 'false eye' pattern as Northern Pygmy-owl. VOICE: A prolonged series of *whoip* notes. HABITAT: Saguaro deserts and open woodland. DISTRIBUTION: S Arizona and S Texas.

8 ELF OWL *Micrathene whitneyi* 14–15cm FIELD NOTES: Hunts at dusk and at night, mainly feeding on insects. VOICE: A sharp *pew* and a series of *pe pe pe* notes; also a descending, whistled *meeeew*. HABITAT: Deserts, riparian woods, dry woods and wooded canyons. DISTRIBUTION: Summers in extreme SW USA.

9 BURROWING OWL *Athene cunicularia* 23–25cm FIELD NOTES: Nocturnal, but hunts diurnally during breeding season, often by walking or hopping after prey on the ground. Regularly perches, in daylight, at the entrance to burrow. VOICE: A soft, high-pitched *coo-cooo*; utters a clucking chatter when alarmed. HABITAT: Open country, including grassland, prairie and golf courses. DISTRIBUTION: Summers in W USA and just over the border into Canada; also resident in Florida, Texas and California.

10 BOREAL OWL (TENGMALM'S OWL) *Aegolius funereus* 24–26cm FIELD NOTES: Nocturnal. Roosts in dense cover or cavities. VOICE: A soft, rapid *po-po-po-po-po-po...*; also a nasal *hoooa*. HABITAT: Mixed conifer and deciduous forests. DISTRIBUTION: Boreal Canada and Alaska; also scattered locations in W USA.

11 NORTHERN SAW-WHET OWL *Aegolius acadicus* 19–21cm FIELD NOTES: Mainly nocturnal. Roosts in dense cover or cavities. A. *f. brooksi* (fig 11b) occurs on Queen Charlotte Island. VOICE: A repeated, low *poo poo poo*; also a nasal *pew* and a soft whistled *eeeooi*. HABITAT: Dense conifer and mixed forests, wooded swamps and in winter a wider range of woodland, even in suburban areas. DISTRIBUTION: Mountainous regions of W North America, south from S Alaska, across S Canada and northern E USA. Most Canadian birds winter in E and W USA.

54 NIGHTJARS AND NIGHTHAWKS

1 LESSER NIGHTHAWK (TRILLING NIGHTHAWK) *Chordeiles acutipennis*
19–23cm FIELD NOTES: At rest, tail reaches the end of primaries. In flight, male shows white patch on primaries (nearer to wing-tip than patch on Common Nighthawk), also white subterminal bar on underside of tail. Female lacks tail bar and primary patch smaller and more buff. VOICE: A toad-like trill *urrrr....* HABITAT: Dry open country, scrubland and desert. DISTRIBUTION: Summers in the S USA border states.

2 COMMON NIGHTHAWK *Chordeiles minor* 23–25cm FIELD NOTES: At rest, tail shorter than primary tips. In flight, male shows a prominent white patch at base of primaries and white subterminal band on underside of tail. Female lacks white in the tail. There is also a rufous morph in the SE. VOICE: A descending, buzzy *BEEErzh.* HABITAT: Open woodland or scrub, also suburbs. DISTRIBUTION: Summers over most of North America south of the tundra areas.

3 ANTILLEAN NIGHTHAWK *Chordeiles gundlachii* 20–21cm FIELD NOTES: At rest, tail just reaches primary tips. Flight pattern very similar to Lesser Nighthawk, although underwing less clearly marked with buff bars. VOICE: A descending, spluttering *pity-pit-pit* or *bztbztbzt.* HABITAT: Open or semi-open arid country. DISTRIBUTION: Summer in S Florida.

4 PAURAQUE (COMMON PAURAQUE) *Nyctidromus albicollis* 28cm
FIELD NOTES: In flight, male shows white bar on primaries and extensive white on tail. Female has buff primary bar and white on tail corners. VOICE: A buzzy *purwizheeeeer;* also a slurred *po po po po po po puppurrEEyeeeeeeerrrr.* HABITAT: Woodland clearings with dense bushy cover. DISTRIBUTION: S Texas.

5 POORWILL (COMMON POORWILL) *Phalaenoptilus nuttallii* 18–21cm
FIELD NOTES: In flight, male shows white corners on tail, smaller and duller on female. Some birds lighter than that shown. VOICE: A low, whistled *poor-will-ip.* HABITAT: Arid or semiarid country with scattered vegetation. DISTRIBUTION: Summers in W half of the USA and S Canada. Resident along much of the US-Mexican border.

6 BUFF-COLLARED NIGHTJAR (RIDGWAY'S WHIP-POOR-WILL)
Caprimulgus ridgway 21–25cm FIELD NOTES: In flight, male shows white corners on tail, female tail shows buff corners. VOICE: An accelerating *cuk cuk cuk cuk cuk cuka-cheea* or an accelerating and rising *tok tok tek tek tek teeka-teea.* HABITAT: Rocky arid or semiarid scrubland. DISTRIBUTION: Summers in S Arizona and S New Mexico.

7 CHUCK-WILLS-WIDOW (CAROLINA CHUCK-WILL) *Caprimulgus carolinensis* 27–34cm FIELD NOTES: In flight, males show white webs on inner webs of outer tail feathers, female has buffy tips on tail corners. Generally more rufous than other nightjars. VOICE: A loud *chuk weeo weeo* or similar. In flight utters clucks, growls or deep *quok* calls. HABITAT: Deciduous and mixed woodland, oak groves, open country and suburban areas. DISTRIBUTION: Summers in the SE half of E USA, resident in Florida.

8 GREY NIGHTJAR (JUNGLE NIGHTJAR) *Caprimulgus indicus* 28–32cm
FIELD NOTES: In flight, male has large white patch on primaries and white corners on tail. Female wing and tail patches are tawny-buff. VOICE: A rapid *tuk tuk tuk tuk tuk....* HABITAT: Clearings in mountain or hill woodland. DISTRIBUTION: Very rare vagrant from E Asia to the Aleutians.

9 WHIP-POOR-WILL *Caprimulgus vociferus* 22–27cm FIELD NOTES: In flight, male shows large white patches on tail corners, female tail corners smaller and buffy. Some birds are slightly more rufous than depicted. It is expected that SW birds will become a full species, known as Mexican Whip-poor-will. VOICE: Eastern birds give a loud *whip-poor-will* or *WHIP puwiwWEEW,* south-western birds have a more blurred *g-prrip prrEE.* HABITAT: Eastern birds occur in mature woods and south-western birds are found in mountain woodlands. DISTRIBUTION: Summers over much of E USA and SC and SE Canada, although only a migrant in SE USA; another population summers in SW USA.

55 SWIFTS

1 BLACK SWIFT *Cypseloides niger* 15–18cm FIELD NOTES: Gregarious, often occurs in large flocks feeding high in the air. Flight less erratic than smaller swifts, wing-beats shallow. VOICE: A soft *chip-chip* or *plik-plik-plik-plik*. HABITAT: Sea-cliffs, mountain canyons, often near waterfalls. DISTRIBUTION: Summers in scattered locations in W North America, from Alaska south to California and Colorado.

2 WHITE-COLLARED SWIFT (COLLARED SWIFT) *Streptoprocne zonaris* 20–22cm FIELD NOTES: Flight rapid and agile. In natural range, gregarious and often associated with Vaux's Swift. VOICE: A shrill *scree-scree*; also a rapid *chip-chip-chip*. HABITAT: Usually mountain forest areas, lower in bad weather. DISTRIBUTION: Rare vagrant from Mexico or the West Indies.

3 CHIMNEY SWIFT *Chaetura pelagica* 12–14cm FIELD NOTES: Usually gregarious. Wing-beats rapid and with a bat-like fluttering when feeding low down. VOICE: A chattering *chip chip chip chip....* HABITAT: Urban areas, farmland and woodland. DISTRIBUTION: Summers in USA and S Canada east of the Rockies.

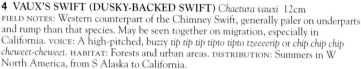

4 VAUX'S SWIFT (DUSKY-BACKED SWIFT) *Chaetura vauxi* 12cm FIELD NOTES: Western counterpart of the Chimney Swift, generally paler on underparts and rump than that species. May be seen together on migration, especially in California. VOICE: A high-pitched, buzzy *tip tip tip tipto tipto tzeeeerip* or *chip chip chip cheweet-cheweet*. HABITAT: Forests and urban areas. DISTRIBUTION: Summers in W North America, from S Alaska to California.

5 WHITE-THROATED NEEDLETAIL (NEEDLE-TAILED SWIFT) *Hirundapus caudacutus* 19–20cm FIELD NOTES: Flight fast and powerful. Below shows a white throat and a large white horseshoe-shaped area from tail to flank. VOICE: A high-pitched twittering. HABITAT: Wooded lowlands, thinly vegetated hills, feeds over river valleys and pastures. DISTRIBUTION: Very rare vagrant from Asia, recorded from the Aleutians.

6 SWIFT (COMMON or EUROPEAN SWIFT) *Apus apus* 16–17cm FIELD NOTES: Flight fast and powerful interspersed with long glides. The forked tail is not always noticeable during fast, direct flight. VOICE: A screaming *srrreeee*. HABITAT: Cities, towns, villages and cliffs, feeds over a variety of locations, especially lakes. DISTRIBUTION: Very rare vagrant from Europe.

7 FORK-TAILED SWIFT (PACIFIC SWIFT or NORTHERN WHITE-RUMPED SWIFT) *Apus pacificus* 17–18cm FIELD NOTES: Underparts show pale fringes, especially on belly and under-tail coverts. Usually in flocks mixed with other swift species. VOICE: A high-pitched *skree-ee-ee*. HABITAT: Sea and inland cliffs, mountains and urban areas. DISTRIBUTION: Rare vagrant from Asia, recorded from Alaskan islands.

8 WHITE-THROATED SWIFT *Aeronautes saxatalis* 15–18cm FIELD NOTES: Gregarious. Fast, dashing flight with swoops and quick changes in direction. White trailing edge to secondaries. VOICE: A descending *ki ki ki kir kir kiir kiir kirsh krrsh krrsh*. HABITAT: Mountains, cliffs and rocky canyons. DISTRIBUTION: Summers in W USA, north into S British Columbia. Resident SW USA.

9 ANTILLEAN PALM SWIFT *Tachornis phoenicobia* 10–11cm FIELD NOTES: Flight rapid and bat-like interspersed with glides. In natural range usually in small groups, which are occasionally mixed with swallows and martins. VOICE: A constant, high-pitched, weak twittering. HABITAT: Open cultivated and urban areas, usually with nearby palms. DISTRIBUTION: Very rare vagrant from the West Indies.

56 HUMMINGBIRDS

1 GREEN VIOLET-EAR (MEXICAN VIOLET-EAR) *Colibri thalassinus* 11–12cm
FIELD NOTES: Black band on tail. Can appear uniformly green. Female and juvenile
duller. VOICE: A repeated *chip-tsirr, tsip-tsup* or *chitik-chitik*. HABITAT: Woods with
clearings. DISTRIBUTION: Rare vagrant from Mexico, recorded mainly in Texas.

2 GREEN-BREASTED MANGO *Anthracothorax prevostii* 11–12cm FIELD NOTES:
In natural range feeds mainly at flowering trees, although often fly-catches, sallying
from a perch or by hovering and then darting after insect prey. VOICE: A repeated
chipping, a high-pitched shrill note and a series of thin *see* notes. HABITAT: Coastal
areas with scattered bushes and trees. DISTRIBUTION: Rare vagrant from Mexico.

3 BROAD-BILLED HUMMINGBIRD *Cynanthus latirostris* 9–10cm
FIELD NOTES: White mark behind eye on male often hidden. Juvenile males similar to
adult female, but with some blue feathers on throat and breast. VOICE: A chattering
je-dit, tetek or *tek*, similar to call of Ruby-crowned Kinglet. HABITAT: Rocky canyons
where springs or streams allow the growth of sycamore and mesquite. DISTRIBUTION:
Summers in SE Arizona and SW New Mexico.

4 WHITE-EARED HUMMINGBIRD *Hylocharis leucotis* 9–10cm
FIELD NOTES: Both sexes have a much bolder, white head stripe than shown by Broad-
billed Hummingbird. VOICE: A clear, repeated *tink tink tink....* HABITAT: Mountain
canyons. DISTRIBUTION: Rare summer visitor in SE Arizona.

5 XANTU'S HUMMINGBIRD (BLACK-THROATED HUMMINGBIRD)
Hylocharis xantusii 8–9cm FIELD NOTES: Unmistakeable. Gleans insects from trees as
well as feeding from blossoms. VOICE: A dry, chattering rattle and a high *chi-ti* or *ti-tink*.
HABITAT: Arid scrub and brushy woodlands. DISTRIBUTION: Very rare vagrant from
Baja California.

6 BERYLLINE HUMMINGBIRD *Amazilia beryllina* 8–10cm FIELD NOTES: Rufous
in wings best distinguishing feature from similar Buff-bellied Hummingbird. Upper tail
coverts dark violet. VOICE: A buzzy *drrzzzt* or *dzzzzir*; also a loud *bob-o-lek* or similar.
HABITAT: Mountain oak woods. DISTRIBUTION: Rare summer visitor to SW USA.

7 BUFF-BELLIED HUMMINGBIRD (FAWN-BRESTED HUMMINGBIRD)
Amazilia yucatanensis 10–11cm FIELD NOTES: Green-bronze upper tail coverts and
plain, dark wings. Can sometimes appear quite dark. VOICE: Hard chips that sometimes
run into a rattle. HABITAT: Lowland scrub. DISTRIBUTION: Summers in the Rio Grande
valley, Texas. Vagrant along Gulf coast.

8 CINNAMON HUMMINGBIRD *Amazilia rutila* 10–11cm FIELD NOTES: Female
similar to male but has red only on lower mandible. VOICE: Squeaky, chipping notes,
trills and thin chips. HABITAT: Arid scrub, pastures, second-growth woodland and forest
edge. DISTRIBUTION: Very rare vagrant from Mexico.

9 VIOLET-CROWNED HUMMINGBIRD *Amazilia violiceps* 10–11cm
FIELD NOTES: Unmistakeable. Crown often looks black. Juvenile crown brownish.
VOICE: A dry *tak* and a descending *seew seew seew....* HABITAT: Canyons with mesquite,
sycamore or oak. DISTRIBUTION: Summer visitor to SE Arizona and SW New Mexico.

10 BLUE-THROATED HUMMINGBIRD *Lampornis clemenciae* 13cm
FIELD NOTES: Large size, bronzy rump and dark bill separate from female of Broad-billed
Hummingbird. VOICE: A repeated, quiet, hissing rattle *situtee trrrrrrttt*; also a clear,
monotonous *seek*. HABITAT: Wooded canyons, especially near streams. DISTRIBUTION:
Summers in SE Arizona and SW Mew Mexico.

11 MAGNIFICENT HUMMINGBIRD (RIVOLI'S HUMMINGBIRD)
Eugenes fulgens 11–13cm FIELD NOTES: Male often appears all black. Juvenile male
similar to adult female but green below with pale fringes. VOICE: A sharp *chip-chip*; also
a buzzy warble. HABITAT: Pine-oak forests. DISTRIBUTION: Summer in SE Arizona, SW
New Mexico and SW Texas.

57 HUMMINGBIRDS

1 PLAIN-CAPPED STARTHROAT *Heliomaster constantii* 11.5–12.5cm
FIELD NOTES: Often makes low sallies to capture flying insects. VOICE: A loud *peek*; song transcribed as *chip chip chip chip pi-chip chip chip...*, or *chi chi chi chi whit-it chi....* HABITAT: Shrubby, arid woodland, woodland edge and thickets. DISTRIBUTION: Rare vagrant from Mexico.

2 BAHAMA WOODSTAR *Calliphlox evelynae* 8–9.5cm FIELD NOTES: Female has buff tips on outermost tail feathers. Feeds on nectar and by hawked insects. VOICE: A dry *prititidee prititidee prititidee*; also a sharp *tit titit tit titit*, which often speeds into a rattle. HABITAT: Mixed pine forests, forest edge, clearings, scrub and large gardens. DISTRIBUTION: Very rare vagrant from the Bahamas.

3 LUCIFER HUMMINGBIRD *Calothorax lucifer* 9–10cm FIELD NOTES: Male has a forked tail. Feeds on nectar and insects which are obtained by brief fly-catching sallies. VOICE: Twittering chips. HABITAT: Desert areas with agave, mountain slopes and canyons. DISTRIBUTION: Summers in SW Texas and S Arizona.

4 RUBY-THROATED HUMMINGBIRD *Archilochus colubris* 8–9.5cm
FIELD NOTES: Feeds on nectar; insects are taken during fly-catching sallies. VOICE: A squeaking *cric-cric*. HABITAT: Woodland edge, copse and gardens. DISTRIBUTION: Summers in E USA and S Canada, from Alberta eastwards.

5 BLACK-CHINNED HUMMINGBIRD *Archilochus alexandri* 10cm FIELD NOTES: Female very similar to Ruby-throated Hummingbird. VOICE: A husky *tiup, tiv* or *tipip*. Song is a weak warble. HABITAT: Dry scrub. DISTRIBUTION: Summers in W and SW USA.

6 ANNA'S HUMMINGBIRD *Calypte anna* 10–11cm FIELD NOTES: Feeds on nectar and insects, which are gleaned or hawked. VOICE: Song is jumble of squeaks and raspy notes. Call is a sharp *chick*. HABITAT: Chaparral, canyons, woodlands and coastal scrub. DISTRIBUTION: Extreme W North America, from British Columbia southwards.

7 COSTA'S HUMMINGBIRD *Calypte costae* 7.5–8.5cm FIELD NOTES: As well as nectar, takes insects by hawking or hovering. VOICE: A high, light, sharp *tik* or *tip*, often repeated to form a twitter. Song, a thin high, rising and falling buzz. HABITAT: Dry areas with sages, ocotillo and yuccas. DISTRIBUTION: Summers in extreme SW USA. Winters in S California and SW Arizona.

8 CALLIOPE HUMMINGBIRD *Stellula calliope* 8cm FIELD NOTES: Tends to feed on lower blossoms when taking nectar from plants. VOICE: A soft *tsip*. Song is a thin *tseeeee-ew*. HABITAT: Mountain glades and canyons. DISTRIBUTION: Summers in W mountain area from SW Canada south to California and S Colorado.

9 BUMBLEBEE HUMMINGBIRD *Atthis heloisa* 7.5cm FIELD NOTES: Bumblebee-like flight. Feeds mainly on nectar. VOICE: High chips. Song is a high, thin *sssssssssssiu* or *seeuuuuu*, fading at the end. HABITAT: Forest edge and clearings. DISTRIBUTION: Very rare vagrant from Mexico.

10 BROAD-TAILED HUMMINGBIRD *Selasphorus platycercus* 10cm
FIELD NOTES: Feeds on nectar and insects, which are gleaned or hawked. Male wings produce a loud trilling whistle. VOICE: A sharp chip. HABITAT: Pine and juniper forests, riparian and dry pine-oak forest. DISTRIBUTION: Summers in USA in the S and W Rockies and the Great Basin mountains.

11 RUFOUS HUMMINGBIRD *Selasphorus rufus* 10cm FIELD NOTES: A small number of males have a green upper back, making them virtually identical to Allen's Hummingbird. VOICE: A hard *tyuk*, an excited *zee-chupity-chup* and various chipping and buzzing notes. HABITAT: Coniferous forests, forest edge, clearings and mountain meadows. DISTRIBUTION: Summers in the far west, from S Alaska south to N California.

12 ALLEN'S HUMMINGBIRD *Selasphorus sasin* 10cm FIELD NOTES: Feeds on nectar and insects, which are hawked or gleaned. Female virtually identical to Rufous Hummingbird. VOICE: Similar to Rufous Hummingbird. HABITAT: Canyons, coastal chaparral, scrub and bushy slopes. DISTRIBUTION: Summers on Pacific coast from S Oregon to California.

58 PARAKEETS, TROGONS AND KINGFISHERS

1 BUDGERIGAR *Melopsittacus undulatus* 18cm FIELD NOTES: Popular cage bird that occurs in a variety of colours. In flight shows a yellow wing bar. VOICE: A subdued screech and a pleasant warble, the latter often uttered in flight. HABITAT: Grassland and suburban areas. DISTRIBUTION: Introduced populations in Florida.

2 GREEN PARAKEET (GREEN CONURE) *Aratinga holochlora* 32cm
FIELD NOTES: May or may not show the odd red feather on head or breast. VOICE: A raucous, shriek *krreh-krreh* or *kee-ik krii-krii kriir*; also a deeper *kreh kreh....* HABITAT: Forests, plantations and arid pine-oak forests. DISTRIBUTION: S Texas, some may be vagrants from Mexico.

3 CANARY-WINGED PARAKEET (WHITE-WINGED PARAKEET)
Brotogeris versicolurus 23cm FIELD NOTES: Gregarious. Upperwing shows white inner primaries and secondaries with yellow secondary coverts. Underwing also shows white inner primaries and secondaries. The very similar Yellow-chevroned Parakeet (not shown) lacks the white in wings. VOICE: A high, scratchy *krere-krere*; feeding flocks utter a high-pitched chattering. HABITAT: Residential areas. DISTRIBUTION: Introduced populations in Florida and California.

4 MONK PARAKEET (QUAKER or GREY-BREASTED PARAKEET)
Myiopsitta monachus 28–29cm FIELD NOTES: Gregarious and noisy. Flight swift with rapid wing-beats. VOICE: A loud, staccato shriek and a high-pitched chattering. HABITAT: Cultivated areas, orchards and suburban areas. DISTRIBUTION: Introduced populations in Florida, Oregon, Texas, Illinois and many areas in Atlantic coast states.

5 RED-CROWNED PARROT (RED-CROWNED or GREEN-CHEEKED AMAZON) *Amazona viridigenalis* 30–33cm FIELD NOTES: In flight shows distinct red patch on secondaries. VOICE: A harsh *kee-craw craw craw*. HABITAT: Suburban areas, wet forests and scrub. DISTRIBUTION: Introduced in various southern cities; birds from Texas may be genuine vagrants from Mexico.

6 ELEGANT TROGON (COPPERY-TAILED TROGON) *Trogon elegans* 32cm
FIELD NOTES: Sits quietly with short sallies to catch insects or pick fruit. Underside of tail finely barred black and white, with white tips. Juvenile similar to adult female but with white spots on wing coverts. VOICE: A soft, chattering brr *brr brr brr...*; also a monotonous, croaking *co-ah*. HABITAT: Dry woodland. DISTRIBUTION: Summers in SE Arizona.

7 EARED TROGON (EARED QUETZAL) *Euptilotis neoxenus* 33–35cm
FIELD NOTES: More mobile than Elegant Trogon, pairs move through trees in search of food. Underside of tail black with large white tips. VOICE: A squeal, with a rising end note *kweeeeeee-chk*. HABITAT: Montane pine forests. DISTRIBUTION: Rare vagrant from Mexico to S Arizona.

8 GREEN KINGFISHER *Chloroceryle americana* 22cm FIELD NOTES: Feeds by diving from a waterside perch, sometimes hovers. Regularly bobs head and pumps tail. VOICE: A clicking, similar to 2 pebbles being struck together; also a rapid, subdued ticking. HABITAT: Various freshwater and brackish water situations. DISTRIBUTION: SW Texas.

9 BELTED KINGFISHER *Megaceryle alcyon* 28–33cm FIELD NOTES: Usually feeds by diving from a perch but also hovers and dives in search of fish. VOICE: A harsh, rattling *kekity-kek-kek-kek-tk-ticky-kek*. HABITAT: Rivers, lakes, marshes, ponds and estuaries. DISTRIBUTION: Widespread in North America (only in winter in SW USA), south of the Arctic. Northern and central birds move south in winter.

10 RINGED KINGFISHER *Megaceryle torquata* 40cm
FIELD NOTES: Unmistakeable. Often uses the same perch for up to 2 hours. Also hovers when searching for fish prey. VOICE: A loud *kek*, *klek* or *klek-klek*; when alarmed, gives a rattling *klek-klek-klek-klek-klek....* HABITAT: Large rivers, ponds, coastal lagoons and estuaries. DISTRIBUTION: S Texas.

blue form

1

yellow form

♂

2

3

4

5

6

7

♀

♀

♂

♀

8

♂

9

♂

10

♀

♂

59 WRYNECK AND WOODPECKERS

1 WRYNECK (EURASIAN WRYNECK) *Jynx torquilla* 16–17cm
FIELD NOTES: Forages mainly on the ground in search of ants. VOICE: A plaintive *quee-quee-quee-quee* and a hard *teck* when alarmed. HABITAT: Open woodland edges and clearings, orchards, parks and large gardens. DISTRIBUTION: Very rare vagrant from Europe.

2 RED-HEADED WOODPECKER *Melanerpes erythrocephalus* 23–25cm
FIELD NOTES: Forages on trees and on the ground; also takes insects by making fly-catching sallies. In flight shows striking white secondaries and rump. Juvenile has a brown head, lightly streaked underparts and a black bar on secondaries. VOICE: A loud *queark, queeeah* or *krrrrr*. Drumming weak and short. HABITAT: Mature lowland forest, with open understorey, open woods, orchards, parks and gardens. DISTRIBUTION: Most of E USA and extreme S Canada, absent from SW Texas. Western and northern birds move south and east in winter.

3 LEWIS'S WOODPECKER *Melanerpes lewis* 26–28cm FIELD NOTES: Regularly makes sallies from a prominent perch to catch insects; also takes insects from the ground or gleans from trees or bushes. Often forms large flocks in winter. Juvenile lacks red face and is generally grey below. VOICE: A weak *teef*. Drumming weak, a roll followed by 3 or 4 taps. HABITAT: Open woodland, orchards and farmland with trees. DISTRIBUTION: W North America from British Columbia southward. Northern birds move south in winter.

4 ACORN WOODPECKER *Melanerpes formicivorus* 23cm FIELD NOTES: In flight shows white patch on primaries and a white rump. Feeds mainly in treetops, regularly makes fly-catching sallies. Drills holes in trees and posts to store acorns. VOICE: Noisy, rattling, whinnying and laughing calls; commonest being a nasal *whaaka-whaaka*. Drumming short with 2–20 evenly spaced taps. HABITAT: Oak and mixed pine-oak woodland. DISTRIBUTION: California and SW states of the USA.

5 GOLDEN-FRONTED WOODPECKER *Melanerpes aurifrons* 22–26cm
FIELD NOTES: In flight shows white rump and a small white area at the base of primaries. Feeds mainly in trees, also indulges in fly-catching sallies. VOICE: Contact call is a harsh *kirr*; also utters a rolling *churr-churr* and a cackling *kek-kek-kek-kek*. Drumming consists of a series of short rolls preceded by 1–4 taps. HABITAT: Dry woodlands, groves and mesquite bush. DISTRIBUTION: C Texas and SW Oklahoma.

6 GILA WOODPECKER *Melanerpes uropygialis* 21–25cm FIELD NOTES: In flight shows a barred rump and a white patch at base of primaries. Forages at all levels, from treetops to ground. VOICE: A loud, rolling *churr-ur-rr*, a laughing *geet geet geet geet geet* and a nasal, squeaky *kee-u kee-u kee-u*. Drums occasionally, with long regular rolls. HABITAT: Arid areas with scattered trees and large cacti, riparian woodland and around habitations. DISTRIBUTION: SE California, extreme S Nevada, S Arizona and SW New Mexico.

7 RED-BELLIED WOODPECKER *Melanerpes carolinus* 24cm FIELD NOTES: In flight shows a white rump, with a few black spots or bars and a white area at the base of primaries. Central tail feathers black in S Florida birds. Feeds in trees, mainly by gleaning; occasionally uses fly-catching to capture insects. VOICE: A loud, rolling *churr* or *churr churr churr*; also a chuckling, descending *chig chigh chchchchchch*. Drumming weak, rolls with a steady rhythm. HABITAT: Various open woodland, deciduous, mixed and swampy woodlands, also groves and trees in suburban areas. DISTRIBUTION: Widespread in E USA.

8 GREAT SPOTTED WOODPECKER *Dendrocopus major* 22–23cm
FIELD NOTES: Forages mainly in upper branches of trees; agile, often clinging acrobatically to extricate prey. Juvenile has a red crown. VOICE: A high-pitched *kik* or *chik*. Drumming rapid and far-carrying. HABITAT: Many types of woodland and forest, copses, parkland and gardens. DISTRIBUTION: Very rare vagrant from Europe–Asia.

60 WOODPECKERS

1 LADDER-BACKED WOODPECKER *Picoides scalaris* 17–19cm
FIELD NOTES: Forages in small trees, rarely on the ground. VOICE: A sharp *pwick*; also a rattling *cheekeekeekeekeekikk*. Drums with fast, short rolls. HABITAT: Dry semi-desert brushland, mesquite, cactus country and urban areas. DISTRIBUTION: Mexican border states, north into SE Colorado, S Nevada, SW Utah.

2 NUTTALL'S WOODPECKER *Picoides nuttallii* 18–19cm FIELD NOTES: Forages mainly in trees, occasionally feeds on the ground or by fly-catching sallies. VOICE: A *pitit* or *pit*; also a rattling *itititititit*. Drumming rolls last 1–3 seconds. HABITAT: Mainly open oak woods. DISTRIBUTION: California.

3 DOWNY WOODPECKER *Picoides pubescens* 15–17cm FIELD NOTES: Smaller than Hairy Woodpecker; outer tail feathers usually show black spots. Pacific coast birds *P. p. gairdnerii* (fig 3b) generally more buff. Juvenile has red crown. Forages mainly in trees, often visits garden feeding stations. VOICE: A short, soft *pik*; also a prolonged *peet-peet-peet-peet-peet-pit-pit-pitpit*. Drums in short, slow rolls. HABITAT: Deciduous and mixed forest, woods, parks and gardens. DISTRIBUTION: Widespread in North America, apart from Arctic areas and mountain areas in SW USA.

4 HAIRY WOODPECKER *Picoides villosus* 23–25cm FIELD NOTES: Larger than Downy Woodpecker, outer tail feathers generally unmarked white. Pacific coastal race *P. v. harrisi* (fig 4b) more buff, birds from Queen Charlotte Island, *P. v. picoideus*, similar but underparts lightly streaked. Juvenile has a red crown. Forages mainly in trees, occasionally on the ground. VOICE: A loud *keek* and a rapid whinny. Drumming fast, short rolls tending to slow towards the end. HABITAT: Wide range of dense mature woods. DISTRIBUTION: Most of North America south of Arctic areas, apart from parts of SW USA and Florida.

5 ARIZONA WOODPECKER (STRICKLAND'S or BROWN-BACKED WOODPECKER) *Picoides arizonae* 18–20cm FIELD NOTES: Juvenile has a red crown. Feeds mainly on tree trunks, occasionally makes fly-catching sallies. VOICE: A sharp *peep* or *keech*; also a descending rattle. Drumming long and loud. HABITAT: Pine-oak woodland or riparian woodland. DISTRIBUTION: SE Arizona and SW New Mexico.

6 RED-COCKADED WOODPECKER *Picoides borealis* 22cm FIELD NOTES: Juvenile has a red forehead. Forages mostly on tree trunks, often in small groups, occasionally makes fly-catching sallies. VOICE: A raspy, nasal *sripp*, *shrrit* or high-pitched *tsick*; also a rattling *shirrp-chrchrchrchr....* HABITAT: Mature pine forests. DISTRIBUTION: SE USA.

7 WHITE-HEADED WOODPECKER *Picoides albolarvatus* 24cm FIELD NOTES: In flight shows a white patch at base of primaries. Forages mainly on lower trunk of conifers with visits to needle clusters and cones, occasionally makes fly-catching sallies. Juvenile has a red crown. VOICE: A sharp *chick-chick* or *pitik*; also a rattling *peekikikikikik*. Drumming fairly long with varying tempo. HABITAT: Mixed conifer forests, in mountains. DISTRIBUTION: Pacific states of the USA and extreme S British Columbia.

8 AMERICAN THREE-TOED WOODPECKER *Picoides dorsalis* 21–23cm
FIELD NOTES: Primarily arboreal. Depicted are the nominate from the Rockies and dark race (fig 8b) *P. d. bacatus* from the east. NW race *P. d. fasciatus* has centre of back white, narrowly barred black. VOICE: A high-pitched *kip*; also a rattling *kliklikikli*. Drumming rolls slow, faster at end. HABITAT: Mature montane and boreal conifer forests, partial to burned areas. DISTRIBUTION: Boreal band from Alaska east to the Atlantic coast, also occurs on the Rockies, south to New Mexico.

9 BLACK-BACKED WOODPECKER *Picoides arcticus* 24cm FIELD NOTES: Mainly arboreal. Tends to forage on dead conifers and in less dense woodland than American Three-toed Woodpecker. VOICE: A sharp *kik*; also a grating variably pitched snarl. Drumming rolls long, accelerating at the end. HABITAT: Conifer forests, partial to burnt and windfall areas. DISTRIBUTION: Very similar to American Three-toed Woodpecker, although confined mainly to the N part of the US Rockies.

61 SAPSUCKERS, FLICKERS AND WOODPECKERS

1 WILLIAMSON'S SAPSUCKER *Sphyrapicus thyroideus* 21–23cm FIELD NOTES: In flight, male shows white rump and large white wing-patch, female shows a white rump. Mainly arboreal. Juvenile male has a white throat. VOICE: A strong *queeeah*; also a low-pitched *k-k-r-r-r*. Drumming begins with a roll followed by 2–4 slow taps. HABITAT: Pine forests. DISTRIBUTION: W North America, south from S British Columbia. Northern and eastern birds migrate south.

2 YELLOW-BELLIED SAPSUCKER (COMMON SAPSUCKER)
Sphyrapicus varius 19–21cm FIELD NOTES: In flight shows white rump and large white patch on upperwing. Juvenile generally brownish with a pale throat, crown brown with pale feather tips. Like others of the genus drills a series of shallow holes to form sap wells. VOICE: A nasal, squealing *neeah*; also a hoarse *wik-a-wika....* Drumming consists of about 5 rapid taps then slower with the odd double tap. HABITAT: Woodlands, aspen groves and orchards. DISTRIBUTION: Most of boreal Canada and NE USA, migrates to SE USA for the winter.

3 RED-NAPED SAPSUCKER *Sphyrapicus nuchalis* 19–21cm FIELD NOTES: Often considered as a race of Yellow-bellied Sapsucker, with which, apart from the red nape, which is sometimes absent, it is very similar. VOICE: Calls and drumming similar to Yellow-bellied Sapsucker. HABITAT: Forests, especially if containing aspen, aspen groves. DISTRIBUTION: Summers in W North America, from British Columbia and SW Alberta south to mid-western USA, with isolated populations in California, Colorado, Arizona and New Mexico. Winters in California, Arizona and New Mexico.

4 RED-BREASTED SAPSUCKER *Sphyrapicus ruber* 20–22cm
FIELD NOTES: Southern race *S. r. daggetti* (fig 4b) occurs from S Oregon southwards. Actions and habits similar to Yellow-bellied Sapsucker. VOICE: Calls and drumming similar to Yellow-bellied Sapsucker. HABITAT: Mixed deciduous and conifer forest, especially if aspen or ponderosa pine is present. DISTRIBUTION: Summers in coastal Pacific, from S Alaska to California; northern birds migrate south for the winter.

5 GILDED FLICKER *Colaptes chrysoides* 26–30cm FIELD NOTES: In flight shows a white rump and yellow underwing. Frequently feeds on the ground. Often considered a race of Northern Flicker, with which it is known to hybridise. VOICE: A descending *peah* or *klee-yer*; also a soft *wicka wicka wicka...* and a long *whit whit whit whit whit...* series. Drumming moderate to fast. HABITAT: Arid scrub and desert, with large cacti and yucca, also riverside woodlands. DISTRIBUTION: Extreme SE California and S Arizona.

6 NORTHERN FLICKER (COMMON or YELLOW-SHAFTED FLICKER)
Colaptes auratus 31–33cm FIELD NOTES: In flight shows a white rump and yellow underwing. Western race, Red-shafted Flicker *C. a. cafer* (fig 6b) has reddish underwing and grey face. Mainly arboreal, although will descend to forage or dust bathe on the ground. VOICE: Calls and drumming similar to Gilded Flicker, although the former a little lower-pitched. HABITAT: Open woodland, forest edge, open country with scattered trees, parks and gardens. DISTRIBUTION: Much of North America, apart from Arctic areas, SW Texas, extreme SE California and S Arizona. Winters in S British Columbia, extreme SW Alberta, throughout USA apart from NC states.

7 PILEATED WOODPECKER *Dryocopus pileatus* 40–43cm FIELD NOTES: In flight, from above, primaries show white bases, underwing white with black tips to primaries and secondaries. VOICE: A deep *wek* or *wuk* often given in flight, also given in series. Drumming slow and powerful, accelerating and fading at end. HABITAT: Mature forests. DISTRIBUTION: Across S Canada, E and Pacific states of USA.

8 IVORY-BILLED WOODPECKER *Campephilus principalis* 48–53cm
FIELD NOTES: In flight from above, shows distinctive white secondaries and inner primaries, underwing also shows white coverts. VOICE: A high-pitched, nasal *yank*. HABITAT: Mature, inaccessible forests. DISTRIBUTION: SE USA. Almost certainly extinct, recent sightings are disputed.

62 BECARD AND TYRANT FLYCATCHERS

1 ROSE-THROATED BECARD *Pachyramphus aglaiae* 18–19cm FIELD NOTES: Makes fly-catching sallies to glean from leaves or to take insects in mid-air. VOICE: A down-slurred *t-sseu*; also a squeaky chatter, ending with a thin, descending note. HABITAT: Riparian woods. DISTRIBUTION: Summer in extreme SE Arizona and extreme S Texas.

2 NORTHERN BEARDLESS-TYRANNULET *Camptostoma imberbe* 11cm FIELD NOTES: Secretive, best located by voice. Often flicks tail and wings. Feeds mainly by gleaning. VOICE: A thin, whistled *fleeceer* or *fleeeee-rit*; also a descending *piti pi pi PEEE dee dee*. HABITAT: Dense bushes or trees, usually near water. DISTRIBUTION: S Arizona and S Texas, the Arizona birds depart post breeding.

3 VARIEGATED FLYCATCHER *Empidonomus varius* 18–19cm FIELD NOTES: Hawks insects and hover-gleans from vegetation. VOICE: A harsh *chee-chee-chu*; also a thin, nasal *zreee* or *zreeetee*. HABITAT: Light woodland and forest edge. DISTRIBUTION: Very rare vagrant from South America.

4 PIRATIC FLYCATCHER *Legatus leucophaius* 15cm FIELD NOTES: May perch on high, exposed branch. Mainly fruit feeder. VOICE: Clear *tee-u* followed by a trill. HABITAT: Humid woodland and forest borders. DISTRIBUTION: Very rare vagrant from Mexico.

5 CROWNED SLATY FLYCATCHER *Empidonomus aurantioatrocristatus* 18cm FIELD NOTES: Usually perches and fly-catches from exposed branch at top of bushes or small trees. VOICE: A low *pree-ee-ee-er*, but generally silent after breeding. HABITAT: Forest edge and pastures with scattered trees. DISTRIBUTION: Very rare vagrant from South America.

6 GREENISH ELAENIA *Myiopagis viridicata* 13.5cm FIELD NOTES: Lively, makes short aerial sallies and hover-gleans. VOICE: A buzzy *cheerip*. HABITAT: Light woodland, scrub and plantations. DISTRIBUTION: Very rare vagrant from Mexico.

7 WHITE-CRESTED ELAENIA *Elaenia albiceps* 15cm FIELD NOTES: Often sits motionless for long periods in dense foliage. Gleans, including hover gleaning, for berries, nectar and insects. VOICE: Generally silent post breeding. HABITAT: Woodland borders and scrub. DISTRIBUTION: Very rare vagrant from South America.

8 TUFTED FLYCATCHER *Mitrephanes phaeocercus* 12–13.5cm FIELD NOTES: Makes fly-catching sallies, regularly returning to the same perch, often shivers tail on landing. VOICE: A bright *tchwee-tchwee* or *turree-turree*. HABITAT: Forest edge and clearings. DISTRIBUTION: Very rare vagrant from Mexico.

9 OLIVE-SIDED FLYCATCHER *Contopus cooperi* 18–19cm FIELD NOTES: Makes fly-catching sallies, often uses the same perch for weeks. VOICE: A sharp *quick three bears*; also a low *pep pep pep* or similar. HABITAT: Coniferous forests. DISTRIBUTION: Summers in the boreal zone from Alaska to Newfoundland, including area around Great Lakes and south through W mountains.

10 GREATER PEWEE *Contopus pertinax* 20cm FIELD NOTES: Makes aerial sallies, generally returning to same exposed perch. VOICE: A clear *ho-say ma-re-ah*; also a low *pip-pip-pip*. HABITAT: Mountain pine-oak woodlands. DISTRIBUTION: Summers in SE Arizona.

11 CUBAN PEWEE (CRESCENT-EYED PEWEE) *Contopus caribaeus* 15–16.5cm FIELD NOTES: Depicted is a bird from the Bahamas, Cuban birds brighter ochre below. VOICE: A prolonged thin whistle and a squeaky *eeah ooweeah dee-dee*. HABITAT: Forest, forest edge, bushy scrub. DISTRIBUTION: Very rare vagrant from the West Indies.

12 WESTERN WOOD-PEWEE *Contopus sordidulus* 15–17cm FIELD NOTES: Only reliably distinguished from Eastern Wood-pewee by voice. Makes sallies from perch to catch insects in the air or from foliage, returning to the same or a nearby perch. VOICE: A nasal, descending *peeyee* or *peeer*. HABITAT: Deciduous woods, woodland edge. DISTRIBUTION: Summers in W North America, from Alaska southward.

13 EASTERN WOOD-PEWEE *Contopus virens* 16cm FIELD NOTES: Feeding actions very similar to Western Wood-pewee. Voice only sure way to differentiate. VOICE: A plaintive *pee-a-wee*, which slurs down then up; also an up-slurred *pawee* or a down-slurred *peeaaa*. HABITAT: Woods and woodland edge. DISTRIBUTION: E USA and adjacent Canada.

63 TYRANT FLYCATCHERS

1 YELLOW-BELLIED FLYCATCHER *Empidonax flaviventris* 15cm FIELD NOTES: Distinct eye ring. Makes sallies from a low perch, taking insects in the air or from foliage, occasionally takes prey from the ground. VOICE: A liquid *che-lek*, a mournful *per-wee* and a loud *chew*. HABITAT: Spruce woodland on migration, often low down in shady woods. DISTRIBUTION: Summers in boreal Canada and NE USA.

2 ACADIAN FLYCATCHER *Empidonax virescens* 12–14cm FIELD NOTES: Long primary projection. Feeding actions similar to Yellow-bellied Flycatcher. VOICE: A loud *spit a KEET*, a loud flat *peek* and a slow whistled *pwipwipwipwipwipwipwi*. HABITAT: Deep, shady, wooded swamps. DISTRIBUTION: Summers in much of E USA.

3 ALDER FLYCATCHER *Empidonax alnorum* 15cm FIELD NOTES: Similar to Willow Flycatcher, best identified by voice. Feeding actions much as Yellow-bellied Flycatcher. VOICE: A harsh *rreeBEEa*, *fee-beeo* or *rrreep*; a clear *pew* or *peewi* and a flat *pip*. HABITAT: Alder and birch thickets in boggy areas. DISTRIBUTION: Summers in boreal areas from Alaska across Canada and in NE USA.

4 WILLOW FLYCATCHER *Empidonax traillii* 14–15cm FIELD NOTES: Shorter primary projection than Acadian Flycatcher. Distinguished from Alder Flycatcher by voice. VOICE: A harsh *BRRITZbeyew* or *rrreep-yew*; also a liquid *whit*. HABITAT: Low bushy areas, usually near water. DISTRIBUTION: Summers in S British Columbia and across much of N and C USA.

5 LEAST FLYCATCHER *Empidonax minimus* 12.5–14cm FIELD NOTES: Distinct eye ring and short primary projection. Feeding actions similar to Yellow-bellied Flycatcher. VOICE: A sharp, dry *pwit* or *pit*; also an emphatic, repeated *CHEbek* or *cheBIK*. HABITAT: Mature forests, forest clearings and edge and sugar maple woods. DISTRIBUTION: Summers across N USA and Canada, east of the Rockies and south of the Arctic.

6 HAMMOND'S FLYCATCHER *Empidonax hammondii* 12.5–14.5cm FIELD NOTES: Similar to Dusky Flycatcher, best distinguished by voice and habitat. Feeding actions as Yellow-bellied Flycatcher. VOICE: A 3-phrase *tsi-pik swi-vrk grr-vik*; also a sharp *peek* and a low *weew*. HABITAT: Mountain conifers. DISTRIBUTION: Summers in W mountains, from Alaska south to California and New Mexico.

7 DUSKY FLYCATCHER *Empidonax oberholseri* 13–15cm FIELD NOTES: Distinguished from Hammond's Flycatcher by voice and habitat. VOICE: A 3-phrase *sibip quwerrrp psuweet*; also a soft, dry *whit* or fuller *twip*. HABITAT: Low chaparral, brush and small trees. DISTRIBUTION: Summers in W North America, from S British Columbia to New Mexico.

8 GREY FLYCATCHER (WRIGHT'S FLYCATCHER) *Empidonax wrightii* 14–15.5cm FIELD NOTES: Gentle downward tail-wag is unique in the genus, others flick tails, quickly upward. Feeding actions as Yellow-bellied Flycatcher. VOICE: A 2-phrase *jr-vrip tidoo*; also a sharp *chivip* a low *weew* and a dry *whit*. HABITAT: Arid woodland, brushland and open pine forests. DISTRIBUTION: Summers in W North America, disjointedly south from British Columbia.

9 PACIFIC-SLOPE FLYCATCHER *Empidonax difficilis* 14–17cm FIELD NOTES: Virtually identical to Cordilleran Flycatcher, best distinguished by voice. Channel Island birds generally greyer than mainland birds. VOICE: A 3-phrase *tsip kiseewii pTIK*. HABITAT: Shady forest, often near water courses. DISTRIBUTION: Summers in Pacific coastal areas, from British Columbia to California.

10 CORDILLERAN FLYCATCHER *Empidonax occidentalis* 13–17cm FIELD NOTES: Virtually identical to Pacific-slope Flycatcher, from which it has been split. Voice only sure way to differentiate. VOICE: A 3-phrase *tsip kiseewii Ptik*. HABITAT: Forests and woods. DISTRIBUTION: Summers in the US Rockies.

11 BUFF-BREASTED FLYCATCHER *Empidonax fulvifrons* 11.5–13cm FIELD NOTES: Distinctive little flycatcher, feeding methods similar to Yellow-bellied Flycatcher. Juvenile much brighter orange-buff below. VOICE: A sharp, musical *PIdew piDEW PIdew piDEW*; a rolling *prrrew* or *pijrr* and a dry, sharp *pit*. HABITAT: Open pine forests. DISTRIBUTION: Summers in SE Arizona.

64 TYRANT FLYCATCHERS

1 EASTERN PHOEBE *Sayornis phoebe* 16.5–18cm FIELD NOTES: Makes frequent fly-catching sallies from a prominent perch. Persistently pumps and spreads tail. VOICE: A distinctive *fee-be* and a sharp *chip* or *tsyp*. HABITAT: Woodland, woodland edge, farmland, stream sides and farm and suburban buildings. DISTRIBUTION: Summers over most of E USA, apart from SE where mainly a winter resident, and C Canada.

2 BLACK PHOEBE *Sayornis nigricans* 15–18cm FIELD NOTES: Actions and habits similar to Eastern Phoebe. Juvenile has cinnamon fringes to body feathers and cinnamon wing bars. VOICE: 2, usually alternated, high whistled phrases *sisee sitsew sisee sitsew...*, also a thin *tseew*. HABITAT: Semi-open and shaded areas near water. DISTRIBUTION: California and SW USA, east to Texas.

3 SAY'S PHOEBE *Sayornis saya* 17–19.5cm FIELD NOTES: Pumps and spreads tail. Perches on or near ground, makes sallies to capture insects from air, foliage or the ground. VOICE: A plaintive *pe-ee*; also a low *pidiweew pidireep pidiweew pidireep....* HABITAT: Open dry areas, including prairie, sagebrush and barren foothills. DISTRIBUTION: Summers in W North America, from Alaska to California, usually away from coastal areas; winters from California across SW USA to Texas.

4 VERMILION FLYCATCHER *Pyrocephalus rubinus* 15cm FIELD NOTES: Pumps and spreads tail while perched. Juvenile very similar to female, streaking stronger below and undertail white. VOICE: A sharp *tsik*, *pees* or *peent*; also a tinkling repeated *pit-a-zee* or *p-p-pik-zee*. HABITAT: Bushes and trees, usually near water. DISTRIBUTION: Summers in US-Mexican border states, winters in S Texas.

5 DUSKY-CAPPED FLYCATCHER *Myiarchus tuberculifer* 18cm FIELD NOTES: Little or no rufous on tail. Inconspicuous wing bars. Fly-catches or hover-gleans from foliage. VOICE: A plaintive whistle and a rolling *pree-pree-prrreeit*. HABITAT: Shady woods, especially oak and sycamore in canyons. DISTRIBUTION: Summers in SE Arizona and SW New Mexico.

6 ASH-THROATED FLYCATCHER *Myiarchus cinerascens* 19–20.5cm FIELD NOTES: Very pale yellow below. Inner webs of tail rufous, shows when tail spread. Juvenile shows much rufous on tail. VOICE: A sharp *bik*, a *ki-brrrnk-brr* and a short *ka-wheer*. Song often transcribed as *tea-for-two*. HABITAT: Thorn scrub, open woodland and brushy pastureland. DISTRIBUTION: Summers in SW USA, from Oregon across to Texas.

7 NUTTING'S FLYCATCHER *Myiarchus nuttingi* 18–19cm FIELD NOTES: Very like Ash-throated Flycatcher although secondaries generally brighter, best distinguished by voice. VOICE: A sharp *wheek*, *wheep*, *wih-ik whi-ik* or *kwee-week*. HABITAT: Arid or semiarid scrubby woodland, thorn forests and semi-open areas with small trees and bushes. DISTRIBUTION: Very rare vagrant from Mexico.

8 GREAT-CRESTED FLYCATCHER *Myiarchus crinitus* 20.5–22cm FIELD NOTES: Shows much rufous in tail. Rarely occurs in same habitat as similar looking Ash-throated or Nutting's Flycatcher. VOICE: A rising *wheep*, often repeated; also an alternating *quitta queetoquitta queeto....* HABITAT: Deciduous woods, orchards, wooded pastures, parks and urban areas. DISTRIBUTION: Summers in E USA into adjacent Canada, resident in S Florida.

9 BROWN-CRESTED FLYCATCHER *Myiarchus tyrannulus* 20cm FIELD NOTES: Heavy bill, rufous on inner webs of tail shows when tail spread. VOICE: A sharp *h-whik*, *ha-wik* or *hwuik*, a longer *kir-ir-ik* and a rolling *prEErrr-prdrdrrr wrrp-didider....* HABITAT: Riparian woodland, thorn woodland and saguaro desert. DISTRIBUTION: Summers in SE California, S Nevada, SW Utah, S Arizona, SW New Mexico and S Texas.

10 LA SAGRA'S FLYCATCHER *Myiarchus sagrae* 19–22cm FIELD NOTES: Little or no yellow on underparts. Generally more grey. Captures insects and caterpillars during hovering flight, usually in the understorey. VOICE: A plaintive *huit* and a rolling *brr-r-r*. HABITAT: Pine woods, mixed woodland, thickets and scrub. DISTRIBUTION: Rare vagrant from the West Indies, recorded in Florida.

65 TYRANT FLYCATCHERS

1 TROPICAL KINGBIRD *Tyrannus melancholicus* 18–23cm FIELD NOTES: Longer billed than Couch's Kingbird, but best distinguished by voice. Red crown patch usually concealed. Uses a prominent perch from which it launches aerial sallies after insects, usually returns to the same perch or one nearby. VOICE: A twittering *tzitzitzitzitzi* or *pip-pip-pip-pip*. HABITAT: Often near water in open and semiarid scrubland with scattered trees, dry forest borders and areas of human disturbance, such as golf courses. DISTRIBUTION: Summers in S Arizona, resident in extreme S Texas.

2 COUCH'S KINGBIRD *Tyrannus couchii* 20–24cm FIELD NOTES: Shorter billed than Tropical Kingbird, but best distinguished by voice. Red crown patch usually concealed. Feeding technique similar to Tropical Kingbird. VOICE: A nasal *pik* and a buzzy *kweeeerz, brrrear* or *brreeah*; also an insect-like *dik dik dikweeeerz*. HABITAT: Scrubby woodland, forest edge and plantations, often near water. DISTRIBUTION: Summers in S Texas, resident in the Rio Grande valley.

3 CASSIN'S KINGBIRD *Tyrannus vociferans* 20.5–23cm FIELD NOTES: Pale tip to tail. Dark grey breast. Red crown patch usually concealed. Hawks insects from an exposed perch, often at the topmost branches of a tree. Also feeds at fruiting trees and shrubs. VOICE: A rough *sh-beehr, CHI-Vrrr* or *chi-bew*; also a nasal *breeahr breeahr....* HABITAT: Varied, including open country with scattered trees, dry country thickets and pastures. DISTRIBUTION: Summers in SW USA, extreme E Wyoming, SE Montana and parts of S Dakota and Nebraska.

4 WESTERN KINGBIRD *Tyrannus verticalis* 21–22cm FIELD NOTES: White outer tail feathers. Red crown patch is usually concealed. Feeding methods similar to Cassin's Kingbird. VOICE: A sharp *whit* or *kit*; also a rapid, rising *widik-pik-widi-pik-pik-pik* and a lower *kdew-kdew-kdew-kdew*. HABITAT: Variety of open areas, including grassland, sagebrush and urban areas with trees. DISTRIBUTION: Widespread in summer in W USA, north into adjacent Canada.

5 THICK-BILLED KINGBIRD *Tyrannus crassirostris* 20.5–24cm FIELD NOTES: Juvenile brighter yellow from belly to undertail and with rufous fringes to wing feathers. Red crown patch usually concealed. Hawks insects, often from a high, exposed perch. VOICE: A nasal *di-didweek, kidi-wik*, a buzzy *chweeer*, repeated and sometimes interspersed with clipped, nasal and bickering calls; also a stuttering *ki-di di-di di-di-dee-yew* or similar. HABITAT: Cottonwoods and mesquite, usually near water. DISTRIBUTION: Summer in extreme S Arizona.

6 GREY KINGBIRD *Tyrannus dominicensis* 21–23cm FIELD NOTES: Slightly forked tail. Red crown patch often concealed. Regularly uses bare treetops, telephone posts and wires from which to hawk for flying insects. VOICE: A chattering *pit-piteerri-ri-ree, tik-teeerr* or *preeerr-krrr*, and a trilled *tril-il-il-it*. HABITAT: Open areas with scattered trees, mangroves and scrub. DISTRIBUTION: Summers in Florida and SE Georgia.

7 EASTERN KINGBIRD *Tyrannus tyrannus* 19–23cm FIELD NOTES: White-tipped tail. Red crown patch usually concealed. Frequently perches in tall trees, hawks after flying insects. VOICE: A buzzy *kzeer*, and a series of spluttering notes ending in a descending buzz *kdik kdik kdik PIKa PIKa PIKa kzeeeer*. Early morning song is a rapid rattling, building to a crescendo *kiu kitttttttttiu didite*. HABITAT: Semi-open woodland, pastures with scattered shrubs and trees, orchards, shelterbelts, parks and gardens; often near water. DISTRIBUTION: Summers over most of North America, apart from Arctic, far W and SW areas.

8 LOGGERHEAD KINGBIRD *Tyrannus caudifasciatus* 24–26cm FIELD NOTES: Races shown are the nominate from Cuba and the buff-vented race *T. c. bahamensis* from the Bahamas (fig 8b). Orangey crown patch usually concealed. Feeding actions similar to others of the genus. VOICE: A variable loud chattering such as *jo-bee-beep*; also a bubbling, repeated *p-p-q*. HABITAT: Forests, mangroves and swamp edges. DISTRIBUTION: Very rare vagrant from the West Indies.

66 TYRANT FLYCATCHERS, TITYRA AND SHRIKES

1 SCISSOR-TAILED FLYCATCHER *Tyrannus forficatus* 31–38cm
FIELD NOTES: Underwing coverts bright pinkish-orange, juvenile has underwing coverts buffy and a shorter tail. Feeds by hawking flying insects, although tends to take prey from the ground more often. VOICE: A low, flat *pik, pik-prrr* or *kopik*. At dawn utters *pup-pup-pup-pup-pup-perleep*. HABITAT: Open areas with scattered bushes. DISTRIBUTION: Summers in SC states of USA.

2 FORK-TAILED FLYCATCHER *Tyrannus savana* 33–41cm FIELD NOTES:
Underwing coverts white. Female and juvenile shorter tailed. Uses exposed perch to launch sallies in pursuit of flying insects; occasionally takes insects from the ground or surface of water; also feeds on berries and fruits. VOICE: A very high-pitched *tik-tik-krkrkr....* HABITAT: Open savannah. DISTRIBUTION: Regular vagrant from South America.

3 GREAT KISKADEE (KISKADEE FLYCATCHER) *Pitangus sulphuratus* 25cm
FIELD NOTES: Uses exposed, low perch to hawk flying insects, pick prey from the ground and even catch fish like a kingfisher. VOICE: A loud *kis-ka-dee*, a loud *k-reah* or *kih-kerrr*. Dawn song is raucous *kyah k-yah zzk-zzik ky-ar*. HABITAT: Waterside woodland. DISTRIBUTION: S Texas.

4 SOCIAL FLYCATCHER *Myiozetetes similis* 16–18cm FIELD NOTES: Regularly perches with a half-cocked tail. Forages from treetops to ground, hawks for flying insects, drops to ground to collect prey and takes tadpoles from water. VOICE: A shrill, screamed *seea, tcheea* or *see-yh*. HABITAT: Semi-open areas with scattered trees, forest edge and plantations. DISTRIBUTION: Very rare vagrant from Mexico.

5 SULPHUR-BELLIED FLYCATCHER *Myiodynastes luteiventris* 19–22cm
FIELD NOTES: Frequently perches high in canopy. Hawks flying insects or makes sallies to glean insects from foliage. In flight shows a distinctive rufous tail. VOICE: A *wee iz-uh* or *weez-ih* that sounds much like a squeezy toy; also a squeaky series *whee whee-whee-whee-whee-i-eezk*. HABITAT: Broadleaf trees along mountain streams. DISTRIBUTION: SE Arizona.

6 MASKED TITYRA *Tityra semifasciata* 20–24cm FIELD NOTES: Often perches on a bare, exposed branch, feeds primarily on fruit; also pursues large insects in the air or from foliage. VOICE: A nasal, buzzing *zzzu rrk, zzr zzzrt* or *rr-rr-rrk*. HABITAT: Forest edge, forest clearings, semi-open areas with scattered trees. DISTRIBUTION: Very rare vagrant from Mexico.

7 BROWN SHRIKE *Lanius cristatus* 17cm FIELD NOTES: Usually perches prominently on bush tops or other vantage points from where it can pounce on large insects or small vertebrates. VOICE: A harsh *shack* or *shack-shack* and a trilling *jun-jun-jun*, *kichi-kichi-kichi* or *gey gey gey*. HABITAT: Open cultivation, open mixed forest and forest edge. DISTRIBUTION: Rare vagrant from E Europe and Asia.

8 GREAT GREY SHRIKE (NORTHERN SHRIKE) *Lanius excubitor* 24cm
FIELD NOTES: In flight shows large white patch at the base of the primaries. Perches prominently, often using the same vantage point for long periods, often hovers when searching for small vertebrate prey. Regularly pumps tail. VOICE: A harsh *shraaaa*; also a repeated *kdldi kdldi kdldi....* HABITAT: Open scrub, western birds favouring feltleaf willow. DISTRIBUTION: In the east summers in C and N Quebec, in the west from Alaska across N Canada to Hudson Bay, migrates south to winter from S Alaska, S Canada and much of N USA.

9 LOGGERHEAD SHRIKE *Lanius ludovicianus* 23cm FIELD NOTES: In flight shows large, white patch at base of primaries. Uses exposed perches from which to drop on to quarry; sometimes hovers while searching for prey. VOICE: A harsh *jaaa* and grating *teen raad raad raad raad raad*; song, a sharp *krrDI krrDI krrDI....* HABITAT: Quite variable, including open areas with low vegetation, small shrubs and trees, pastures, woodland edge. DISTRIBUTION: Widespread through the USA north into C Canada; central birds leave for the south in winter.

67 VIREOS

1 WHITE-EYED VIREO *Vireo griseus* 12.5cm FIELD NOTES: Sluggish and rather secretive when moving around in dense vegetation. Juvenile duller with darker eyes. VOICE: The song is a repeated *chip-a-tee-weeo-chip* or similar; calls include a *rik* or *rikrikrikrik-rik-rik-rik-rik*. Often includes the calls of other species into its song. HABITAT: Bushy woodlands, undergrowth, scrub and coastal thickets. DISTRIBUTION: Summers over most of E USA, resident in Florida and along Gulf coast.

2 THICK-BILLED VIREO *Vireo crassirostris* 13cm FIELD NOTES: Slow and secretive, more often heard than seen. Underparts vary from yellow to grey. VOICE: Song and calls are very similar to those of the White-eyed Vireo, but generally slower; the calls are usually longer. HABITAT: Woodland edge, bushes and undergrowth. DISTRIBUTION: Rare vagrant from the West Indies.

3 BELL'S VIREO *Vireo bellii* 12cm FIELD NOTES: Flicks and bobs tail in a nervous manner. Depicted are the eastern race and the duller western race *V. b. arizonae* (fig 3b); the race from California *V. b. pusillus* lacks yellow tone on underparts (not shown). VOICE: A nasal, rapid *sheh-sheh* or *chih-chih*. Song is a chatty *chewed jechewide cheedle jeeew*. HABITAT: Dense, low bush near water. DISTRIBUTION: Summers in SW and C USA.

4 GREY VIREO *Vireo vicinior* 14cm FIELD NOTES: Distinct pale eye ring. Active forager, flicks tail as it moves through foliage. VOICE: A low, rasping *charr, jerr* or *jerr-jerr-jerr-jerr*; also rough *cherrcherr....* Song is a hesitant *ch-ree ch-ruh chee-r ch-ree....* HABITAT: Primarily dry hillsides with scattered juniper-pinyon areas. DISTRIBUTION: Summers patchily in SW USA.

5 YELLOW-THROATED VIREO *Vireo flavifrons* 13cm FIELD NOTES: Bright yellow eye ring. Usually forages alone in treetops. VOICE: Song is a slow, slurred *rrreeyoo rreeoooe three-eight* or *de-ar-ie come-here three-eight*, on average repeated every 3 seconds. Call is a harsh, descending *chi-chi-chur-chur-chur-chur* or *ship-shep-shep-shep-shep-shep-shep*. HABITAT: Various types of forest, woodland, second growth and scrub. DISTRIBUTION: Widespread in summer in the USA.

6 PLUMBEOUS VIREO *Vireo plumbeus* 15cm FIELD NOTES: Feeds steadily in high parts of trees and shrubs. Originally considered part of the Solitary Vireo group, along with Blue-headed and Cassin's Vireo. VOICE: Call and song similar to Yellow-throated Vireo, the former often ending with a rising *zink*. HABITAT: Deciduous and mixed woods. DISTRIBUTION: Summers in WC USA.

7 CASSIN'S VIREO *Vireo cassinii* 14cm FIELD NOTES: Actions and habits similar to Plumbeous Vireo. VOICE: Song like Plumbeous Vireo, but slightly higher-pitched. Calls like Yellow-throated Vireo. HABITAT: Deciduous and mixed woods. DISTRIBUTION: Summers in SW Canada (British Columbia and SE Alberta) and W USA (NW Montana, N Idaho, N and W Oregon, Washington and California).

8 BLUE-HEADED VIREO (SOLITARY VIREO) *Vireo solitarius* 14cm FIELD NOTES: Habits and action similar to Plumbeous Vireo. VOICE: Song, a high-pitched, clear *see you cheerio be-seein-u so-long seeya* given, on average, every 2.5 seconds. HABITAT: Deciduous and mixed woods. DISTRIBUTION: Summers in the boreal zone of Canada and NE USA, south along the Appalachians; winters in Florida, the Gulf coast and Atlantic coast north to Virginia.

1

2

grey form

buff form

yellow form

3b

3

4

5

6

7

8

68 VIREOS

1 HUTTON'S VIREO *Vireo huttoni* 13cm FIELD NOTES: Incomplete eye ring. Looks like a chunky Ruby-crowned Kinglet. Often part of mixed species feeding parties, foraging in mid- to upper levels. VOICE: A rising, nasal *reeee dee de* or laughing *rrrreeeeee-dee-dee-dee-dee*; also a high, harsh mewing *shhhhhrii shhhri shhr shhr* and a dry *pik*. Song is a simple mix of 2 phrases: *trrweer trrweer trrweer - tsuwiif tsuwiif....* HABITAT: Moist woodlands, especially oak. DISTRIBUTION: Resident along the Pacific from SW British Columbia to California, also SE Arizona, SW New Mexico and SW Texas.

2 BLACK-CAPPED VIREO *Vireo atricapillus* 11cm FIELD NOTES: Distinctive head pattern. Active and acrobatic, although often hard to see when foraging in tangled understorey. VOICE: A harsh, rising *zhreee*, *sherr-sherr* or *dr-dr-dri*; also a dry *tidik*. Song consists of hurried, scratchy, warbled phrases. HABITAT: Semiarid scrub in oak-juniper stands. DISTRIBUTION: Summers through C Texas to C Oklahoma.

3 WARBLING VIREO *Vireo gilvus* 13–15cm FIELD NOTES: Forages in mixed species groups, from low down to upper levels. Western birds can be dingier on underparts. VOICE: A harsh, nasal mewing *meeerish*, *nyeeah* or *rreih*; also a dry *ch* or *ch-ch-ch....* Song is a long, rapid husky warble. HABITAT: Deciduous and mixed woodland. DISTRIBUTION: Widespread in W Canada, south of Arctic, most of USA apart from much of Texas and the SE.

4 PHILADELPHIA VIREO *Vireo philadelphicus* 13cm FIELD NOTES: Some birds can be less bright than that shown, when they can look very similar to Warbling Vireo. Forages in the low to middle level in trees; recorded hovering, or fluttering to pick insects from vegetation. VOICE: A descending *weeej weeezh weeezh weeezh*. Song very similar to Red-eyed Vireo but weaker and higher-pitched. HABITAT: Broadleaf forests, especially edges and clearings, also thickets and parkland. DISTRIBUTION: Summers across S Canada, east from NE British Columbia and adjacent areas in NE USA.

5 YELLOW-GREEN VIREO *Vireo flavoviridis* 14–15cm FIELD NOTES: Sluggish, forages in trees at the mid- to upper levels. VOICE: Song like Red-eyed Vireo but shorter and more rapid. Calls include a dry chatter and a rough mewing. HABITAT: Woodland, scrubby forest edge and plantations. DISTRIBUTION: Vagrant from Mexico.

6 RED-EYED VIREO *Vireo olivaceus* 14–15cm FIELD NOTES: Active but with 'heavy' movements; forages primarily in the tree canopy. Red eye only visible at close range. VOICE: The song consists of rambling, warbling phrases that often end abruptly *teeduee-tueed-teeudeeu...*, or *here-I-am-in-the-tree look-up at-the-top...*, each phrase given every 2 seconds. Calls include a soft mewing *meerf* and a nasal *tshay*. HABITAT: Forests, open woodlands, scrub and gardens. DISTRIBUTION: Summers in E USA extending west into NW USA and north into the boreal zone of Canada.

7 BLACK-WHISKERED VIREO *Vireo altiloquus* 15–16cm FIELD NOTES: Often sits motionless, best located by song. VOICE: Song is a monotonous *chip-john-phillip chip-phillip...chillip phillip*. Calls include a nasal mew, a thin *tsit* and a nasal chatter. HABITAT: Mainly broadleaf trees, including mangroves. DISTRIBUTION: Summers in coastal Florida.

8 YUCATAN VIREO *Vireo magister* 15cm FIELD NOTES: Forages slowly in thick vegetation, more often heard than seen. VOICE: Song consists of varied rich phrases, given in a tentative manner *chu-ree chu-i-chu ch-weet ch ee chu ch oo choo-choo....* Calls include a soft, dry chatter *shit chi-chi-chi-ch...*, a sharp *peek*, *beenk* or *peenk peenk*. HABITAT: Scrubby woodland, woodland edge and mangroves. DISTRIBUTION: Very rare vagrant from Mexico.

69 JAYS

1 GREY JAY (CANADA JAY) *Perisoreus canadensis* 27–31cm
FIELD NOTES: Generally in pairs or small groups, can become quite bold. Depicted are the nominate; also the US west coast race *P. c. obscurus* (fig 1b) and *P. c. capitalis* (fig 1c) from the US Rockies. VOICE: A soft, whistled *wheeeoo* and *weef weef weef*; also a musical, husky *chuf-chuf-weeff* and a harsh, grating *cha-cha-cha-cha* given in alarm. HABITAT: Primarily conifer forest, sometimes in mixed forest. DISTRIBUTION: Boreal Alaska and Canada south through the Rockies and the Cascades, also into NE USA.

2 STELLER'S JAY *Cyanocitta stelleri* 28–32cm FIELD NOTES: Forages in pairs or small groups, usually shy and wary although can be quite tame around campsites. Depicted are the nominate, the Queen Charlotte Island race *C. s. carlottae* (fig 2b) and the Rocky Mountain race *C. s. macrolopha* (fig 2c). VOICE: Very varied, including a harsh *shaaak shaaak*, a mellow *klook klook* and a mewing *hidoo*. HABITAT: Open conifer and mixed pine-oak forests. DISTRIBUTION: W mountain areas from S Alaska to California.

3 BLUE JAY *Cyanocitta cristata* 26–28cm FIELD NOTES: Unmistakeable. Usually forages alone or in pairs; may form small flocks post breeding. VOICE: Very varied, including a short, shrill *peeeah peeeah* and a high-pitched *too-doodle-up-to*. HABITAT: Deciduous and mixed woodland, parks and gardens. DISTRIBUTION: E USA, CS and NE Canada.

4 GREEN JAY *Cyanocorax yncas* 25–28cm FIELD NOTES: Unmistakeable. Generally shy, but can be quite bold and inquisitive, especially when in groups. VOICE: Very varied, including mewing, chattering, rattling, buzzing and squeaking notes. HABITAT: Bushy thickets, shrubby woodland and forest edge. DISTRIBUTION: S Texas.

5 BROWN JAY *Cyanocorax morio* 38–44cm FIELD NOTES: Juvenile a little paler with a yellow bill. Forages in small groups. VOICE: A high-pitched, nasal *peeeeah*; also makes a clicking or hiccupping sound. HABITAT: Open woodland and riverine forest. DISTRIBUTION: Extreme S Texas.

6 FLORIDA SCRUB-JAY *Aphelocoma coerulescens* 26cm FIELD NOTES: Usually encountered in pairs or small family parties. Feeds mainly on the ground near cover. Juvenile duller with a greyish head, blue confined to tail and flight feathers. VOICE: Calls include a low *kereep*, a sweet *ch-leep* and a rising *kreesh*. HABITAT: Scrubby oak thickets. DISTRIBUTION: C Florida.

7 ISLAND SCRUB-JAY *Aphelocoma insularis* 33cm FIELD NOTES: Unmistakeable, only jay on Santa Cruz Island. Juvenile greyer with blue confined to flight feathers and tail. VOICE: Very similar to Western Scrub-jay. HABITAT: Low growing oak chaparral, oak woodland and relict pine forest. DISTRIBUTION: Santa Cruz Island, off SW California.

8 WESTERN SCRUB-JAY *Aphelocoma californica* 28–30cm FIELD NOTES: Nominate birds usually more bold than those from the interior, interior race shown is *A. c. woodhouseeii* (fig 8b) from SC USA. Juvenile grey, with blue confined to tail and flight feathers. VOICE: A harsh, rising *shreeeenk*, a rapid *wenk wenk wenk...* or *kkew kkew kkew...*; also a pounding *sheeyuk sheeyuk*. HABITAT: Mixed oak, pine and juniper woodlands, scrubland and chaparral. DISTRIBUTION: Much of WC and SW USA.

9 MEXICAN JAY (GREY-BREASTED JAY) *Aphelocoma ultramarina* 28–30cm
FIELD NOTES: Often encountered in noisy groups, feeding among leaf litter. Juvenile generally duller greyish, blue confined to tail and flight feathers. VOICE: A ringing *wink-wink-wink....* Texas birds also give a mechanical rattle. HABITAT: Mountainsides and canyons with oak or pine-oak woodlands. DISTRIBUTION: SE Arizona and extreme SW Texas.

10 PINYON JAY *Gymnorhinus cyanocephalus* 25–27cm FIELD NOTES: Gregarious, often forages in large flocks. Juvenile dull greyish blue. VOICE: Varied, including a high-pitched *kwa-kwa-kwa-kwa*, a slow *kura kura kura* and a mewing *kraa-aha*. HABITAT: Pinyon-juniper forests. DISTRIBUTION: Mountain and plateau areas of interior W USA.

70 NUTCRACKER, CROWS AND RAVENS

1 CLARK'S NUTCRACKER *Nucifraga columbiana* 29–31cm FIELD NOTES: In flight shows black wings with white secondaries and black tail with extensive white on outer feathers. VOICE: A nasal *kraaaa kraaa kraaaa*. HABITAT: Mountain conifer forests. DISTRIBUTION: Mountain areas in W USA and SW Canada.

2 BLACK-BILLED MAGPIE *Pica hudsonia* 45–60cm FIELD NOTES: In flight, primaries white with black tips. Southern birds show bare grey-black skin around eye. VOICE: Various chattering and rattling calls. HABITAT: Open country with scattered trees. DISTRIBUTION: S Alaska, through W and S Canada and inland W USA, south to northern areas of Arizona, New Mexico and Oklahoma.

3 YELLOW-BILLED MAGPIE *Pica nuttalli* 43–54cm FIELD NOTES: Apart from yellow bill and facial skin, very similar in all aspects to Black-billed Magpie. VOICE: Very similar to Black-billed Magpie. HABITAT: Wooded rangelands and foothills. DISTRIBUTION: C California.

4 JACKDAW (WESTERN or EURASIAN JACKDAW) *Corvus monedula* 34cm FIELD NOTES: Juvenile has dark eyes. Often associates with other crows. VOICE: An abrupt, often repeated *chjak*. HABITAT: Open country with scattered trees, parkland and towns. DISTRIBUTION: Rare vagrant from Europe, mainly on the eastern seaboard.

5 CARRION CROW *Corvus corone* 48–56cm FIELD NOTES: Slightly larger than American Crow, best distinguished by voice. The Hooded Crow *C. c. cornix* (fig 5b) considered by most authorities a full species, although hybridises freely with Carrion Crow. VOICE: A vibrant *kraaa*. HABITAT: Varied, including farmland, open woodland and coastal cliffs. DISTRIBUTION: Very rare vagrant from Europe.

6 NORTHWESTERN CROW *Corvus caurinus* 42–45cm FIELD NOTES: Very sociable. Only reliably identified by range. VOICE: As American Crow, maybe slightly lower and hoarser. HABITAT: Shorelines, islands and coastal villages. DISTRIBUTION: Pacific coast, from Alaska to S Washington.

7 ROOK *Corvus frugilegus* 47cm FIELD NOTES: Loose thighs compared to crows. Juvenile lacks pale 'face'. VOICE: A dry *kraah*, higher-pitched *kraa* and various cawing, chuckling, gurgling and clicking noises. HABITAT: Primarily farmland with stands of trees. DISTRIBUTION: Very rare vagrant from Europe, recorded from Greenland.

8 TAMAULIPAS CROW (MEXICAN CROW) *Corvus imparatus* 37cm FIELD NOTES: Small size, the larger Chihuahuan Raven is the only other regular black crow in the area. VOICE: A frog-like *braarp*, *nark* or *gar*, often repeated. HABITAT: Open brushland and rangeland. DISTRIBUTION: S Texas.

9 AMERICAN CROW *Corvus brachyrhynchos* 43–53cm FIELD NOTES: Most widespread crow, usually in pairs or small parties, may form larger groups at good food source. VOICE: A short *ahhh*, *caaw* or *carr*, a rapid, rattling *tatatato* and a soft *prrrk*. HABITAT: Varied, including cities, farmland, woodland and shorelines. DISTRIBUTION: Most of North America south of the sub-tundra zone, apart from much of SW USA. Northern birds move south in winter.

10 FISH CROW *Corvus ossifragus* 36–41cm FIELD NOTES: Usually gregarious. Very similar to American Crow, best distinguished by voice. VOICE: A short, nasal *cah* or *cah-ah*; also a throaty rattle, higher pitched than American Crow. HABITAT: Coastal marshes, riversides and seashores. DISTRIBUTION: Coastal and river system areas from New England to Texas.

11 RAVEN (NORTHERN RAVEN) *Corvus corax* 58–69cm FIELD NOTES: In flight shows distinctive wedge-shaped tail. VOICE: Varied, including a deep hollow *pruk-pruk-pruk*, a hoarse *kraaah* and a low *brrronk*. HABITAT: Mountains, tundra and forests. DISTRIBUTION: W USA, W and E Greenland, Alaska and Canada, apart from the prairies.

12 CHIHUAHUAN RAVEN *Corvus cryptoleucus* 48–50cm FIELD NOTES: In flight shows slight wedged tail. Sometimes white feather bases show when preening or in a wind. VOICE: A rising *graak*, usually higher pitched than Raven. HABITAT: Primarily flat, arid grasslands. DISTRIBUTION: CS USA.

71 LARKS, PIPITS AND ACCENTOR

1 SKYLARK *Alauda arvensis* 16–18cm FIELD NOTES: Wings show a white trailing edge, tail has white outer feathers. Variable, from rufous-brown to grey-brown depending on wear. VOICE: Various warbling and trilling phrases mixed with mimicry and the odd call note, given from a high display-flight or low perch. Calls include a liquid *chirrup* and a short *preet*. HABITAT: Mainly open grassy areas. DISTRIBUTION: Introduced to Vancouver Island. Rare vagrant to W Alaska.

2 HORNED LARK (SHORE LARK) *Eremophila alpestris* 16–19cm FIELD NOTES: Variable, depicted are the nominate from E Canada, *E. a. adusta* (fig 2b) from S Arizona and *E. a. arcticola* (fig 2c) from Alaska and NW Canada. VOICE: Rippling trills followed by a short chatter, given from a perch or in flight. Calls include a short *tsee-titi* or *see-tu*. HABITAT: Barren areas with short grass or scattered bushes, winters on fields and shorelines. DISTRIBUTION: Virtually the whole of North America, apart from C Canada and SE USA, although occurs there in winter. Northern birds migrate to USA in winter.

3 TREE PIPIT *Anthus trivialis* 15cm FIELD NOTES: Walks with a slower, more deliberate gait than Meadow Pipit. VOICE: A thin, hoarse *tzeez*, when alarmed utters a *seet-seet-seet*. HABITAT: Woodland, woodland edge and grassland with scrub and trees. DISTRIBUTION: Very rare vagrant from Europe.

4 MEADOW PIPIT *Anthus pratensis* 15cm FIELD NOTES: Forages by walking or running, with slight tail-wagging. Overall colour varies (mainly due to wear) from that shown, to pale olive-buff above and whiter below. VOICE: A squeaky *seep* or *seep-seep-seep*. Song is a mixture of accelerating *seep* and *tseut* notes, gaining in pitch and ending in a long trill. HABITAT: Open grassy areas. DISTRIBUTION: W Greenland.

5 PECHORA PIPIT *Anthus gustavi* 14cm FIELD NOTES: Mouse-like skulker; often flies off without calling. VOICE: A *tsip* or *tsip-tsip-tsip-tsip*. HABITAT: Wet shrubby tundra, marshes and wet meadows. DISTRIBUTION: Rare vagrant from E Europe.

6 RED-THROATED PIPIT *Anthus cervinus* 14cm FIELD NOTES: Rufous areas on head can be less intense, or lacking altogether. Actions and habits similar to Meadow pipit. VOICE: A short *tew* or high-pitched *pseeeu*. Song consists of variable notes followed by thin rattling and buzzing notes, usually given during a display-flight. HABITAT: Breeds in marshy tundra. DISTRIBUTION: Summers in NW Alaska.

7 OLIVE-BACKED PIPIT (OLIVE TREE PIPIT) *Anthus hodgsoni* 14cm FIELD NOTES: Actions and habits similar to Tree Pipit. VOICE: A drawn-out *tseez* and when alarmed utters a weak *sit*. HABITAT: Mixed dense forest and open lowland forest. DISTRIBUTION: Vagrant from E Europe, mainly on Bering Sea islands.

8 BUFF-BELLIED PIPIT (AMERICAN PIPIT) *Anthus rubescens* 16cm FIELD NOTES: Walks with a light, dainty gait and bobbing tail. Birds from the Rockies have underparts deeper buff with little or no streaking. VOICE: A high-pitched *slip* or *slip-ip*, when flushed a higher *tseep* or *tsitiip*. Song, given in flight, consists of high jingling phrases. HABITAT: Open tundra, fields and shores. DISTRIBUTION: Summers in Alaska, N, NE and W Canada, also patchily in W USA. Winters across S USA.

9 SPRAGUE'S PIPIT *Anthus spragueii* 16cm FIELD NOTES: Does not bob tail. Usually solitary and secretive. VOICE: A high-pitched *squeet* or *squeet-squeet....* Song, given during a high display-flight, is a descending series of rattling, harsh metallic notes. HABITAT: Grassy plains, open grassy, weedy areas. DISTRIBUTION: The N Great Plains of Canada and USA; winters in Texas and adjacent states.

10 SIBERIAN ACCENTOR *Prunella montanella* 15cm FIELD NOTES: Twitches wings as it creeps, mouse-like, in undergrowth. VOICE: A ringing *tsee-ree-see*. HABITAT: Stunted birch and conifer woodlands, also waterside thickets. DISTRIBUTION: Rare vagrant from Siberia.

72 WAGTAILS AND DIPPER

1 EASTERN YELLOW WAGTAIL (YELLOW or ALASKAN YELLOW WAGTAIL) *Motacilla (flava) tshutshensis* 16cm FIELD NOTES: Actions and habits similar to Citrine Wagtail. Juvenile greyer above, with a black moustachial streak and upper breast-band, *see* Citrine Wagtail for juvenile comparison. Asian race of Yellow Wagtail, a vagrant to the Pribilofs and Aleutians, is very similar but lacks the smudgy breast marks. Many authors regard Eastern Yellow Wagtail as just one of the myriad of races of the Yellow Wagtail. VOICE: In flight gives a vibrant *tzeer, tsewee* or a clear *tzeen tzeen tzeen*. Song notes similar to calls, but repeated *tzeeu tzeeu tzeek*.... HABITAT: Tundra, marsh edge and bushy fields. DISTRIBUTION: Summers in N and W Alaska.

2 CITRINE WAGTAIL (YELLOW-HOODED WAGTAIL) *Motacilla citreola* 17cm FIELD NOTES: Tail wagging less pronounced than that of White Wagtail. Often perches on vegetation, posts, mounds, bushes or wires. Juvenile very similar to juvenile Eastern Yellow Wagtail, but pale eye-brow is broader, wing bars are broader and edges of secondaries are white rather than yellowish. VOICE: A sharp *tzreep, tcheep* or *tchreep*. Song similar to Eastern Yellow Wagtail, but usually more varied; *tzreeep – tchip-tchip... tzreeep...tzreep...tzreep-tcheree-tche-tche...tzreeep...tcherewe-tche-tche*. HABITAT: Similar to Eastern Yellow Wagtail. DISTRIBUTION: Very rare vagrant from Siberia.

3 GREY WAGTAIL *Motacilla cinerea* 19cm FIELD NOTES: Constantly pumps rear body and tail. In flight, underwing shows a wide white wing bar. Often perches on trees and bushes overhanging water. VOICE: A high-pitched *zit, zit-zit* or *tzi-tzi-tzit*; when alarmed utters a rapid *tzihihihihihi*. HABITAT: Primarily by fast-flowing hill streams and rivers in wooded areas; on migration and in winter spreads to various water-edge places. DISTRIBUTION: Rare vagrant from Europe.

4 WHITE WAGTAIL (SWINHOE'S WHITE WAGTAIL) *Motacilla alba ocularis* 17cm FIELD NOTES: Non-breeding female has a greyish-white throat. Walks with a nodding head while wagging tail up and down. Agile insect feeder using running, jumping or acrobatic short fluttering flights to capture prey. Often perches on bushes, trees, fences, buildings wires etc. Also depicted is M. *a. lugens* Black-backed Wagtail (fig 4b), a vagrant from Siberia, that is often considered a full species. VOICE: A *tslee-wee, tslee-vit* or similar, often repeated. Song consists of a single repeated note *tchelee, psiwip, psilii* or similar, or a complex twittering interspersed with call notes. HABITAT: Open areas, usually near water. DISTRIBUTION: Summers in extreme NW Alaska.

5 AMERICAN DIPPER *Cinclus mexicanus* 19cm FIELD NOTES: Bobs whole body while perched. Swims and walks underwater, feeding on stream or river bottoms. Juvenile has a pale yellowish bill and pale feather fringes on underparts, wings and tail coverts. VOICE: A metallic *zeet* or a rapid *dzik-dzik*. Song is a bubbling *k-tee k-tee wij-ij-ij treeoo treeoo tsebrr tsebrr tsebrr tsebrr*.... HABITAT: Fast-flowing rivers or streams. DISTRIBUTION: Resident in W North America, from the Aleutians, much of Alaska and then south along the Rockies and coastal mountains.

1

♀

♂

2

♀

♂

3

♂ n-br

♂ br

4

4b

♀ br

♂ n-br

4b

♂ br

♀ br

♂ br

5

73 MARTINS AND SWALLOW

1 PURPLE MARTIN *Progne subis* 19–22cm FIELD NOTES: Western females are paler below and have a whitish collar. Forages high in the air, frequently at 50m or more. Less manoeuvrable than smaller swallows, alternates flapping flight with gliding on outstretched wings. VOICE: A rich *cherr* and a melodious whistle; also a gurgling croak uttered by the male, while the female gives various chortles. HABITAT: Open areas, often near water; also villages and towns. DISTRIBUTION: Summers in E USA, the Canadian prairies and along the Pacific coast, south from British Columbia; patchy breeder in the Rockies, occurring in Arizona, W New Mexico, W Colorado and N Utah.

2 CUBAN MARTIN *Progne cryptoleuca* 18–19cm FIELD NOTES: Foraging techniques similar to Purple Martin, which means high-flying birds are virtually impossible to identify. Often considered to be a race of Purple Martin. VOICE: A melodious warble and a gurgling that includes a high-pitched *twick-twick* similar to, but said to be distinct from, those of Purple Martin. HABITAT: Lowland open areas, swamp borders, towns and cities. DISTRIBUTION: Very rare vagrant from Cuba.

3 SOUTHERN MARTIN *Progne elegans* 17cm FIELD NOTES: Forages alone or in small groups, at high or low level. Flight is slow and weak with much gliding. VOICE: Calls similar to Purple Martin. HABITAT: Grasslands, dry forest and around human habitations. DISTRIBUTION: Very rare vagrant from South America.

4 GREY-BREASTED MARTIN (WHITE-BELLIED MARTIN) *Progne chalybea* 16–18cm FIELD NOTES: Forages at medium heights; spends much time gliding, interspersed with fast flapping when chasing insects; also recorded feeding on the ground when there is an abundant source of insects. VOICE: Variable, including a *cheur*, a rattle and a *zurr*. HABITAT: Lowland woodland, forest clearings, savannah, farmland, coastal mangroves around human habitations. DISTRIBUTION: Very rare vagrant from Mexico.

5 BROWN-CHESTED MARTIN *Progne tapera* 16cm FIELD NOTES: Forages alone or in small groups. Flight is fast and low over vegetation or water, slower and weaker around trees or open ground. VOICE: A *chu-chu-chip* contact call. HABITAT: Open or semi-open areas with trees, often near water; also around human habitations. DISTRIBUTION: Very rare vagrant from South America.

6 SWALLOW (BARN SWALLOW) *Hirundo rustica* 15–19cm FIELD NOTES: Flight is fast and agile, with twist and turns when chasing flying insects. Regularly forages in flocks over open areas. Female and juvenile generally paler below, the latter with much shorter outer tail feathers. VOICE: A thin *vit* or *vit*; also a sharper *vit-VEET* given when alarmed. Song is a melodious twittering interspersed with a grating rattle, given in flight or when perched. HABITAT: Primarily open country where buildings are available for nest sites. DISTRIBUTION: Summers in North America north to the tree line, apart from S Florida and extreme SW USA.

7 HOUSE MARTIN (COMMON or NORTHERN HOUSE MARTIN)
Delichon urbica 13cm FIELD NOTES: In flight shows a conspicuous white rump. Less twisting flight than Swallow, more gliding and soaring, often at a great height. VOICE: An abrupt *prrt* or longer *pri-pit*. Song consists of a soft, rapid twittering interspersed with a dry rattling. HABITAT: Around buildings in towns, villages or farms. DISTRIBUTION: Rare vagrant from Europe.

74 SWALLOWS

1 TREE SWALLOW *Tachycineta bicolor* 13–15cm FIELD NOTES: Usually alone or in small groups. Flight light, often straight and direct with sudden dips or turns to catch prey. VOICE: A high chirping or twittering; when alarmed, a harsh chatter. Song starts with 3 descending notes followed by a liquid warble. HABITAT: Open woodlands, near water. Needs dead trees for nest holes. DISTRIBUTION: Widespread in summer over much of North America, from C Alaska, Canada, north to the tree line, N USA south to Tennessee in the east and C California in the west. Winters in S California, W Arizona and coastally from S Texas to Virginia.

2 MANGROVE SWALLOW *Tachycineta albilinea* 11–12cm FIELD NOTES: Feeds alone or in pairs. Flight generally direct with fast wing-beats and some gliding, normally low over water. VOICE: A chirping *chiri-chrit*, *chrit* or *chriet*. HABITAT: Coastal areas, including beaches and mangroves, inland over various water bodies such as lakes, marshes and rivers. DISTRIBUTION: Very rare vagrant from Mexico.

3 BAHAMA SWALLOW *Tachycineta cyaneoviridis* 15cm FIELD NOTES: Active mainly in the evening or during overcast weather, chasing insects either high up, where gliding flight seems to be the norm, or low over the ground in a rapid darting flight. VOICE: A metallic *chep* or *chi-chep* and a plaintive *seew-seew-seew-sew*. HABITAT: Pine forests, woodland clearings, open fields and urban areas. DISTRIBUTION: Rare vagrant from the Bahamas, primarily to Florida.

4 VIOLET-GREEN SWALLOW *Tachycineta thalassina* 12–13cm FIELD NOTES: Females generally duller than males, juvenile grey above with a dusky face. Flight rapid and direct including some gliding. Forages in small groups or loose flocks. VOICE: A *chee-che*, *chilip* or *chip-lip*; also a creaking *twee tsip-tsip-tsip*.... HABITAT: Open coniferous, deciduous or mixed woodland and around human habitations; feeds over open country, water or forest canopy. DISTRIBUTION: Summers in W North America, from Alaska south to Mexico.

5 NORTHERN ROUGH-WINGED SWALLOW *Stelgidopteryx serripennis* 13cm FIELD NOTES: Flight direct with leisurely, purposeful wing-beats; usually forages low over water or land. Juveniles have bright cinnamon wing bars on upperwing coverts. VOICE: A low, harsh *prrit*. Song is a rising *frrip-frrip-frrip*.... HABITAT: Open areas near water; requires banks for nest holes. DISTRIBUTION: Widespread in summer in the USA and S Canada.

6 SAND MARTIN (BANK SWALLOW) *Riparia riparia* 12cm FIELD NOTES: Rapid, light flight usually low over water or ground. Nests colonially. VOICE: A short, harsh, often repeated *tschr*, *chirr* or *shrrit*. Song is a repeated *wit wit dreee drr drr drr*. HABITAT: Open lowland country, especially near water; requires banks for nest holes. DISTRIBUTION: Widespread in summer in North America, apart from the far north and S USA.

7 CLIFF SWALLOW (AMERICAN CLIFF SWALLOW) *Petrochelidon pyrrhonota* 13–15cm FIELD NOTES: Usually encountered in flocks, hawking insects both high in the air and near to the ground; frequently soars and glides. Nests colonially. VOICE: A soft, husky *verr*, *purr* or *chur*. The song is a creaky twittering. HABITAT: Farms, towns and cliffs. DISTRIBUTION: Widespread in summer over North America, apart from the Arctic north and SE USA.

8 CAVE SWALLOW *Petrochelidon fulva* 12.5–14cm FIELD NOTES: Usually in loose, small or large flocks; flight strong with frequent periods of gliding. Nests colonially. A few birds may show a dark spot on throat. VOICE: Calls include a *chu-chu*, *weet*, *cheweet* and a short *choo*. Song is a series of squeaks and a warble ending with a series of 2-toned notes. HABITAT: Caves or artificial structures, such as bridges or churches. DISTRIBUTION: Summers in S New Mexico and Texas and in S Florida.

75 VERDIN, BUSHTIT AND CHICKADEES

1 VERDIN *Auriparus flaviceps* 10–11cm FIELD NOTES: Active, usually forages alone but also in pairs or family parties. Juvenile lacks yellow, head grey contiguous with rest of upperparts, throat and underparts pale grey. VOICE: A sharp *tschep*, *tschik* or *chip*, the latter often repeated. Song is a whistled *chee-chee-chee...* or similar. HABITAT: Dry scrubland. DISTRIBUTION: SW USA, from SE California to Texas.

2 BUSHTIT *Psaltriparus minimus* 11cm FIELD NOTES: Active and confiding. Forms small to large flocks after breeding. Depicted are: the nominate Pacific race; the interior race *P. m. plumbeus* (fig 2b); and the SW Texas form '*P. m. lloydi*' (fig 2c), not all of which have a full black mask, some forms having only black ear-coverts and various intermediates occur. There is much variation, with intermediates where ranges meet. VOICE: An emphatic *pit* or *tsit*, a *skrrti ti ti*; travelling groups sometimes utter a trilling *pit pit pit sre-e-e-e-e-e* or *srrit srrit srrit sisisi*, the latter given when anxious. HABITAT: Dry open woodland, woodland edge scrub and chaparral. DISTRIBUTION: SW British Columbia south to California, then east to W Texas.

3 CAROLINA CHICKADEE *Poecile carolinensis* 11–12cm FIELD NOTES: Very similar to Black-capped Chickadee, but is smaller headed, shorter tailed, has less distinct pale wing edges and is usually duller. VOICE: Call is a high-pitched, rapid *chikadeedeedeedee*. Song is a *fee-bee fee-bay*, *sufee-subee* or similar. HABITAT: Broadleaf woodlands, especially along watercourses, swamp forest, parks and wooded gardens. DISTRIBUTION: SE USA.

4 BLACK-CAPPED CHICKADEE *Poecile atricapilla* 13–15cm FIELD NOTES: Large headed with distinct whitish wing edges. Birds from the NW *P. a. turneri* (fig 4b) have greyer flanks. Tame and confiding; regular member of winter mixed species flocks. VOICE: A sharp *chik* leading to a slow *chick-a-dee-dee-dee*. Song is a *fee-bee* or *fee-bee-ee*. HABITAT: Open woodlands, clearings, parks and gardens. DISTRIBUTION: Boreal Alaska and Canada southward over N half of USA.

5 MOUNTAIN CHICKADEE *Poecile gambeli* 13cm FIELD NOTES: When worn, white eye-brow can become indistinct. Pacific coast birds from W Canada and NW USA *P. g. baileyae* (fig 5b) are generally greyer. VOICE: A harsh *chick-adee-adee-adee*. Typical song is a *fee-bee-bay* or *fee-bee fee-bee*. HABITAT: Montane conifer forest; moves to lower level forest or scrub in winter. DISTRIBUTION: Mountainous areas of W North America.

6 MEXICAN CHICKADEE *Poecile sclateri* 13cm FIELD NOTES: Large black bib and dark grey flanks. VOICE: A buzzy *sschleeeer*, also buzzy trills followed by a hissing *tzee tzee tzee shhhh shhhh*. In song gives a *peeta peeta peeta*. HABITAT: Open montane conifer forests and deciduous woodland. DISTRIBUTION: Extreme SE Arizona and SW New Mexico.

7 CHESTNUT-BACKED CHICKADEE *Poecile rufescens* 12cm FIELD NOTES: Distinctive. The greyer flanked race *P. r. barlowi* (fig 7b) occurs in S coastal California. VOICE: A rapid, hoarse *tseek-a-dee-dee*, a nasal *tsidi-tsidi-tsidi-cheer-cheer* and a weak *tsity ti jee jee*. HABITAT: Coniferous and mixed woods. DISTRIBUTION: Extreme W North America, from Alaska to California.

8 BOREAL CHICKADEE *Poecile hudsonica* 14cm FIELD NOTES: Grey rear cheeks. Occurs in small flocks after breeding, often part of mixed species flocks. VOICE: A nasal *tseek-a-day-day*, *tsi-jaaaay* or *tsi ti jaaaay jaaay*. Song is a simple trill *p-twee-titititititititititi*. HABITAT: Primarily dense boreal conifer forest. DISTRIBUTION: Boreal Alaska, Canada and far north of E USA.

9 SIBERIAN TIT (GREY-HEADED CHICKADEE) *Poecile cincta* 14cm FIELD NOTES: Very similar to Boreal Chickadee, but longer tailed and rear of cheeks white. VOICE: Calls, which are lower than Boreal Chickadee, include a thin *chit-sit*, *si-si*, *tsit* and a sharp *chik*, like tapping stones together. HABITAT: Mature willows along watercourses, spruce forest and in winter in aspen and alder. DISTRIBUTION: N Alaska and extreme NW Canada.

1 BRIDLED TITMOUSE *Baeolophus wollweberi* 13cm FIELD NOTES: Unmistakeable. Forms small parties after breeding; also occurs in mixed species flocks. VOICE: A rapid, harsh chatter *ji ji ji ji ji* or *jededededed*. Song is a rapid, whistled *pidi pidi pidi pidi pidi* or *pipipipi....* HABITAT: Primarily mountain evergreen oak, pine and juniper woods. DISTRIBUTION: S Arizona and SW New Mexico.

2 OAK TITMOUSE *Baeolophus inornatus* 15cm FIELD NOTES: More often heard than seen. Generally forages in the upper storey. Originally lumped with Juniper Titmouse under the name Plain Titmouse. VOICE: A *si si si chrr* or *pi pi pi peeew*. Song variable, including a *chuwi-chuwi-chuwi-chuw* and a *chit it-chit it-chit it....* HABITAT: Dry open woods, especially of oak. DISTRIBUTION: SW Oregon south to S California.

3 JUNIPER TITMOUSE *Baeolophus ridgwayi* 15cm FIELD NOTES: Action and habits similar to Oak Titmouse. VOICE: A rapid *sisisi-ch-ch-ch-ch*, *si-ch-ch-ch* or similar. Song lower and faster than Oak Titmouse *jijiji jijiji jijiji....* HABITAT: Juniper-pinyon woodland, scrub oak and ponderosa pine, alder and willow in winter. DISTRIBUTION: Inland in SW USA.

4 TUFTED TITMOUSE *Baeolophus bicolor* 17cm FIELD NOTES: Generally occurs singly or in pairs, foraging at all levels, including on the ground. VOICE: Calls include a *chick-a-dee*, a harsh *tsee-day-day-day* and when excited a *sit-sit-sit*. Song is a fast or slow *peter-peter-peter-peter* or variants. HABITAT: Deciduous and mixed woodland, wooded farmland, parks and suburban gardens. DISTRIBUTION: E USA.

5 BLACK-CRESTED TITMOUSE *Baeolophus atlicristatus* 17cm FIELD NOTES: Often considered a race of Tufted Titmouse, actions and habits similar; intergrades occur where ranges overlap, showing dark grey crown. VOICE: Similar to Tufted Titmouse, but generally louder and more nasal. Calls include a *si-si-cha-cha*, *pete-chee-chee-chee* and a scolding *cher-cher-cher-cher....* Song is a slurred *peew peew peew peew peew....* HABITAT: Dry forest and scrub. DISTRIBUTION: C Texas, from the Mexican border into SW Oklahoma.

6 BROWN CREEPER *Certhia americana* 13–15cm FIELD NOTES: Forages, with a jerky creeping action, from base of trees upwards. Occurs in brown and greyish morphs. VOICE: A thin *seee* or *sreee*, western birds utter a buzzier *teeesee*. Song variable, often transcribed as *trees trees pretty little trees.* HABITAT: Coniferous, mixed and deciduous forests. DISTRIBUTION: Resident across North America in conifer zone and south into mountainous regions of W and E USA. Winters throughout the rest of the USA.

7 RED-BREASTED NUTHATCH *Sitta canadensis* 11.5cm FIELD NOTES: Female duller on crown and flanks. Often forages head-down on trunks and branches, regularly gleans from outer twigs. VOICE: A nasal *ink*; also a hoarse *iik iik iik*. Song is a clear, rising *eeeen eeeen eeeen....* HABITAT: Coniferous and mixed forest. DISTRIBUTION: Resident across most of S Canada, NE USA and the mountainous regions of W and E USA. Winters over the whole of the USA.

8 WHITE-BREASTED NUTHATCH *Sitta carolinensis* 13–15cm FIELD NOTES: Female has a greyer crown. Western birds have darker grey flanks. VOICE: Call variable, eastern birds utter a *yenk*, western birds a *eeern* and interior birds a *yidi-yidi-yidi*. Song is a soft *whi-whi-whi....* HABITAT: Open woodland, especially oak and pine. DISTRIBUTION: Resident in S Canada and USA, except where forests are absent.

9 PYGMY NUTHATCH *Sitta pygmaea* 11cm FIELD NOTES: Restless forager. Occurs in small to large flocks after breeding. VOICE: High pitched, including *bip-bip-bip*, *kip* and a *wee-bee*. HABITAT: Pine forests, especially ponderosa pines. DISTRIBUTION: W mountain regions, south from S British Columbia.

10 BROWN-HEADED NUTHATCH *Sitta pusilla* 11cm FIELD NOTES: Actions and habits similar to Pygmy Nuthatch. VOICE: A hard sharp *pik*; also nasal *KEWde* or *KEWdodododo tew*. HABITAT: Pine woodland, especially loblolly. DISTRIBUTION: SE USA.

162

77 WRENS

1 CACTUS WREN *Campylorhynchus brunneicapillus* 18–19cm FIELD NOTES: Forages low in vegetation or on the ground. Race *C. b. sandiegense* (fig 1b) occurs in coastal S California. VOICE: A staccato *tek tek tek tek....* Song, a harsh *cha cha cha....* HABITAT: Arid areas with cacti. DISTRIBUTION: US-Mexican border states.

2 ROCK WREN *Salpinctes obsoletus* 14–15cm FIELD NOTES: Forages among rocks, habitually bobs up and down. VOICE: A buzzy, trilled *dee-dee, dee-dr-dr-dr-dr-dr*. Song consists of variable phrases, e.g. *cheer-cheer-cheer-cheer, deedle-deedle-deedle-deedle, tur-tur-tur-tur*. HABITAT: Rocky hillsides and gullies. DISTRIBUTION: W USA and adjacent Canada. Northern birds move to winter in SW USA.

3 CANYON WREN *Catherpes mexicanus* 13–15cm FIELD NOTES: Unobtrusive forager among rock crevices. VOICE: A loud, buzzy *jeet*. Song is a series of clear descending and slowing whistles followed by a nasal hissing. HABITAT: Mainly canyons. DISTRIBUTION: W mountain regions from S British Columbia southward.

4 CAROLINA WREN *Thryothorus ludovicianus* 13–14cm FIELD NOTES: Forages in undergrowth. Race *T. l. lomitensis* (fig 4b) occurs in Texas. VOICE: A harsh *zhwee zhwee ...*, a low *dip* or *didip* and a descending trill. Song is a loud, ringing *tea-kettle tea-kettle tea-kettle* or similar. HABITAT: Woodlands, forest edge and urban areas. DISTRIBUTION: Much of E USA, north to SE Canada.

5 BEWICK'S WREN *Thryomanes bewickii* 13cm FIELD NOTES: Forages low, in vegetation or on the ground. Race *T. b. eremophilus* (fig 5b) occurs in interior SW USA. VOICE: A scolding buzzy *shreee*, a soft *wijo* and a high-pitched, rising *zrink*. Song is variable, incorporating a high-pitched, thin buzzing and slow trills. HABITAT: Dense brushy places, including thickets, woodland clearings and suburban areas. DISTRIBUTION: Pacific coastal states from British Columbia southward and SC USA (east to S Appalachians). Easternmost birds move west and south in winter.

6 HOUSE WREN *Troglodytes aedon* 11–13cm FIELD NOTES: Variable, from greyish to rufous. VOICE: Variable, including a mewing *merrrrr*, harsh, rising *sshhhhp* and a low *chek*. Song is a cascade of bubbling whistled notes. HABITAT: Brushy woodland, hedgerows, and well-vegetated suburban areas. DISTRIBUTION: Summers over much of S Canada and USA, away from SC and SE areas of USA, where only occurs in winter.

7 WINTER WREN *Troglodytes hiemalis* 10cm FIELD NOTES: Secretive. Forages in woodland undergrowth. Eastern birds slightly paler than western birds; Bering Sea race *T. t. alascensis* (fig 7b) larger and greyer expected to become a full species, Pacific Wren. VOICE: Eastern birds give a hard *jip-jip*, western birds a sharp *chat-chat*; also a rapid series of staccato notes when alarmed. Song is a series of high trills and thin buzzes. HABITAT: Wet coniferous woods with dense undergrowth. DISTRIBUTION: Summers in boreal Canada, NW and NE USA, resident along Pacific coasts and in the Appalachians. Canadian birds move south to winter in SE USA.

8 SEDGE WREN *Cistothorus platensis* 11cm FIELD NOTES: Very secretive, best located by song. VOICE: A rich *chip* or *chip-chip*; also a sharp *chadt*. Song is a sharp staccato trill or chatter. HABITAT: Tall-grass meadows with scattered bushes. DISTRIBUTION: Summers in Canadian Prairies and northern half of E USA. Winters in SE USA, from Texas east to Atlantic.

9 MARSH WREN *Cistothorus palustris* 11.5–12.5cm FIELD NOTES: Secretive, forages low in marsh vegetation. Western birds slightly paler. Race *C. p. griseus* (fig 9b) occurs on the coast of Georgia and S Carolina. VOICE: A sharp *tek*. Song consists of gurgling, rattling, buzzing and trilling notes, introduced by a few *tek* notes. Song of eastern birds less varied. HABITAT: Reed swamps. DISTRIBUTION: Summers, in suitable habitats, over much of C and W North America. Winters in S USA and on E and W coasts.

grey morph
6

rufous morph

78 OLD WORLD WARBLERS AND GNATCATCHERS

1 MIDDENDORFF'S GRASSHOPPER WARBLER *Locustella ochotensis* 15cm
FIELD NOTES: Skulking. VOICE: A jarring, short warble. HABITAT: Waterside scrub, reed-beds and thickets in damp grassland. DISTRIBUTION: Very rare vagrant from E Asia.

2 LANCEOLATED WARBLER *Locustella lanceolata* 12cm FIELD NOTES: Shy. Juvenile may have unstreaked flanks. VOICE: A soft *tak* and a *chi-chirr* or *chirr-chirr*. HABITAT: Damp areas with scattered scrub or small trees. DISTRIBUTION: Very rare vagrant from C Europe.

3 SEDGE WARBLER *Acrocephalus schoenobaenus* 13cm FIELD NOTES: Furtive but active forager in vegetation. VOICE: A sharp *tuc* or *tuc-tuc* and a soft *churr*. HABITAT: Dense vegetation, usually near water. DISTRIBUTION: Very rare vagrant from Europe.

4 WILLOW WARBLER *Phylloscopus trochilus* 11.5cm FIELD NOTES: Active. Flicks wings and tail while foraging. VOICE: A disyllabic *hoo-eet*. HABITAT: Open woods, thickets and hedgerows. DISTRIBUTION: Very rare vagrant from Europe.

5 ARCTIC WARBLER *Phylloscopus borealis* 12cm FIELD NOTES: Alaskan birds are more yellow below. Twitches wings and tail. VOICE: A sharp *dzik*. A shivering trill, often interspersed with call notes. HABITAT: Tundra thickets. DISTRIBUTION: Summers in W Alaska and vagrant from N Europe.

6 DUSKY WARBLER *Phylloscopus fuscatus* 11.5cm FIELD NOTES: Skulking, active forager, mainly in low vegetation. VOICE: A sharp, repeated *chett*. HABITAT: Thickets, often near water. DISTRIBUTION: Rare vagrant from E Asia.

7 YELLOW-BROWED WARBLER *Phylloscopus inornatus* 10cm FIELD NOTES: Actions and habits much as Willow Warbler. VOICE: A high *tswe-eet* or *tsuee-eep*. HABITAT: Conifer, deciduous or mixed forest, often near water. DISTRIBUTION: Rare vagrant from E Europe.

8 PALLAS'S WARBLER (PALLAS'S LEAF WARBLER) *Phylloscopus proregulus* 10cm FIELD NOTES: Pale crown stripe. Flicks wings and tail, often hover-gleans. VOICE: A soft, nasal *due*; also a soft *wseep*. HABITAT: Conifer and mixed forest. DISTRIBUTION: Very rare vagrant from E Asia.

9 WOOD WARBLER *Phylloscopus sibilatrix* 12.5cm FIELD NOTES: Distinct yellow throat and breast. Forages mainly in tree canopy. VOICE: A plaintive *pew* and a soft *wit-wit-wit*. HABITAT: Mature forests. DISTRIBUTION: Very rare vagrant from Europe.

10 BLACKCAP *Sylvia atricapilla* 13cm FIELD NOTES: Usually revealed by call. Shy and skulking. VOICE: A *tac-tac*, *churr* and a *teck-teck-teck-teckcherr*. HABITAT: Thickets and forest undergrowth. DISTRIBUTION: Rare vagrant from Europe, recorded from Greenland.

11 LESSER WHITETHROAT *Sylvia curruca* 12.5cm FIELD NOTES: Very skulking. Dark mask. VOICE: A hard *tac-tac* and a scolding *churr*. HABITAT: Bushy areas. DISTRIBUTION: Very rare vagrant from Europe.

12 BLACK-TAILED GNATCATCHER *Polioptila melanura* 11cm
FIELD NOTES: Note undertail pattern. Active, often hovers to glean insects. VOICE: Various, including a *psssh*, *gee-gee* and a *ch-ch-ch-ch....* HABITAT: Arid brush. DISTRIBUTION: Along the Mexican border of the USA.

13 CALIFORNIA GNATCATCHER *Polioptila californica* 11cm FIELD NOTES: Note undertail pattern. Actions as Black-tailed Gnatcatcher. VOICE: A mewing *mee-eew*; a soft *dear dear...* and a harsh *tssshh*. HABITAT: Coastal brush. DISTRIBUTION: SW California.

14 BLACK-CAPPED GNATCATCHER *Polioptila nigriceps* 11cm
FIELD NOTES: Note undertail pattern. Actions as other gnatcatchers. VOICE: A buzzy *jehrr* and a sharp *chip chip chip*. HABITAT: Thickets along desert streams. DISTRIBUTION: Rare vagrant from Mexico, has bred in Arizona.

15 BLUE-GREY GNATCATCHER *Polioptila caerulea* 11cm FIELD NOTES: Active forager in trees and tall bushes, often fly-catches by making short flits from branches. Western birds slightly darker, especially on the crown. VOICE: A thin *zpee-zpee*, *pwee* or *zeef-zeef*. Song is a wheezy series with high chips and slurs. HABITAT: Woodlands and scrub. DISTRIBUTION: Summers in E USA and S parts of W USA.

yakutensis

nominate

79 KINGLETS, WRENTIT AND OLD WORLD FLYCATCHERS

1 GOLDEN-CROWNED KINGLET *Regulus satrapa* 10cm FIELD NOTES: When foraging, constantly on the move, flitting from twig to twig. Juvenile has a greyish centre crown stripe. VOICE: Very high-pitched *see-see-see*. Song rising then ending in a tumbling chatter *see see see si si si tititichichichichi*. HABITAT: Primarily coniferous woodlands. DISTRIBUTION: Boreal Canada, S Alaska, W and E North American mountain regions and C N USA. Canadian birds move south in winter to become widespread in the USA.

2 RUBY-CROWNED KINGLET *Regulus calendula* 10cm FIELD NOTES: Restless acrobatic forager. Females and juveniles lack the red crown patch, although in the male it is usually concealed. VOICE: A dry *jidit, jit* or *jit jit jit...* when alarmed. Song is a series of high, then descending notes ending in a warble, transcribed as *sii si sisisi berr berr pudi pudi pudi see*. HABITAT: Woodlands, thickets and scrub. DISTRIBUTION: Boreal Canada and Alaska extending south down the US Rockies. Northern birds migrate to winter in S, E and W USA.

3 NARCISSUS FLYCATCHER *Ficedula narcissina* 13cm FIELD NOTES: Makes fly-catching sallies from the middle or upper storey. VOICE: Repeated warbles and whistles, transcribed as *o-shin-tsuk-tsuk*. HABITAT: Deciduous, conifer or mixed forest with dense undergrowth. DISTRIBUTION: Very rare vagrant from Kuril Islands.

4 MUGIMAKI FLYCATCHER *Ficedula mugimaki* 13cm FIELD NOTES: Flicks and spreads tail. Forages in the middle or upper storey. VOICE: A soft, rattled *trrrrr*. Song is a fast twittering warble. HABITAT: Mature mixed forest. DISTRIBUTION: Very rare vagrant from the E Palearctic.

5 TAIGA FLYCATCHER (RED-THROATED FLYCATCHER) *Ficedula albicilla* 13cm FIELD NOTES: In flight, white outer tail bases distinctive. Forages by flitting from bush to bush, gleaning insects from foliage or the ground; also makes short aerial sallies. Constantly cocks and jerks tail. VOICE: A creaking *trrrrr*. HABITAT: Deciduous and mixed taiga forests. DISTRIBUTION: Rare vagrant from Europe.

6 BROWN FLYCATCHER (ASIAN BROWN FLYCATCHER) *Muscicapa daurica* 13cm FIELD NOTES: No streaking on underparts. When making fly-catching sallies, returns to the same or nearby perch. VOICE: A short, thin *tzi*, a soft *churr* and a rattling *tze-te-te-te-te* when alarmed. HABITAT: Glades in deciduous and mixed woodland. DISTRIBUTION: Very rare vagrant from the E Palearctic.

7 DARK-SIDED FLYCATCHER (SIBERIAN or SOOTY FLYCATCHER) *Muscicapa sibirica* 13cm FIELD NOTES: Diffuse streaking on breast and flanks. Actions as Brown Flycatcher. VOICE: A tinkling *chi-up-chi-up-chi-up*. HABITAT: Coniferous, deciduous and mixed forest. DISTRIBUTION: Very rare vagrant from the E Palearctic.

8 GREY-STREAKED FLYCATCHER (GREY-SPOTTED FLYCATCHER) *Muscicapa griseisticta* 14cm FIELD NOTES: Distinct streaking on breast and flanks. Actions much as Brown Flycatcher. VOICE: A loud, melodious *chipee tee-tee*. HABITAT: Open forests, plantations and urban parks. DISTRIBUTION: Rare vagrant from the E Palearctic.

9 SPOTTED FLYCATCHER *Muscicapa striata* 14cm FIELD NOTES: Discreetly streaked crown, throat and breast. Fly-catching sallies take the bird out in a sweeping circle, returning to same or nearby perch. VOICE: A squeaky *zeee, chick* or *zee-zuck* when agitated. HABITAT: Open deciduous or conifer woodland, woodland edge, glades, parks and large gardens. DISTRIBUTION: Very rare vagrant from Europe.

10 WRENTIT *Chamaea fasciata* 16–17cm FIELD NOTES: Often heard prior to being seen. Pale eye. Tail often cocked as it hops from twig to twig, much like a wren. Pumps tail as it makes short, weak flights from bush to bush. Variable, 2 extremes depicted. VOICE: A dry *trrrk*. Song consists of a series of accelerating, staccato notes developing into a descending trill. HABITAT: Dense chaparral, bushy forest margins, parks and gardens. DISTRIBUTION: Pacific coast of the USA.

1 SIBERIAN RUBYTHROAT *Luscinia calliope* 15cm FIELD NOTES: Skulks in dense vegetation. Often cocks tail. VOICE: A *chak-chak* and a whistled *ee-uk*. HABITAT: Thickets and scrub. DISTRIBUTION: Rare vagrant from the Palearctic.

2 SIBERIAN BLUE ROBIN *Luscinia cyane* 14cm FIELD NOTES: Skulks in cover. Shivers tail. Female shows dull blue on rump. VOICE: A subdued *tak, se-ic* and a *chuck-chuck-chuck* when alarmed. HABITAT: Coniferous and mixed forest with dense shrubs and undergrowth. DISTRIBUTION: Very rare vagrant from the E Palearctic.

3 BLUETHROAT (RED-SPOTTED BLUETHROAT) *Luscinia svecica* 14cm FIELD NOTES: Chestnut outer tail bases 'flash' as bird flits into cover. VOICE: A *tacc-tacc*, a croaky *turrc-turrc* and a plaintive *hweet*. Song is vigorous with bell-like notes and a throaty *torr-torr-torr*; also mimics birds and insects. HABITAT: Arctic scrub. DISTRIBUTION: Summers in N Alaska.

4 RED-FLANKED BLUETAIL (ORANGE-FLANKED BUSH ROBIN) *Tarsiger cyanurus* 14cm FIELD NOTES: Cover-loving. Regularly jerks tail downwards. VOICE: A *tic-tic*; also a soft *huit* and a guttural *kerrr*. HABITAT: Moist mixed and coniferous forest with undergrowth; on migration uses all types of woodlands. DISTRIBUTION: Rare vagrant from the Palearctic.

5 STONECHAT *Saxicola torquatus* 13cm FIELD NOTES: Sits atop a prominent perch, flicking wings and tail; usually drops to the ground to pick up food and then returns to the same perch or one nearby. The race shown is the 'Siberian Stonechat' *S. t. maurus*. VOICE: A *chak* or *wheet*, often combined as *wheet-chak-chak*. HABITAT: Open areas with low scrub. DISTRIBUTION: Rare vagrant from the Palearctic.

6 WHEATEAR (NORTHERN WHEATEAR) *Oenanthe oenanthe* 14.5–15.5cm FIELD NOTES: In flight shows white rump and white bases to outer tail feathers. Always appears alert. Regularly flicks wings and tail. VOICE: A hard *chak* and a *wheet*, often combined as *wheet-chak-chak*. Song is a brief scratchy warble interspersed with chacking, creaking and fluty notes. HABITAT: Tundra and rocky slopes. DISTRIBUTION: Summers in Greenland, Alaska and NW and NE Canada.

7 MOUNTAIN BLUEBIRD *Sialia currucoides* 17–18cm FIELD NOTES: Makes darting flights from branch or rock perch to catch flying insects; also hovers in pursuit of insect prey. VOICE: A soft *feeer* or muffled *perf*; also a harsh *chik* or *chak*. Song is a short clear warble. HABITAT: High elevation open areas with scattered trees. DISTRIBUTION: W North America, from C Alaska south to Arizona and New Mexico. Northern birds winter in SW USA.

8 EASTERN BLUEBIRD *Sialia sialis* 15–16.5cm FIELD NOTES: Uses an exposed perch to pounce upon insects on the ground; occasionally makes short fly-catching sallies. VOICE: A musical *chur-lee, tu-a-wee* or *jeew wiwi*. Song consists of soft mellow whistles. HABITAT: Open country with hedgerows, woodland edge and roadsides. DISTRIBUTION: E USA and adjacent states in Canada; northern birds move to winter in SE USA.

9 WESTERN BLUEBIRD *Sialia mexicana* 17–18cm FIELD NOTES: Actions much as Eastern Bluebird. VOICE: A hard, low *jewf*, or *pew pew pew*; also a dry chatter. Song is a series of call notes. HABITAT: Open park-like woodlands, trees in foothills and mountains, farmland and orchards. DISTRIBUTION: W North America, from British Columbia southward. Northern inland birds move to SW USA in winter.

10 TOWNSEND'S SOLITAIRE *Myadestes townsendi* 21–23cm FIELD NOTES: In flight shows white outer tail feathers and buff wing bar. Makes darting fly-catching sallies from a high perch. VOICE: A high pitched *eek* or *heeh*. Song is a complex, prolonged warble, very finch-like in quality. HABITAT: Montane coniferous forests. DISTRIBUTION: W mountain areas, from C Alaska south to Arizona and New Mexico. Northern birds move south in winter.

81 THRUSHES

1 VARIED THRUSH *Ixoreus naevius* 23cm FIELD NOTES: Shy, feeds low down or on the ground in dark shaded areas. VOICE: A weak *chuk*; also a thin *woooeee*. Song consists of vibrant, eerie, melancholic and sustained notes, varying rapidly from high to low pitch; also buzzing trill. HABITAT: Dense coniferous forests with undergrowth of dogwood and wild current. DISTRIBUTION: W America, from Alaska to N California. In the winter, Alaskan and Canadian birds move south, as far as S California.

2 AZTEC THRUSH *Ridgwayia pinicola* 24cm FIELD NOTES: Forages on the ground or low down in bushes or thick vegetation. Best detected by call. VOICE: A thin, slightly quavering *wheeerr*; also an upslurred, buzzing *zrrip*, *prrip* or *prreep* and a nasal *sweee-uh*. HABITAT: Pine or pin-oak forests in ravines. DISTRIBUTION: Rare vagrant from Mexico.

3 EYE-BROWED THRUSH *Turdus obscurus* 22cm FIELD NOTES: Feeds on the ground or in trees bearing berries or fruit. VOICE: A soft *chuk*, a hard *tack-tack*; also a *shree* and a *dzee* flight call. HABITAT: Birch forests; open forests and open country on migration. DISTRIBUTION: Rare vagrant from E Palearctic.

4 BLACKBIRD (EURASIAN BLACKBIRD) *Turdus merula* 27cm FIELD NOTES: Feeds on the ground and in fruiting bushes and trees. Juvenile like female but mottled with darkish spots below. VOICE: A low *chuck-chuck-chuck*, rapidly repeated when alarmed; also a drawn-out *tseee*. Song consists of rich, fluty notes that merge into short, continuous phrases. HABITAT: Variable, including woodlands, scrub, farmland and gardens. DISTRIBUTION: Very rare vagrant from Europe.

5 NAUMANN'S THRUSH (DUSKY THRUSH) *Turdus naumanni* 23cm FIELD NOTES: Mainly a ground feeder. 'Dusky Thrush' *T. n. eunomus* (fig 5b) is a rare vagrant to NW North America; the nominate race may occur, tagged on to other thrush visitors. VOICE: A shrill *cheeh-cheeh*, often repeated; also a harsh *ket-ket-ket* and a chuckling *chak-chak*. HABITAT: Woodland edge, scrub, fields and urban areas. DISTRIBUTION: Rare vagrant from the E Palearctic.

6 CLAY-COLOURED THRUSH (CLAY-COLOURED ROBIN) *Turdus grayi* 23cm FIELD NOTES: Shy, forages in dense thickets and brush. VOICE: A slurred, mewing *quire*, *hoouree*, *sreer*, *keyaah* or similar; also a *tock tock* and chuckling notes. Song is a slow, low-pitched warbling. HABITAT: Moist, damp or wet woodland. DISTRIBUTION: Rare breeder in S Texas.

7 RUFOUS-BACKED THRUSH (RUFOUS-BACKED ROBIN) *Turdus rufopalliatus* 23.5cm FIELD NOTES: Forages on the ground and in fruiting trees. VOICE: A plaintive, mellow *peeeoooo*, *cheeoo* or *teeeuu*; also a throaty *chuck chuck chuck*. Song is a slow series of rich, warbled notes. HABITAT: Deciduous and mixed forest, woodland edge, scrub and large gardens. DISTRIBUTION: Vagrant from Mexico to US border states.

8 WHITE-THROATED THRUSH (WHITE-THROATED ROBIN) *Turdus assimilis* 22–26.5cm FIELD NOTES: Shy. Forages mainly in mid-level or tree canopy of fruiting trees, much less so on the ground. VOICE: A nasal *rreeuh* or *rreuh*; also a clucking *ch-uhk* and a thin *ssi* given in flight. Song is a rich warble with repeated phrases. HABITAT: Forest, forest edge and plantations. DISTRIBUTION: Rare vagrant from Mexico.

9 AMERICAN ROBIN *Turdus migratorius* 23–25cm FIELD NOTES: Feeds mainly on the ground but also in trees and bushes where attracted to berries and fruit. Juvenile duller with dark- spotted underparts and pale fringes on wings and mantle. NE Canadian birds generally darker. VOICE: A *tut-tut-tut*; also a descending *shheerr* and an excited *kli quiquiquiqui....* Song is loud, liquid, often transcribed as *cheerily cheer-up cheerio* or *cheerily-cheery-cheerily-cheery*. HABITAT: Forests, woods, thickets, meadows with hedges and urban areas. DISTRIBUTION: North America, apart from the extreme N tundra areas. Alaskan, Canadian and northern-most US birds move south to winter in the USA.

82 THRUSHES

1 FIELDFARE *Turdus pilaris* 25cm FIELD NOTES: White underwing coverts. Feeds on the ground, also attracted to fruiting trees and bushes. VOICE: A *chach-chack*, a nasal *tseee* and, when anxious, a *chetchetchetje* or *trt- trrrrt-trrt*. HABITAT: Open conifer, deciduous or mixed forest and tundra scrub. Winters in more open areas. DISTRIBUTION: Possible small population in Greenland, otherwise vagrant from Europe.

2 REDWING *Turdus iliacus* 21cm FIELD NOTES: Rusty underwing coverts. Feeds on the ground and in fruiting trees. VOICE: A thin *seee*; when alarmed gives a rattling *trrrt-trrrt-trrrt* or *jip-jip*. HABITAT: Birch woodland, scrub, urban areas. DISTRIBUTION: Rare vagrant from Europe; has bred in Greenland.

3 SONG THRUSH *Turdus philomelos* 22cm FIELD NOTES: Ochre underwing coverts. Feeds largely on the ground. VOICE: A *sip* and a loud *chick* given in alarm. HABITAT: Open woodland, urban areas. DISTRIBUTION: Very rare vagrant from Europe.

4 VEERY *Catharus fuscescens* 17cm FIELD NOTES: Secretive. Forages primarily on the ground. Western birds are more earthy above, with darker spotting on breast. VOICE: A fluted *phew*, *whee-uu* and a slow, slurred *wee-oo*. Song is a descending *da-vee-ur - vee-ur - veer - veer*. HABITAT: Undergrowth in deciduous or mixed forests. DISTRIBUTION: Summers across the centre of North America and south down the Rockies and Appalachians.

5 GREY-CHEEKED THRUSH *Catharus minimus* 16–20cm FIELD NOTES: Wary, forages on or near the ground. VOICE: A down-slurred *wee-ah*; also a short *chuck* and a light *pheeeu*. Song is a series of high-pitched, repeated notes interspersed with a sharp *chee-chee* and ending with a descending *wee-oh wee-oh*. HABITAT: Dense conifer, mixed and open forest, also shrubby thickets. DISTRIBUTION: Summers in the northern Taiga region, from Alaska to Newfoundland.

6 BICKNELL'S THRUSH *Catharus bicknelli* 16–17cm FIELD NOTES: Wary, forages on or near the ground. VOICE: A *wee-oo*, *psee-uuu* or *peeez*. Song like Grey-cheeked Thrush, but higher pitched. HABITAT: Stunted conifer forests on mountain slopes and hill-tops. DISTRIBUTION: Summers in E Canada and NE USA.

7 SWAINSON'S THRUSH *Catharus ustulatus* 16–20cm FIELD NOTES: Shy. Forages on the ground and in fruiting trees. Western coastal birds slightly more rufous above. VOICE: A liquid *whit* and a soft *whup*. Song is a musical *whip-poor-will-a-will-e-zee-zee-zee*. HABITAT: Shaded or damp understorey of dense spruce forests. DISTRIBUTION: Summers in North American boreal and W mountain zones.

8 HERMIT THRUSH *Catharus guttatus* 19cm FIELD NOTES: Shy. Forages on the ground, constantly flicks wings and tail. Birds from the Rockies *C. g. auduboni* (fig 8b) are greyer. VOICE: A low *chuck*, a ringing *cheeee* and a harsh *pay*. Song is a series of different pitched flute-like notes. HABITAT: Mixed or coniferous forest, forest clearings with shrubby undergrowth. DISTRIBUTION: Summers in North American boreal zone and along the Rockies. Winters in the USA, on Pacific and Atlantic coasts and in southern states.

9 ORANGE-BILLED NIGHTINGALE-THRUSH *Catharus aurantiirostris* 15–17cm FIELD NOTES: Shy. Usually forages in thick undergrowth. VOICE: A scratchy *mew* and a nasal *waaa-a-a-a*, often prolonged into a chatter. HABITAT: Brushy understorey and dense thickets. DISTRIBUTION: Very rare vagrant from Mexico.

10 BLACK-HEADED NIGHTINGALE-THRUSH *Catharus mexicanus* 15–16.5cm FIELD NOTES: Forages among low branches or on the ground, where it progresses using a series of springing hops. VOICE: Sharp ascending *seeet*, plaintive mewing, rising *chowr* and a buzzing *chrrr* when alarmed. HABITAT: Forest undergrowth. DISTRIBUTION: Very rare vagrant from Mexico.

11 WOOD THRUSH *Hylocichla mustelina* 20cm FIELD NOTES: Distinctive. Generally a shy and retiring ground feeder. Frequently flicks wings. VOICE: A *pit-pit-pit* and a low *tuck-tuck*. Song consists of fluty phrases interspersed with call notes, ending with a soft trill. HABITAT: Woodland undergrowth; also urban areas. DISTRIBUTION: Summers in E USA.

83 MOCKINGBIRDS AND THRASHERS

1 BAHAMA MOCKINGBIRD *Mimus gundlachii* 28cm FIELD NOTES: Juvenile uniform above with less distinct flank streaks. VOICE: A series of repeated phrases. HABITAT: Woodlands, semiarid scrub and urban areas. DISTRIBUTION: Rare vagrant to Florida from the Bahamas.

2 NORTHERN MOCKINGBIRD *Mimus polyglottos* 24–28cm FIELD NOTES: Conspicuous and often aggressive. In flight shows large white wing-patch and white outer tail feathers. VOICE: A series of melodious phrases, each repeated several times; often mimics the calls of other birds. When agitated, a harsh *tchack*. HABITAT: Thickets, copses, shelterbelts and gardens. DISTRIBUTION: Resident across S and NE USA.

3 BLUE MOCKINGBIRD *Melanotis caerulescens* 24–26.5cm FIELD NOTES: Usually stays well hidden, foraging on ground or in low vegetation. VOICE: A rich *choo*. HABITAT: Scrubby woodland. DISTRIBUTION: Very rare vagrant from Mexico.

4 SAGE THRASHER *Oreoscoptes montanus* 20–23cm FIELD NOTES: Forages on the ground. Sings from the tops of bushes. VOICE: A low *chup*, a high *churr* and a whistled *whee-er*. Song is a continuous series of warbled phrases. HABITAT: Sagebrush plains. DISTRIBUTION: Summers over most of W USA and parts of extreme S Canada. Winters in SW USA.

5 BROWN THRASHER *Toxostoma rufum* 28cm FIELD NOTES: Forages primarily in leaf litter under bushes and trees. VOICE: A loud *tschek* or *chip*. Song consists of rich musical phrases; also a quieter low warble. HABITAT: Bushy woods, shelterbelts, copses and shrubby gardens. DISTRIBUTION: Summers in E USA as far west as the Rockies and north into adjacent Canadian states. Winters SE and E coast of USA.

6 LONG-BILLED THRASHER *Toxostoma longirostre* 26–29cm FIELD NOTES: Grey faced. Slight down-curved bill. Actions similar to Brown Thrasher. VOICE: A sharp *chak*, a mellow *cheeop* and a rattled *chttr*. Song consists of rich musical phrases, harsher and less rambling than Brown Thrasher. HABITAT: Dense thickets. DISTRIBUTION: Resident in S Texas.

7 BENDIRE'S THRASHER *Toxostoma bendirei* 23–25cm FIELD NOTES: Yellow eyes. Forages mainly on the ground. Often cocks tail when running. VOICE: A low *chuk*. Song is a continuous, flowing, sweet and husky warble. HABITAT: Open farmland, grassland and brushy desert. DISTRIBUTION: Summers inland in southern SW USA, resident in SE Arizona.

8 CURVE-BILLED THRASHER *Toxostoma curvirostre* 26–28cm FIELD NOTES: Orange eye. Forages primarily on the ground. Plumage variable; depicted are *T. c. oberholseri* from S Texas and *T. c. palmeri* (fig 8b) from SW and C Arizona. VOICE: A sharp, liquid *wit-WEET-wit*; also a dry *pitpitpitpit* and a low *chuk*. Song consists of trills, warbles and rattles. HABITAT: Open desert with emergent trees, cacti and thorn scrub. DISTRIBUTION: Resident in central SW USA.

9 CALIFORNIA THRASHER *Toxostoma redivivum* 28–32cm FIELD NOTES: Forages on the ground, usually under cover of shrubs and around fallen branches. Runs swiftly between feeding sites, with tail slightly raised. VOICE: A loud *churreep*, a soft *shtupp* and when alarmed a sharp *chack*. Song is a series of variable, harsh and mellow phrases. HABITAT: Primarily chaparral-covered slopes. DISTRIBUTION: Resident in W California.

10 CRISSAL THRASHER *Toxostoma dorsale* 26–29cm FIELD NOTES: Distinctive. Forages on the ground, usually under bushes. VOICE: A far-carrying *choit* and a rolling *chideery-chideery* or *pjurre-durrre*. Song consists of strong and melodious phrases, with little repetition. HABITAT: Low scrubby vegetation along streams and washes. DISTRIBUTION: Resident inland in extreme SW USA.

11 LE CONTE'S THRASHER *Toxostoma lecontei* 24–28cm FIELD NOTES: Forages on the ground. VOICE: A sharp *quit* and a whistled *tew-eep*. Song, soft and husky with long slurred notes. HABITAT: Open semi-desert. DISTRIBUTION: Resident in S California, S Nevada and SW Arizona.

84 CATBIRD, STARLING, MYNAS, BULBUL, WAXWINGS AND SILKY FLYCATCHERS

1 GREY CATBIRD *Dumetella carolinensis* 23cm FIELD NOTES: Skulks in thick cover, near or on the ground. More often heard than seen. VOICE: An explosive *kak-kak-kak* and a soft, cat-like *mew*. Song consists of sweet, varied phrases interspersed with mewing and harsh notes. HABITAT: Dense, low, streamside thickets, woodland and garden shrubbery. DISTRIBUTION: Summers across S Canada and USA, apart from the SW quarter, Florida and the Gulf coast. Winters in the USA in Florida and on the E and Gulf coasts.

2 STARLING (COMMON or EUROPEAN STARLING) *Sturnus vulgaris* 22cm FIELD NOTES: Gregarious at all times, forms very large winter flocks. Juvenile grey-brown above, slightly paler below, especially on throat. Bill dark. VOICE: Various harsh and grating notes. Song is a medley of clicks, chirrups, warbles etc., interspersed with drawn-out whistles and mimicry. HABITAT: Very varied, including farmland, woodland edge, villages and cities. DISTRIBUTION: Widespread in North America away from Arctic areas. Northern birds move south to USA in the winter.

3 HILL MYNA *Gracula religiosa* 30cm FIELD NOTES: Unmistakeable. In flight shows large white patch on base of primaries. VOICE: Various whistles, squawks and chirps; can also mimic virtually any sound. HABITAT: Open woodland and suburban areas. DISTRIBUTION: Introduced in California and Florida.

4 COMMON MYNA (INDIAN MYNA) *Acridotheres tristis* 23cm FIELD NOTES: Tame, can become a pest. VOICE: A grouchy *kwerrh*. Song consists of tuneless gurgled and whistled phrases. HABITAT: Urban and suburban areas. DISTRIBUTION: Introduced in Florida.

5 RED-WHISKERED BULBUL *Pycnonotus jocosus* 20cm FIELD NOTES: Juvenile lacks red ear-patch, has browner crown and pinkish under-tail coverts. Occurs in small flocks. VOICE: A rolling *prroop* and staccato *kink-a-jou*. Song lively with variable musical phrases. HABITAT: Suburban areas with lush vegetation. DISTRIBUTION: Introduced in S Florida.

6 WAXWING (BOHEMIAN WAXWING) *Bombycilla garrulus* 20cm FIELD NOTES: White tips to wing feathers. Juvenile duller, lacks black throat and has a shorter crest. Forms flocks in winter. VOICE: A ringing *sirrrr*. Song consists of quiet trilled phrases. HABITAT: Breeds in conifer woods. In winter spreads to a wide variety of woodland, including parks and gardens, in search of berries. DISTRIBUTION: Summers in Alaska and W Canada. Winters from British Columbia across C North America to Newfoundland.

7 CEDAR WAXWING *Bombycilla cedrorum* 18cm FIELD NOTES: Much plainer wings than Waxwing. White under-tail coverts. Juvenile duller. Forms large flocks in winter. VOICE: A high-pitched *sreee*. Song a series of high *screee* notes in an irregular rhythm. HABITAT: Breeds in conifer and mixed woods. In winter spreads to a wider range of woodland and suburban areas in search of berries. DISTRIBUTION: Breeds across the whole of C North America. Winters throughout the USA.

8 GREY SILKY-FLYCATCHER *Ptilogonys cinereus* 18–21cm FIELD NOTES: Often perches conspicuously on tall trees, makes sallies to catch flying insects. Usually occurs in pairs or small flocks. VOICE: A dry *chi-che-rup che-chep* and a sharp *chureet, chu-leep* and *ch-tuk*. HABITAT: Pine, oak and juniper forest, forest edge and open areas with scattered trees. DISTRIBUTION: Very rare vagrant from Mexico.

9 PHAINOPEPLA *Phainopepla nitens* 18–21cm FIELD NOTES: In flight, male shows extensive white on primaries. Makes sallies, often with erratic changes of direction, after flying insects. VOICE: A soft, rising *wurp*. Song is a short warble. HABITAT: Desert washes with trees and shrubs. DISTRIBUTION: US-Mexican border states, northern birds move south.

85 AMERICAN WARBLERS

1 OLIVE WARBLER *Peucedramus taeniatus* 13cm FIELD NOTES: Often forages in pine needle clumps. VOICE: A soft *teew* or *tewp* and a hard *pit*. Song is a loud, 2-note whistle, transcribed as *pee-ter pee-ter pee-ter pee-ter*. HABITAT: Montane conifer forests. DISTRIBUTION: SE Arizona and SW New Mexico.

2 TENNESSEE WARBLER *Vermivora peregrina* 12cm FIELD NOTES: Usually forages high in the tree canopy, although will descend to feed in bushes; agile and active. VOICE: Calls include a sharp *tsit* and a thin *see*. Song is a series of staccato double and single notes, ending in a trill. HABITAT: Conifer and mixed woodland; on migration occurs in open woodland and thickets. DISTRIBUTION: Summers in the boreal area of Canada, NE Minnesota and extreme NE USA.

3 BACHMAN'S WARBLER *Vermivora bachmanii* 12cm FIELD NOTES: Almost certainly extinct. Often forages high in treetops. VOICE: A buzzy, pulsating trill; only call recorded is a low, hissing *zee-e-eep*. HABITAT: Swampy forests with dense undergrowth, near standing water and canebrakes. DISTRIBUTION: Summers in SE USA (South Carolina).

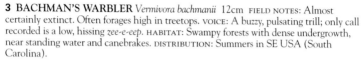

4 BLUE-WINGED WARBLER *Vermivora pinus* 12cm FIELD NOTES: Female duller. Agile acrobatic forager, usually in mid-level. VOICE: A wheezy *beee-bzzz*; also a longer *tsi tsi tsi tsi tsi zweeeeeeezt zt zt zt*. Call is a sharp, dry *nik* or *chik*. HABITAT: Brushy fields, woodland edge and streamside thickets. DISTRIBUTION: Summers in NE USA.

5 GOLDEN-WINGED WARBLER *Vermivora chrysoptera* 12cm FIELD NOTES: Very agile, acrobatically foraging in bushes and trees. VOICE: A soft, buzzy *zee-bee-bee-bee*, occasionally more trilling; also a short *tchip* call. HABITAT: Bushy pastures, woodland edge and clearings, also waterside thickets. DISTRIBUTION: Summers in S Manitoba, NE USA and south along the Appalachians.

6 ORANGE-CROWNED WARBLER *Vermivora celata* 13cm FIELD NOTES: Feeds from low to high levels on insects and small berries. Depicted are the nominate and the NW race *V. c. lutescens* (fig 6b). VOICE: A high-pitched trill followed by a lower, slower trill. Calls include a sharp *chet* and a *see* flight note. HABITAT: Open woodland, forest edge and thickets. DISTRIBUTION: Summers in much of W North America and across the boreal zone to Labrador. Winters in the USA in Florida and on Atlantic, Pacific and Gulf coasts.

7 NASHVILLE WARBLER *Vermivora ruficapilla* 12cm FIELD NOTES: Forages mainly at low levels feeding on insects, nectar and berries. VOICE: Song consists of a series of high-pitched *tsee* notes followed by a low trill. Calls include a metallic *tink* or *spink* and a *swit* or *see* flight note. HABITAT: Open, young deciduous and mixed woodland; also second-growth clearings and spruce bogs. DISTRIBUTION: Summers in W North America, from British Columbia south to California and from Saskatchewan east to Labrador and NE USA. Winters in S Texas.

8 VIRGINIA'S WARBLER *Vermivora virginiae* 12cm FIELD NOTES: Actions and habits similar to Nashville Warbler. VOICE: Song is a series of rapid, accelerating, thin notes ending with several lower notes. Calls similar, although a little rougher to those of Nashville Warbler. HABITAT: Chaparral and pinyon-juniper, yellow pine and scrub oak woodland. DISTRIBUTION: Summers in S Rocky Mountain states.

9 COLIMA WARBLER *Vermivora crissalis* 15cm FIELD NOTES: Forages, with slow deliberate actions, mainly in undergrowth. VOICE: A short, monotonous chattering trill. Call is a sharp, metallic *psit*. HABITAT: Oak woodland. DISTRIBUTION: Summers in the Chisos Mountains of SW Texas.

10 LUCY'S WARBLER *Vermivora luciae* 11cm FIELD NOTES: Rufous rump. Forages at low to mid-levels. VOICE: A short twittering trill followed by lower whistled notes *weeta weeta weeta che che che*. Call is a high-pitched, husky *tzip*. HABITAT: Mesquite woodland and scrub, often near water. DISTRIBUTION: Summers in SW USA.

1 NORTHERN PARULA *Parula americana* 11cm FIELD NOTES: Very agile, often hangs upside down whilst foraging in the tree canopy. VOICE: An ascending buzzing trill, ending with an abrupt *tship*. Calls include a sharp *chip* and a weak *tsif* flight note. HABITAT: Conifer and mixed woods, often near water. DISTRIBUTION: Summers in E USA and adjacent Canadian states. Resident in Florida.

2 TROPICAL PARULA *Parula pitiayumi* 11cm FIELD NOTES: Gleans and hovers to collect insects in the canopy. VOICE: An accelerating buzzy trill, preceded by several high-pitched notes. HABITAT: Deciduous forest, forest edge and clearings. DISTRIBUTION: Resident in the lower Rio Grande, S Texas.

3 CRESCENT-CHESTED WARBLER *Parula superciliosa* 11cm
FIELD NOTES: Forages at mid- to high levels. Juvenile duller, lacks red breast crescent. VOICE: A short buzzy trill. Call is a high-pitched *tchip*. HABITAT: Montane forest. DISTRIBUTION: Rare vagrant from Mexico.

4 YELLOW WARBLER *Dendroica petechia* 13cm FIELD NOTES: Agile, active feeder in trees, bushes and on the ground. VOICE: A high-pitched *sweet-sweet-sweet-I'm-so-sweet*. Calls include a musical *tship* and a buzzy *zzee*. HABITAT: Riparian thickets, bushy areas including gardens. DISTRIBUTION: Widespread in North America, apart from the tundra zone, the Sonoran and Mojave deserts and SW USA, from Texas east to the Carolinas. Winters in S California.

5 CHESTNUT-SIDED WARBLER *Dendroica pensylvanica* 13cm
FIELD NOTES: Agile forager at low to medium levels in shrubs and lower branches of trees. VOICE: Song often transcribed as *pleased-pleased-pleased-to-meecha*. Calls with a low, flat *tchip*; in flight utters a buzzy *jrrt*. HABITAT: Young deciduous forest, bushy thickets; on migration woodland edge and clearings. DISTRIBUTION: Summers in NE USA, WC and SW Canada.

6 YELLOW-RUMPED WARBLER (MYRTLE WARBLER) *Dendroica coronata* 14cm FIELD NOTES: Feeds in low vegetation and bushes as well as treetops. Also shown (fig 6b) is the western race 'Audubon's Warbler' *D. c. auduboni*. VOICE: A slow trill, *uwee-tuwee-tuwee-tuwee-tuwee...*, which often changes pitch at the end. Calls include a sharp *chek* and a thin *tsee* flight note. HABITAT: Open conifer and mixed woodland; after breeding, frequents hedgerows, thickets and gardens. DISTRIBUTION: Widespread in summer in N and W North America. Winters over much of E, S and W coasts of the USA.

7 MAGNOLIA WARBLER *Dendroica magnolia* 13cm FIELD NOTES: Active and agile forager in tree foliage at low to mid-levels. VOICE: A short, musical *weety-weety-wee* or *weety-weety-weety-wee*, last note is occasionally higher. Calls include a full *tship* or *dzip*, a harsh *tshekk* and a buzzy *zee* flight note. HABITAT: Young conifer stands. On migration in other woods and tall scrub. DISTRIBUTION: Summers in boreal North America and south through the Appalachians.

8 CAPE MAY WARBLER *Dendroica tigrina* 13cm FIELD NOTES: Active forager in treetops, gleaning and occasionally using sallies to catch flying insects. VOICE: A high *zi-zi-zi-zi-zi*. Calls include a very high *tsip* and a slightly descending *tsee-tsee*, often given in flight. HABITAT: Coniferous and mixed forest; all types of woodland frequented during migration. DISTRIBUTION: Summers in boreal Canada and extreme N and NE USA.

9 BLACK-THROATED BLUE WARBLER *Dendroica caerulescens* 13cm
FIELD NOTES: Active. Forages from low levels to the canopy, although primarily in the understorey. VOICE: A husky *zweea-zweea-zweea-zwee*. Calls include a dull *stip* or *chup* and a metallic *twik* flight note. HABITAT: Mature deciduous and mixed woodland with rich undergrowth; also woodland clearings and logged areas. DISTRIBUTION: Summers in SE Canada and NE USA extending south through the Appalachians.

1 ♀ ♂

2 ♀ ♂

3

4 ♀ ♂

5 ♂ n-br ♂ br

6 ♂ br
6b

6 ♂ n-br ♂ br

7 ♂ n-br ♂ br

8 ♂ n-br ♂ br

9 ♀ ♂

87 AMERICAN WARBLERS

1 BLACK-THROATED GREY WARBLER *Dendroica nigrescens* 13cm
FIELD NOTES: Forages mainly in the understorey. VOICE: A buzzy *weezy-weezy-weezy-weezy WEE-too*. Calls include a *thick* or *tup* and a high-pitched *see* or *sip* flight note. HABITAT: Dry open woodlands with brushy understorey and chaparral. Occurs in any woodland or scrub during migration. DISTRIBUTION: Summers in much of W USA, north into S British Columbia.

2 GOLDEN-CHEEKED WARBLER *Dendroica chrysoparia* 14cm
FIELD NOTES: Forages mainly at medium to high levels, gleaning or fly-catching for insects. VOICE: A buzzy *bzzzz layzee dazzee*. Call is a high *tchip*. HABITAT: Open scrubby woodland with dense stands of juniper. During migration, frequents mountain woods and forests. DISTRIBUTION: Summers on the Edward's Plateau in Texas.

3 BLACK-THROATED GREEN WARBLER *Dendroica virens* 13cm
FIELD NOTES: Feeds mainly in mid- to high levels, on insects captured by gleaning, hovering or fly-catching. VOICE: A lisping *zee zee zee zo zee*. Calls include a sharp *tsik* or *tek* and a high, rising *swit* flight note. HABITAT: Open conifer and mixed forests and cypress swamps. DISTRIBUTION: Boreal Canada, from NE British Columbia east to Newfoundland, then south along the Appalachians and the Atlantic coast in North and South Carolina. Winters in S Florida and extreme S Texas.

4 TOWNSEND'S WARBLER *Dendroica townsendi* 13cm FIELD NOTES: Actions much as Black-throated Green Warbler. VOICE: Song is a series of *zee* notes followed by 2 or 3 high buzzy notes. Calls include a metallic *tick*. HABITAT: Mature coniferous forests. DISTRIBUTION: Summers in W North America, from SE Alaska south to Oregon and Idaho.

5 HERMIT WARBLER *Dendroica occidentalis* 13cm FIELD NOTES: Active acrobatic forager in treetops. VOICE: Variable, includes a buzzy *ze ze ze ze ze ze zee sitew*, others are longer. Calls like Townsend's Warbler. HABITAT: Mature conifer forests. DISTRIBUTION: Summers along Pacific coast of the USA.

6 BLACKBURNIAN WARBLER *Dendroica fusca* 13cm FIELD NOTES: Tends to forage high in the canopy. VOICE: Variable, consisting of *swee* notes followed by a high-pitched trill. Call, a sharp *tsip*; also a thin *seet* flight note. HABITAT: Coniferous and mixed forest; on migration found in all types of woodland and tall bushes. DISTRIBUTION: Summers in NE USA, the Appalachians and SE Canada west to extreme EC Alberta.

7 YELLOW-THROATED WARBLER *Dendroica dominica* 14cm FIELD NOTES: Often forages nuthatch-like in tree canopy. Eastern interior birds lack yellow on fore of eye-brow. VOICE: A series of descending, whistled notes ending in a flourish. Calls are a sweet *chip* and a high *see* flight note. HABITAT: Oak, pine or cypress woodlands. Any woodland or scrub in winter. DISTRIBUTION: SE USA. Winters in Florida.

8 GRACE'S WARBLER *Dendroica graciae* 13cm FIELD NOTES: Forages in treetops, creeps along branches in search of insects. VOICE: Series of down-slurred whistles, quickening and rising towards the end. Call include a sweet *chirp* and a thin *tss* flight note. HABITAT: Pine-oak forests, especially if containing ponderosa or yellow pine. DISTRIBUTION: Summers in C SW USA.

9 PINE WARBLER *Dendroica pinus* 14cm FIELD NOTES: Acrobatic forager from ground level to treetops. VOICE: A simple 1-pitched trill. Calls include a sharp *chip* and a *zeet* flight note. HABITAT: Pine forests. During migration and in winter also occurs in deciduous wood and thickets. DISTRIBUTION: E USA and adjacent Canada, northern birds winter in SE USA.

10 KIRTLAND'S WARBLER *Dendroica kirtlandii* 15cm FIELD NOTES: Endangered. Usually feeds in low to middle levels, occasionally on the ground. VOICE: An emphatic *flip lip lip-lip-tip-tip* CHIDIP. Calls are a descending *tchip* and a high buzzy flight note. HABITAT: Dense stands of young jack-pines. DISTRIBUTION: Breeds in NC Michigan.

1 PRAIRIE WARBLER *Dendroica discolor* 12cm FIELD NOTES: Forages from low to mid-levels in undergrowth. VOICE: A series of rising buzzy notes. Call is a low, sharp *tchip* or *tsup*. HABITAT: Dry scrubby areas, bushy second growth and mangroves. DISTRIBUTION: Summers over most of E USA, resident in Florida.

2 PALM WARBLER *Dendroica palmarum* 14cm FIELD NOTES: Forages low in vegetation or on the ground; hops. Wags tail. Depicted are the eastern (fig 2b) *D. p. hypochrysea* and the nominate. VOICE: A rising and accelerating buzzy trill. Call, a husky *chik* or *sup*; in flight utters a high *seep*. HABITAT: Damp areas of conifer forests. Post breeding in weedy fields, marshes and urban areas. DISTRIBUTION: Boreal Canada, NE USA and SW of the Great Lakes. Winters in extreme SE USA.

3 BAY-BREASTED WARBLER *Dendroica castanea* 14cm FIELD NOTES: Feeds in mid- to high levels, by gleaning and occasional fly-catching. VOICE: A series of high *si* notes. Calls include a high-pitched *sip* and a loud *chip*. HABITAT: Open conifer and mixed forests; after breeding in any type of woodland. DISTRIBUTION: Summers in boreal Canada and N New England.

4 BLACKPOLL WARBLER *Dendroica striata* 14cm FIELD NOTES: Gleans and occasionally fly-catches at mid- to high levels. VOICE: A series of 1-pitched, high *si* notes. Calls include a thin *ssts* and a high *sip*. HABITAT: Coniferous forests, on migration in any type of woodland. DISTRIBUTION: Summers in boreal Canada, Alaska and N New England.

5 CERULEAN WARBLER *Dendroica cerulea* 12cm FIELD NOTES: Feeds mainly in tree canopy. VOICE: A short series of buzzy notes ending in a high buzzy trill. Call is a sharp *chip*; in flight a loud *zzee*. HABITAT: Mature open deciduous or mixed forest, often near swamps. On migration uses any type of woodland. DISTRIBUTION: Summers in E USA, apart from SE states.

6 PROTHONOTARY WARBLER *Protonotaria citrea* 14cm FIELD NOTES: Forages from low to mid-levels. Action much like Black-and-white Warbler. VOICE: A series of ringing *zweet* notes. Calls include a ringing *tsip*, a soft *psit* and a thin *seet* flight note. HABITAT: Swampy, mature woodlands. DISTRIBUTION: Summers in E USA.

7 BLACK-AND-WHITE WARBLER *Mniotila varia* 13cm FIELD NOTES: Climbs up and down trunks and large branches, nuthatch-like, probing for insects. VOICE: A sharp *tick* and a thin *tsip* or *tzeet*. Song transcribed as *see-wee-see-wee-see-wee-see-wee-see-wee-see-wee-see*. HABITAT: Deciduous and mixed woodland, often in damp areas. DISTRIBUTION: Summers in North America, east of the Rockies and south of Arctic areas. Winters in Florida and the Gulf coast.

8 AMERICAN REDSTART *Setophaga ruticilla* 13cm FIELD NOTES: Very active. Regularly fans wings and tail. VOICE: A sweet *chip* and a high, rising *sweet* flight note. Song variable, usually a high-pitched series ending with an emphatic low note. HABITAT: Open woodland, woodland edge, clearings and tall brush. DISTRIBUTION: Summers over much of North America, apart from the far north, SW USA and extreme SE USA. A few winter in S Florida.

9 SWAINSON'S WARBLER *Limnothlypis swainsonii* 14cm FIELD NOTES: Forages on the ground, in low bushes and on logs. VOICE: 3 loud whistles followed by a slow warble. Call is a strong *sship*. HABITAT: Lowland swamps and canebrakes with dense undergrowth. In the Appalachians utilises rhododendron and laurel thickets. DISTRIBUTION: Summers in SE USA, apart from Florida.

10 WORM-EATING WARBLER *Helmitheros vermivorum* 14cm FIELD NOTES: Forages in undergrowth and in trees, among dead leaf clumps. VOICE: Song is a monotonous 1-pitched trill. Calls include a sharp *tchip* and a buzzy *zeet-zeet*. HABITAT: Wooded hillsides and ravines, with dense undergrowth, often near streams. DISTRIBUTION: Summers in mid-eastern USA.

89 AMERICAN WARBLERS

1 KENTUCKY WARBLER *Oporornis formosus* 13cm FIELD NOTES: Shy and skulking, forages on the ground, where it hops, and in low bushes. VOICE: A low, sharp *tship* and a buzzy *zeep*. Song consists of a series of loud, whistled *churree* notes. HABITAT: Mature deciduous forests with dense undergrowth, often in damp situations. DISTRIBUTION: Summers over most of E USA.

2 CONNECTICUT WARBLER *Oporornis agilis* 13–15cm FIELD NOTES: Forages on the ground, where it walks in a deliberate manner, or in low bushes. VOICE: A metallic *plink* and a high, buzzy *zee* flight note. Song is a loud *wee-cher-cher wee-cher-cher*…. HABITAT: Spruce and tamarack bogs and on dry ridges in open poplar woods. DISTRIBUTION: Summers in boreal Canada and the Great Lakes region in the USA.

3 MOURNING WARBLER *Oporornis philadelphia* 13cm FIELD NOTES: Skulking, forages mainly on the ground, where it hops, or in low, dense undergrowth. VOICE: Song is a rich, churring *churree churree churree turi turi*. Calls include a flat *chip* and a *svit* or *zee* flight note. HABITAT: Second growth, dense understorey of forest edges and clearings, often near damp situations. DISTRIBUTION: Summers in boreal Canada and NE USA.

4 MacGILLIVRAY'S WARBLER *Oporornis tolmiei* 13cm FIELD NOTES: White eye arcs. Feeds in low, dense cover. VOICE: A dry *shik* or *twik*. Song consists of a short series of buzzy notes followed by 2 or 3 lower *teeoo* notes. HABITAT: Open forest, forest edge and mountainside scrub. DISTRIBUTION: Summers in W North America, south from S Yukon.

5 YELLOWTHROAT (COMMON YELLOWTHROAT) *Geothlypis trichas* 13cm FIELD NOTES: Forages in thick vegetation, often with tail cocked. All western birds show a paler head band. VOICE: Song variable, often transcribed as *wichity-wichity-wichity-wich*. Call, a dry *chep* or *tchuk*. HABITAT: Primarily thick waterside vegetation. DISTRIBUTION: Summers in North America, south of tundra areas, resident in extreme SW and SE USA.

6 GREY-CROWNED YELLOWTHROAT *Geothlypis poliocephala* 14.5cm FIELD NOTES: Frequently pumps tail up and down or twitches it from side to side. VOICE: A loud, slapping *chack*. Song is a varied, halting warble. HABITAT: Damp fields, hedgerows and bushy savannahs. DISTRIBUTION: Rare vagrant from Mexico.

7 OVENBIRD *Seiurus aurocapilla* 15cm FIELD NOTES: Forages among forest floor leaf litter. Walks in a jerky manner. VOICE: Song is an emphatic *teecher-teecher-teecher*, rising in pitch and volume. Call is a *chuk* or *tsuk*, often repeated. HABITAT: Mature deciduous and mixed forest, with dense understorey. DISTRIBUTION: Summers in North America, east of the Rockies, although missing from much of the southern states. Winters in Florida.

8 NORTHERN WATERTHRUSH *Seiurus noveboracensis* 12.5–15cm FIELD NOTES: Constantly bobs rear-end as it walks on logs or the ground. Alaskan race (fig 8b) is whiter below and greyer above. VOICE: Song often transcribed as *swee-swee-chi-weedleo*, the last note down-slurred. Call is a loud metallic *chink*. HABITAT: Woodland and thickets, near water. DISTRIBUTION: Summers in boreal Canada, inland NW USA and northern states of E USA. A few birds winter in S Florida.

9 LOUISIANA WATERTHRUSH *Seiurus motacilla* 14.5–16cm FIELD NOTES: Actions and habits similar to Northern Waterthrush. VOICE: Song is loud and consists of a short series of descending notes followed by a warbling twitter. Call is a high-pitched *chink*. HABITAT: Wooded ravines by running water and wooded swamps. DISTRIBUTION: Summers in E USA, apart from Florida and the Gulf coast.

90 AMERICAN WARBLERS

1 WILSON'S WARBLER *Wilsonia pusilla* 12cm FIELD NOTES: Active, constantly flicks wings and tail. Forages in thick undergrowth. VOICE: A staccato *chi-chi-chi-chi-chi-chet-chet*. Call is a loud, low *chet*, a hard *tik* and a down-slurred *tsip* flight note. HABITAT: Various woodland types with thick undergrowth. DISTRIBUTION: Summers in much of Alaska and Canada and south along mountainous areas of W USA. Some birds winter on Gulf coast and S Florida.

2 HOODED WARBLER *Wilsonia citrina* 13cm FIELD NOTES: Constantly flicks wings and spreads tail, the latter reveals the white in the outer feathers. VOICE: A loud *too-ee too-ee too-ee tee-ch*. Calls include a sharp *tchip* or *tchink* and a buzzy *zrr*. HABITAT: Mature deciduous woodland with dense understorey, usually near water. DISTRIBUTION: Summers in E USA, west to Iowa and E Texas; missing from Florida.

3 CANADA WARBLER *Wilsonia canadensis* 13cm FIELD NOTES: Active, often forages with tail cocked. VOICE: Song is a variable warble. Calls include a sharp *chick* or *tyup*; flight call recorded both as a low *plik* or a high *zzee*. HABITAT: Deciduous and mixed forests with dense undergrowth, usually near water. DISTRIBUTION: Summers in boreal Canada and NE USA.

4 RED-FACED WARBLER *Cardellina rubrifrons* 14cm FIELD NOTES: Unmistakeable. Usually forages on higher branches. VOICE: Song is a thin *towee towee towee tsew tsew wetoo weeeeew*. Call, a sharp *tuk* or *tship*. HABITAT: Firs and maples in mountain canyons. DISTRIBUTION: Summers in Arizona and New Mexico.

5 SLATE-THROATED REDSTART (WHITE-THROATED WHITESTART) *Myioborus miniatus* 13–14cm FIELD NOTES: Actions and habits similar to Painted Redstart. VOICE: A simple, rising and accelerating *chee chee chee chee....* Call is a sharp *tic*. HABITAT: Montane pine and pine-oak forest. DISTRIBUTION: Rare vagrant from Mexico.

6 PAINTED REDSTART (PAINTED WHITESTART) *Myioborus pictus* 13–13.5cm FIELD NOTES: Active and acrobatic, constantly flicks and spreads wings and tail. VOICE: A soft, musical warble. Calls include a *chidi-ew*, *chwee*, *tseeoo* and a *bdeeyu*. HABITAT: Pine-oak and oak forests. DISTRIBUTION: Summers in Arizona and SE New Mexico.

7 FAN-TAILED WARBLER *Euthlypis lachrymosa* 15cm FIELD NOTES: Tail is constantly flicked and spread, revealing white tips. Feeds on the ground and low in undergrowth. VOICE: Song variable, a warbled *wee wee wee-wee wee-cher* and an even-pitched series ending in a slow flourish. Call, a low-pitched *tseeng*. HABITAT: Sub-montane forest with thick undergrowth. DISTRIBUTION: Rare vagrant from Mexico.

8 GOLDEN-CROWNED WARBLER *Basileuterus culicivorus* 12.5cm FIELD NOTES: Often flicks wings and cocks tail. VOICE: Song variable, normally a short series of slurred whistles. Call, a hard, dry *tek* and a loose rattle. HABITAT: Sub-montane forest and forest edge. DISTRIBUTION: Rare vagrant from Mexico.

9 RUFOUS-CAPPED WARBLER *Basileuterus rufifrons* 13cm FIELD NOTES: Habitually cocks tail and flicks wings. Generally forages low in scrub. VOICE: Song a series of variable, jumbled notes, starts with chirps and ends in an emphatic whistle. Call, a hard *chek*, often lengthened into a harsh chatter. HABITAT: Scrub, forest edge and brushy ravines. DISTRIBUTION: Rare vagrant from Mexico.

10 YELLOW-BREASTED CHAT *Icteria virens* 19cm FIELD NOTES: Shy and retiring, forages in low dense cover, searching for invertebrates or fruit. VOICE: Song consists of a loud jumble of rattles, cackles, squeals and whistles. Calls include a harsh grating *chack*, a nasal *cheewb* and a soft *tuk*. HABITAT: Dense thickets, scrub and woodland edge. DISTRIBUTION: Summers over most of USA, apart from Great Lakes area and Florida, and in southern quarter of W Canada.

91 BANANAQUIT, TANAGERS, GRASSQUITS AND SEEDEATER

1 BANANAQUIT *Coereba flaveola* 11cm FIELD NOTES: Very active, probes flowers on trees or plants in search of nectar; also eats small berries. VOICE: A metallic *ssint*. Song consists of hissing squeaks and buzzes. HABITAT: Open woods and urban areas with flowering or fruiting trees. DISTRIBUTION: Rare vagrant to Florida from the Bahamas.

2 HEPATIC TANAGER *Piranga flava* 18–20cm FIELD NOTES: Usually unobtrusive, forages in upper branches of tall trees. VOICE: Call, a low *chup*. Song consists of sweet rising and falling phrases. HABITAT: Montane pine-oak forests. DISTRIBUTION: Summers in inland SW USA.

3 SUMMER TANAGER *Piranga rubra* 19cm FIELD NOTES: Mainly arboreal. Often makes sallies after flying insects. VOICE: Song is a thrush-like series of sweet, clear notes. Calls include a *chick* and chattering *pit-a chuck piki-i-tuck* or *piki-i-tuck-i-tuck*. HABITAT: Oak or pine-oak woodland. DISTRIBUTION: Summers in S USA, avoiding much of the S Rockies region.

4 WESTERN TANAGER *Piranga ludoviciana* 18cm FIELD NOTES: Arboreal. Non-breeding male has orange confined to face. VOICE: Song similar to Scarlet Tanager. Calls include a soft, rising rattle and a soft whistled *howee* or *weet* flight note. HABITAT: Coniferous mountain forests. DISTRIBUTION: Summers in most of the mountain areas of W North America, south from SE Northwest Territories.

5 SCARLET TANAGER *Piranga olivacea* 18cm FIELD NOTES: Forages mainly in treetops, but will descend to feed on the ground. VOICE: Song is a raspy *querit-queer-query-querit-queer*. Calls include a hoarse *chip-burr* and a clear *puwi* flight note. HABITAT: Mature deciduous woodland. DISTRIBUTION: Summers in the northern three-quarters of E USA and adjacent Canada.

6 FLAME-COLOURED TANAGER *Piranga bidentata* 18–19cm FIELD NOTES: White tail corners. Forages in mid- to upper levels. VOICE: Song a burry *chik churree chuwee* or *churee chiree ch-ree chiwee....* Calls include a hard *ch-t-ruk*, *p-terruk* and a short *ch-duk*. HABITAT: Oak and pine-oak woods. DISTRIBUTION: Rare vagrant from Mexico.

7 WESTERN SPINDALIS (STRIPE-HEADED TANAGER) *Spindalis zena* 15cm FIELD NOTES: Forages mainly in fruiting trees. The green-backed race *S. z. pretrei* (fig 7b) breeds on Cuba. VOICE: Song is a series of thin, high notes that lead into buzzy phrases. Calls include a descending, high-pitched *see-see-see-see...*, a strong *seee* and a sharp *tit*. HABITAT: Open woodland, gardens with fruiting trees. DISTRIBUTION: Rare vagrant to Florida from the West Indies.

8 YELLOW-FACED GRASSQUIT *Tiaris olivaceus* 11.5cm FIELD NOTES: Female face pattern is faint copy of male's. Forages on grass seed-heads or on the ground. Often sings from a tall grass-spike or similar. VOICE: Song is a weak, rapid trill. Call, a soft *tek*. HABITAT: Open grassy areas. DISTRIBUTION: Rare vagrant from Mexico.

9 BLACK-FACED GRASSQUIT *Tiaris bicolor* 11.5cm FIELD NOTES: Female plain headed, no yellow pattern. Usually forages in pairs or small flocks, searching for seeds and occasionally insects. VOICE: Song is a loud, buzzing *dik-zeezeezee*. Call, a soft, musical *tsip*. HABITAT: Open areas with grasses and shrubs. DISTRIBUTION: Very rare vagrant from the West Indies.

10 WHITE-COLLARED SEEDEATER *Sporophila torqueola* 11.5cm FIELD NOTES: After breeding, often found in company with other seed-eating birds. Sings from fences, trees and wires. VOICE: Song is a series of sweet whistles, *sweet sweet tew tew tew tew sit*. Calls include a husky *quit*, a nasal *cheh* and a loud *seeu*. HABITAT: Dense grass near tall cane, weedy fields and second growth. DISTRIBUTION: Rare in S Texas.

92 TOWHEES AND AMERICAN SPARROWS

1 GREEN-TAILED TOWHEE *Pipilo chlorurus* 18cm FIELD NOTES: Forages on or near the ground. VOICE: A drawn-out *weet-chur*, then whistles followed by a rasping trill. Call, a *meewe*; flight call, a buzzy *zeereesh*. HABITAT: Chaparral, thickets and dense brush. DISTRIBUTION: Summers inland in W USA. Winters along the US-Mexican border.

2 EASTERN TOWHEE *Pipilo erythrophthalmus* 20cm FIELD NOTES: Ground feeder, usually under cover. VOICE: Transcribed as *drink-your-tea-ee-ee-ee-ee*. Call, a rising *tow-whee* or *chee-wink*; also a buzzy *zeeeewee* flight note. HABITAT: Undergrowth, woodland edge and gardens. DISTRIBUTION: E USA and adjacent Canada, northern birds move south in winter.

3 SPOTTED TOWHEE *Pipilo maculatus* 20cm FIELD NOTES: Often combined with Eastern Towhee and called Rufous-sided Towhee. Actions and habits similar. VOICE: A *che che che che che zhree* or similar. Call, a harsh *zhree* or *grreeer*; in flight, a *zeeeewee*. HABITAT: Dense brush, woodland edge and gardens. DISTRIBUTION: W USA and adjacent Canada, north-eastern birds move south or west in winter.

4 CANYON TOWHEE *Pipilo fuscus* 19–24cm FIELD NOTES: Forages by scratching in leaf litter. Originally combined with California Towhee and called Brown Towhee. VOICE: A simple trill, introduced by the call note. Calls include a nasal *kidl*, a dry *ch-ch-ch-ch* and a buzzy *zeee* flight note. DISTRIBUTION: C SW USA.

5 CALIFORNIA TOWHEE *Pipilo crissalis* 21–22cm FIELD NOTES: Habits similar to Canyon Towhee. VOICE: An accelerating series of *teek* notes. Call, a metallic *teek*; flight note, a buzzy *zeee*. HABITAT: Brush and arid scrub. DISTRIBUTION: Coastal California and SW Oregon.

6 ABERT'S TOWHEE *Pipilo aberti* 24cm FIELD NOTES: Habits as Canyon Towhee. VOICE: Variably pitched chipping trill. Calls, a sharp *teek*, a high *seeeep* and a buzzy *zeeoeeet* flight note. HABITAT: Dense scrub, especially near water. DISTRIBUTION: SE California, SW Arizona, SW New Mexico, SE Nevada and SW Utah.

7 OLIVE SPARROW *Arremonops rufivirgatus* 14–16cm FIELD NOTES: Forages on the ground. Often cocks tail. VOICE: An accelerating *tsip tsip tsiptsiptsiptiptiptiptptptptptp*. Call, a high *tsip*, flight note a buzzy *seere*. HABITAT: Woodland with dense undergrowth. DISTRIBUTION: S Texas.

8 RUFOUS-WINGED SPARROW *Aimophila carpalis* 14.5cm FIELD NOTES: Forages on the ground and in bushes. VOICE: Variable; *chip* notes accelerating into a trill. Call, a high *seep*. HABITAT: Desert grassland with mesquite. DISTRIBUTION: SC Arizona.

9 CASSIN'S SPARROW *Aimophila cassinii* 15cm FIELD NOTES: Shy except when singing. Forages on the ground, often under cover. VOICE: Song, generally given during display flight, transcribed as *tsisi seeeeeeee ssootssiit*. Calls include a high *teep* and a loud *chip*. HABITAT: Arid grassland with scattered brush or scrub. DISTRIBUTION: Summers in SC USA. Resident adjacent to Mexican border.

10 BACHMAN'S SPARROW *Aimophila aestivalis* 15cm FIELD NOTES: Forages mainly on the ground. Western birds *A. a. bachmani* (fig 10b) more rufous and paler. VOICE: Simple clear whistle followed by a musical trill. Call high *tsip* notes. HABITAT: Open pine woods with patches of brush or grass. DISTRIBUTION: SE USA, apart from S Florida. Northern interior birds move south in winter.

11 BOTTERI'S SPARROW *Aimophila botterii* 15cm FIELD NOTES: Forages on the ground, often with tail cocked. VOICE: A series of whistles ending in an accelerating trill. Call, a high *chip* or rapid chatter. HABITAT: Grassland with scattered bushes. DISTRIBUTION: SE Arizona and S Texas.

12 RUFOUS-CROWNED SPARROW *Aimophila ruficeps* 15cm FIELD NOTES: Forages on the ground. Paler race *A. r. eremoeca* (fig 12b) occurs inland. VOICE: A jumbled series of *chip* notes. Call, a nasal *chur chur chur*, a chatter and a high *zeeet*. HABITAT: Brush and grassy areas on rocky slopes. DISTRIBUTION: Most of SW USA.

93 AMERICAN SPARROWS

1 FIVE-STRIPED SPARROW *Aimophila quinquestriata* 15cm FIELD NOTES: Forages
on the ground and in bushes. VOICE: Short, repeated, tinkling phrases. Calls, a husky
terp, a soft *tink* and a high *tip*. HABITAT: Dense bush and scrub areas on grassy, rocky
hillsides. DISTRIBUTION: SC Arizona.

2 AMERICAN TREE SPARROW *Spizella arborea* 16–17cm FIELD NOTES: Mainly
terrestrial. Gregarious during winter. VOICE: Clear *seet* notes followed by a rapid,
variable warble. Calls, a *tseet* and a musical *teedle-eet-teedle-eet*. HABITAT: Open scrub
on the edge of tundra, winters in weedy areas. DISTRIBUTION: Alaska and N mainland
Canada. Winters over most of USA and Pacific coast of Canada.

3 CLAY-COLOURED SPARROW *Spizella pallida* 14cm FIELD NOTES: Forages
on the ground and in bushes. In winter often mixes with Chipping Sparrow. VOICE:
A short series of insect-like buzzes. Calls, a weak *chip* and a rising *swit* flight note.
HABITAT: Scrubby grassland, thickets. Winters in open areas with scattered scrub.
DISTRIBUTION: Prairies of Canada and adjacent USA, east through the Great Lakes.
Winters in SW Texas.

4 CHIPPING SPARROW *Spizella passerina* 13cm FIELD NOTES: Feeds on the ground
or in bushes. Associates with other seed-eaters during winter. VOICE: A monotonous,
dry trill. Call, *chip* or *tsip*; flight note a rising *tsisi*. HABITAT: Open conifer or pine-oak
woods, woodland edge and urban bushy areas. Winters in open grassy areas, thickets
and gardens. DISTRIBUTION: Most of temperate North America, winters in S USA.

5 FIELD SPARROW *Spizella pusilla* 14–15cm FIELD NOTES: Pinkish bill. Forages
mainly on the ground. Western race *S. p. arenacea* (fig 5b) occurs from North Dakota
south to Texas. VOICE: Clear whistles accelerating into a short trill. Calls include a
tsip and a *tseew* flight note. HABITAT: Overgrown grassy areas with scattered bushes.
DISTRIBUTION: E USA, northern birds move south in winter.

6 WORTHEN'S SPARROW *Spizella wortheni* 15cm FIELD NOTES: Forages on the
ground. Often considered a race of Field Sparrow, differs in song and habitat. VOICE: A
slow monotonous trill. HABITAT: Mesquite-juniper grassland. DISTRIBUTION: Very rare
vagrant from NE Mexico.

7 BLACK-CHINNED SPARROW *Spizella atrogularis* 15cm FIELD NOTES:
Secretive. Forages on the ground or in bushes. VOICE: Sharp, slurred notes that run into
a rapid trill. Call, a weak *tsip* and a *ssip* flight note. HABITAT: Arid scrub, bushy hillsides
and chaparral. DISTRIBUTION: Extreme SW USA. Winters along US-Mexican border.

8 BREWER'S SPARROW *Spizella breweri* 14cm FIELD NOTES: Forages on ground and
in bushes. Gregarious in winter, regularly associated with other sparrow species. VOICE:
A variable series of buzzes and trills. Calls include a sharp *tsip* and a rising *swit* flight
note. HABITAT: Sagebrush and open scrubby areas. Winters in open, semiarid areas and
grassland. DISTRIBUTION: Interior of W USA and adjacent Canada, isolated population
(Timberland Sparrow) centred in SW Yukon. Winters along US-Mexican border.

9 VESPER SPARROW *Pooecetes gramineus* 16cm FIELD NOTES: Forages on the
ground. In flight shows white outer tail feathers. In worn plumage (autumn), streaking
heavier. VOICE: Melodious, 2 long slurred notes, 2 higher notes then a short series of
descending trills. Calls, a loud *hisp* and a buzzy *seet* flight note. HABITAT: Semiarid
scrub, weedy fields and open grasslands. DISTRIBUTION: Most of temperate North
America, apart from S USA, where it is a winter resident.

10 LARK SPARROW *Chondestes grammacus* 15cm FIELD NOTES: In flight shows
much white on outer tail feathers. VOICE: Long trills and buzzes. Calls include a
metallic *tink* and a high *tsewp*. HABITAT: Open country with scattered bushes and trees.
DISTRIBUTION: Most of USA, west of the Appalachians and SW Canada. Northern
and central birds move south in winter.

94 AMERICAN SPARROWS AND LARK BUNTING

1 BLACK-THROATED SPARROW *Amphispiza bileneata* 14cm FIELD NOTES: Calls constantly and regularly flicks tail. White outer tail feathers. VOICE: Rapid, metallic notes followed by a trill. Call, a high, tinkling *tip*. HABITAT: Arid areas with scattered scrub. DISTRIBUTION: Interior of W USA, winters along US-Mexican border.

2 SAGE SPARROW *Amphispiza belli* 16cm FIELD NOTES: Often runs with tail cocked. Race *A. b. nevadensis* (fig 2b) occurs in the Great Basin. VOICE: Jumbled series of rising and falling phrases. Calls include a high twittering. HABITAT: Chaparral (coastal birds), sagebrush and saltbush. DISTRIBUTION: W USA, northern birds move south in winter.

3 LARK BUNTING *Calamospiza melanocorys* 18–19cm FIELD NOTES: Terrestrial. Forms large winter flocks. VOICE: Varied whistles and trills. Call, a soft *hoo-ee*. HABITAT: Dry grassland, farmland and semiarid areas. DISTRIBUTION: C USA and adjacent Canadian prairies. Winters in Texas and along US-Mexican border.

4 SAVANNAH SPARROW *Passerculus sandwichensis* 14–16cm
FIELD NOTES: Variable, shown are the nominate from Alaska; *P. s. beldingi* (fig 4b), from coastal California; *P. s. princeps* (fig 4c), from Sable Island; *P. s. rostratus* (fig 4d), from extreme SE California. VOICE: A series of *chips*, then a buzzy trill followed by a low trill. Call, a thin *seep*. HABITAT: Grasslands, coastal salt marsh and sand dunes. DISTRIBUTION: Virtually the whole of North America, although only a winter visitor in S USA.

5 GRASSHOPPER SPARROW *Ammodramus savannarum* 13cm
FIELD NOTES: Secretive. Regularly flicks wings and cocks tail. VOICE: A thin, insect-like buzz preceded by 2 *tik* notes; also a high tinkling. Call, a thin *tip* and a rising *tswees* flight note. HABITAT: Weedy fields with tall grass. DISTRIBUTION: Most of USA and adjacent W Canada, although absent from much of the CW USA. Winters along US-Mexican border and SE USA.

6 BAIRD'S SPARROW *Ammodramus bairdii* 14cm FIELD NOTES: Very shy, best observed whilst singing from bush or plant stem. VOICE: *zip* notes, then a warble followed by a short trill. Calls, a high *chip* and a low *tr-r-i-p*. HABITAT: Short grass prairie with scattered bushes. DISTRIBUTION: Canadian and US prairies. Winters on US-Mexican border, from SE Arizona to SW Texas.

7 LE CONTE'S SPARROW *Ammodramus lecontei* 13cm FIELD NOTES: Secretive, only conspicuous while singing, from bush top or plant stem. VOICE: A buzzy *tse-bzzzz*. Call, a short *tseep*. HABITAT: Grasslands and moist meadows. DISTRIBUTION: Canadian prairies, east to C Quebec and NE states of E USA. Winters in SE USA.

8 SALTMARSH SHARP-TAILED SPARROW *Ammodramus caudacutus* 13cm
FIELD NOTES: Shy, forages in dense grass and bushes. VOICE: Rapid sequence of gurgling notes. Call, a hard *tek*. HABITAT: Grassy marshes or meadows. DISTRIBUTION: Summers on Atlantic coast of USA, from Maine to North Carolina, northern birds move south to winter on coast from New Jersey to Florida.

9 NELSON'S SHARP-TAILED SPARROW *Ammodramus nelsoni* 13cm
FIELD NOTES: Shy, forages in dense grass and bushes. Atlantic birds *A. n. subvirgatus* (fig 9b) greyer. VOICE: A soft, fading *pl-tesh hhhhh-ush*. Call, a hard *tek*. HABITAT: Grassy marshes or meadows. DISTRIBUTION: Central North American prairies, along shores of S Hudson Bay and NE Atlantic coast, from the St Lawrence to Maine.

10 HENSLOW'S SPARROW *Ammodramus henslowii* 13cm FIELD NOTES: Forages in dense cover. VOICE: An insect-like *tsillik*. Call, a sharp *tsik*. HABITAT: Weedy fields. DISTRIBUTION: NE USA, winters in SE USA.

11 SEASIDE SPARROW *Ammodramus maritimus* 15cm FIELD NOTES: Variable, shown are the nominate, *A. m. mirabilis* (fig 11b) from the Everglades and *A. m. fisheri* (fig 11c) from the Gulf. VOICE: A muffled *tup teetle-zhrrrr*. Call, a low *tup*. HABITAT: Coastal marshes. DISTRIBUTION: Atlantic and Gulf coasts of USA.

95 AMERICAN SPARROWS AND JUNCOS

1 FOX SPARROW *Passerella iliaca* 18cm FIELD NOTES: Highly variable, 3 extremes shown; nominate, from NE North America; *P. i. unalaschcensis* (fig 1b), from Alaska; *P. i. stephensi* (fig 1c), from S California. VOICE: Melodious notes, slowly rising then falling, often interspersed with buzzy trills. Calls, a *stsssp* and various *chips*. HABITAT: Woodland undergrowth, thickets and chaparral. DISTRIBUTION: Boreal Canada and Alaska, and W mountains of USA. Winters in USA, on Pacific coast and in S states.

2 SONG SPARROW *Melospiza melodia* 16cm FIELD NOTES: Variable, from pale rufous interior SW USA race *M. m. saltonis* (fig 2b), to the dark grey races of NW North America. VOICE: Clear notes followed by a buzzing rattle and trill. Calls, a nasal *tchep* and a thin *tsee*. HABITAT: Open shrubby areas, waterside thickets and urban gardens. DISTRIBUTION: Most of temperate North America, although only a winter visitor to SE USA.

3 LINCOLN'S SPARROW *Melospiza lincolnii* 15cm FIELD NOTES: Forages under cover. VOICE: A jumble of husky, chirping trills. Call, a nasal *tschup*. HABITAT: Moist mountain meadows. In winter favours brushy areas. DISTRIBUTION: Boreal Alaska and Canada, southward in Great Lakes region and along W mountain ranges of USA. Winters in the USA, along Pacific coast and in S states.

4 SWAMP SPARROW *Melospiza georgiana* 15cm FIELD NOTES: Secretive, except when singing. VOICE: A slow 1-pitched trill. Call, a hard *chip*. HABITAT: Well-vegetated marshy areas. DISTRIBUTION: Temperate Canada and NE USA, winters in southern two-thirds of E USA.

5 HARRIS'S SPARROW *Zonotrichia querula* 19cm FIELD NOTES: Unmistakeable. VOICE: High clear *seeeeeeee seee seee*. Call, a harsh *cheek*. HABITAT: Stunted boreal forest, winters in thickets and open woodland. DISTRIBUTION: NC Canada, winters in C USA, south to Texas.

6 GOLDEN-CROWNED SPARROW *Zonotrichia atricapilla* 18cm FIELD NOTES: Head pattern duller in non-breeding plumage. VOICE: Short series of melancholy whistles. Calls, a *chink* and thin *seet*. HABITAT: Meadows, with bushes, in mountain and tundra areas. Winters in dry woodland and thickets. DISTRIBUTION: Alaska and Pacific coast of Canada. Winters on Pacific coast of USA.

7 WHITE-THROATED SPARROW *Zonotrichia albicollis* 16cm FIELD NOTES: Some birds have ochre eye-brow stripe. VOICE: A whistled *dee-dee diddla-diddla-diddla*. Calls, a high *tseet* and a sharp *pink*. HABITAT: Open conifer or mixed woodland, bushy clearings and scrub. Winters in scrub, woodlots and gardens. DISTRIBUTION: Much of temperate and boreal Canada and NE USA. Winters over much of E and S USA.

8 WHITE-CROWNED SPARROW *Zonotrichia leucophrys* 16cm FIELD NOTES: Terrestrial forager. NW and California races lack black lores. VOICE: A sad *more-wet-wetter-chee-zee*. Calls, a *tsit* and high *seet*. HABITAT: Dense brush and scrub. Winters in open woodland, woodland edge and urban areas. DISTRIBUTION: Much of Alaska and N Canada, and south into N and C areas of W USA. Winters along Pacific coast and southern two-thirds of USA.

9 YELLOW-EYED JUNCO *Junco phaeonotus* 16cm FIELD NOTES: Forages on the ground and in bushes. VOICE: A 3-part series of whistles and trills. Calls, a high twittering and a sharp *dit*. HABITAT: Open coniferous or pine-oak forest. DISTRIBUTION: SE Arizona and SW New Mexico.

10 DARK-EYED JUNCO *Junco hyemalis* 16cm FIELD NOTES: Distinctive, but very variable; 5 races shown: nominate; *J. h. aikeni* (fig 10b); *J. h. caniceps* (fig 10c); *J. h. mearnsi* (fig 10d); *J. h. oreganus* (fig 10e). VOICE: Fast musical trill, interspersed with warbles, twitters and *chips*. Calls similar to Yellow-eyed Junco. HABITAT: Clearings and edges in coniferous and mixed woodland. Winters in woodland edge, weedy fields and gardens. DISTRIBUTION: Alaska across to Newfoundland, south down mountain ranges of USA. Winters over most of USA and southern W Canada.

96 DICKCISSEL, OLD WORLD SPARROWS, LONGSPURS AND BUNTINGS

1 DICKCISSEL *Spiza americana* 16cm FIELD NOTES: Feeds on the ground. Regularly perches on wires and fences. Gregarious, regularly mixes with other seed-eaters. VOICE: A staccato *dik-dik-serr-si-si dick-ciss-ciss-ciss* or *chup-chup-klip-klip-klip*. Call, a buzzing *dzzrrrt*. HABITAT: Open country, especially cereal fields and weedy grassland. DISTRIBUTION: Summers from the prairies east to the Appalachians and south to Texas.

2 HOUSE SPARROW (ENGLISH SPARROW) *Passer domesticus* 15cm FIELD NOTES: Forages primarily on the ground, feeding on seeds or virtually any scraps left by man. Usually in small flocks. VOICE: Song, consisting mainly of call notes, is an excited *chirrup-chirrup-cheep-chirp-chirrup....* Calls incude a *chirp*, *chirp*, *chissick* and a soft *swee-swee*; when alarmed a rolling *chur-r-r-it-it-it*. HABITAT: Urban areas, often in grassy areas away from buildings. DISTRIBUTION: Virtually the whole of temperate North America (introduced from Europe).

3 TREE SPARROW (EURASIAN TREE SPARROW) *Passer montanus* 14cm FIELD NOTES: Black cheek-patch. Habits much like House Sparrow. VOICE: Rapid alternating high and low call notes, interspersed with *tsooit*, *tsveet* or *tswee-ip* notes. Calls include a high, abrupt *chip* and a sharp *tet*. HABITAT: Urban areas. DISTRIBUTION: Resident in the St Louis area of Illinois (introduced from Europe).

4 SMITH'S LONGSPUR *Calcarius pictus* 15cm FIELD NOTES: 2 outermost pairs of tail feathers mainly white. Secretive. VOICE: A sweet high, warble *sew seeyu wee tee tee dzee tzeeyu* or similar. In flight gives a clear, descending rattle. HABITAT: Wet sedge meadows in tundra area; grassy areas in mountain passes. In winter, grassy or stubble fields. DISTRIBUTION: NE Alaska across to S Hudson Bay. Isolated population in SE Alaska–NW British Columbia. Winters in SC USA.

5 McCOWN'S LONGSPUR *Calcarius mccownii* 15cm FIELD NOTES: Tail mostly white, centre feathers and tips black. Forms winter flocks, often with Horned Larks and Lapland Buntings. VOICE: An energetic jumble of warbles and twitters, often given during display flight. Calls include a *kittip* and a popping *poik*. HABITAT: Short grass prairie. Winters on barren fields, dry lake beds and areas of short grass. DISTRIBUTION: Prairies, from S Canada to N Colorado. Winters in C S USA.

6 LAPLAND BUNTING (LAPLAND LONGSPUR) *Calcarius lapponicus* 15cm FIELD NOTES: White outer tail feathers. Gregarious after breeding, often with Horned Larks and Snow Buntings. VOICE: A husky, warbled *freew didi freer di fridi fideew*, often given during display flight. Calls include a melodious *tee-uu*, in flight utters a rattle and a high *jeeb*. HABITAT: Arctic tundra, winters on stubble fields, pastures and coastal marshes. DISTRIBUTION: Arctic region of Greenland and North America. Winters over most of C North America.

7 CHESTNUT-COLLARED LONGSPUR *Calcarius ornatus* 14cm FIELD NOTES: Tail white with black central triangle. Forms large winter flocks. VOICE: Pleasant warble, starting high, ending low and buzzy, often given in flight. Flight call is a *cheedle cheedle*; also a soft rattle and a buzz. HABITAT: Short grass plains, dense grasslands and wastelands. Winters in grassy areas. DISTRIBUTION: C North American prairies. Winters SC USA.

8 SNOW BUNTING *Plectrophenax nivalis* 15–18cm FIELD NOTES: Winters in small flocks, often with Horned Larks and Lapland Buntings. VOICE: Husky warbling with repeated phrases, often given in display flight. Calls include a *djee*, *chew* and a rippling *tiririrrit* flight note. HABITAT: Barren tundra, rocky terrain and sea cliffs. Winters on coasts and in open country. DISTRIBUTION: Coastal Alaska, Arctic Canada and Greenland. Winters across C North America and W Alaska.

9 McKAY'S BUNTING *Plectrophenax hyperboreus* 18cm FIELD NOTES: Generally whiter than Snow Bunting. Gregarious after breeding. VOICE: Similar to Snow Bunting. HABITAT: Beaches and inland tundra. DISTRIBUTION: Islands in the Bering Sea. Winters on coast of W Alaska.

97 BUNTINGS, CARDINAL AND PYRRHULOXIA

1 PINE BUNTING *Emberiza leucocephalos* 17cm FIELD NOTES: Distinctive. White on inner webs of outer tail feathers. Often associates with other buntings. VOICE: A soft *ze-ze-ze-ze-ze-ZE-ziiiii*. Calls include a metallic *tsit*, a thin *see* and a clicking *tit-tit-tit-tit*. HABITAT: Open forests; on migration and during winter favours arable fields, orchards and waste ground. DISTRIBUTION: Very rare vagrant from E Palearctic.

2 GREY BUNTING *Emberiza variabilis* 17cm FIELD NOTES: Usually forages on the ground in dense undergrowth. VOICE: A pleasant *hsüüü twis-twis-twis*. Call is a sharp *zhii*. HABITAT: Mainly forest undergrowth. DISTRIBUTION: Very rare vagrant from Asia.

3 LITTLE BUNTING *Emberiza pusilla* 13cm FIELD NOTES: Primarily a ground forager. During migration and winter regularly associates with other ground-feeding species. VOICE: Variable, consists of clear, harsh and rolling notes. Call, a hard *tzik* or *pwick*. HABITAT: Moist taiga. Winters in open areas such as fields, forest edges and marshes. DISTRIBUTION: Rare vagrant to the Aleutians and Alaska from N Palearctic.

4 RUSTIC BUNTING *Emberiza rustica* 14cm FIELD NOTES: Forages on the ground. After breeding usually forms small flocks. VOICE: A hurried, mellow warble *deduleu-dewee-deweea-weeu*. Calls, a sharp *tzik* and a high-pitched *tsiee*. HABITAT: Taiga. During migration and winter occurs in woodland, cultivated land and open areas. DISTRIBUTION: Rare vagrant from N Palearctic.

5 YELLOW-BROWED BUNTING *Emberiza chrysophrys* 15cm FIELD NOTES: Secretive. Often mixes with other buntings in winter. VOICE: A pleasant *sweee swee-swee doe-do-doe dweeeee*. Call, a sharp *tik*. HABITAT: Moist forest. Winters in thickets, woodland edge, scrubby and weedy areas. DISTRIBUTION: Very rare vagrant from C Siberia.

6 YELLOW-BREASTED BUNTING *Emberiza aureola* 15cm FIELD NOTES: Male unmistakeable. White wedge on outer tail feathers. Female underparts washed yellowish. VOICE: A monotonous series of rising, ringing notes that falls at the end. Calls, a sharp *tsik* and an abrupt *chup*. HABITAT: Meadows with scattered bushes, waterside thickets. Winters in weedy cultivation and stubble fields. DISTRIBUTION: Very rare vagrant from the Palearctic.

7 YELLOW-THROATED BUNTING *Emberiza elegans* 15cm FIELD NOTES: Unmistakeable. VOICE: A monotonous twitter. Call, a *tzik-tzik*. HABITAT: Open dry forests. Winters in mixed woodland, forest edge and scrubby areas by rivers. DISTRIBUTION: Very rare vagrant from E Palearctic.

8 PALLAS BUNTING (PALLAS'S REED BUNTING) *Emberiza pallasi* 14cm FIELD NOTES: Wing coverts grey. Generally, both sexes lack warm tones. VOICE: Monotonous, rasping *srih-srih-srih-srih*. Call, a fine *chleep* and a pipit-like *chelup*. HABITAT: Tundra thickets. Winters in reed-beds, wet grassy areas and riverine thickets. DISTRIBUTION: Very rare vagrant from NE Palearctic.

9 REED BUNTING *Emberiza schoeniclus* 14–16cm FIELD NOTES: Chestnut wing coverts. Generally warm toned, but many eastern races (fig 9b) paler and greyer, with paler chestnut wing coverts. VOICE: A simple *zritt-zreet-zreet-zreet-zritt-zriüüü*. Call, a falling *seeoo*. HABITAT: Marshy areas with reeds or scrub. In winter may also occur in areas away from water. DISTRIBUTION: Very rare vagrant from the Palearctic.

10 NORTHERN CARDINAL *Cardinalis cardinalis* 22cm FIELD NOTES: Unmistakeable. Forages on the ground and in trees and shrubs. VOICE: A series of high, clear and slurred whistles, very variable, including *whoit whoit whoit what cheer what cheer wheat wheat* and *purty purty purty*. Calls, a high, hard *tik* and a soft, rising *twik*. HABITAT: Woodland margins, thickets and gardens. DISTRIBUTION: E USA, extending west along Mexican border.

11 PYRRHULOXIA *Cardinalis sinuatus* 22cm FIELD NOTES: Unmistakeable. Habits as Northern Cardinal. VOICE: Loud, rich, repeated whistles. Call, a low *spik* and a chattering *pikpikpikpikpik*. HABITAT: Arid or semiarid scrub. DISTRIBUTION: US-Mexican border states, from Arizona to Texas.

98 GROSBEAKS, *PASSERINA* BUNTINGS AND BLUE BUNTING

1 CRIMSON-COLLARED GROSBEAK Rhodothraupis celaeno 21–22cm
FIELD NOTES: Skulking. In flight, underwing coverts are red in the male and yellowish in the female. VOICE: A husky warble ending in an up-slurred *weeee*. Call, a clear *ssseeuu* and a piercing *seeip seeeiyu*. HABITAT: Brushy woodland. DISTRIBUTION: Rare vagrant from NE Mexico.

2 YELLOW GROSBEAK Pheucticus chrysopeplus 21.5–24cm FIELD NOTES: In flight shows extensive white corners on tail, male has large, white patch at base of primaries, female shows a much smaller patch. VOICE: A variable, short, rich warble, transcribed as *chee wee chee-r weer weeuh* or *toodi todi toweeoo*. Call, a sharp *piik* and a soft *hu-oi* or *whoi*. HABITAT: Oak or waterside woodlands. DISTRIBUTION: Rare vagrant from NW Mexico.

3 ROSE-BREASTED GROSBEAK Pheucticus ludovicianus 19cm
FIELD NOTES: Arboreal. Sluggish forager in bushes and trees. In flight, male shows white upper rump, primary bases and tail corners; underwing coverts red in male, buffy-yellow in female. VOICE: A slow whistled warble, thrush-like. Calls include a squeaky *iik* and a wheezy *wheek* flight note. HABITAT: Open woodland, woodland edge, hedgerows, orchards and large gardens. DISTRIBUTION: Summers in NE USA extending into Canada and west to NE British Columbia.

4 BLACK-HEADED GROSBEAK Pheucticus melanocephalus 21cm FIELD NOTES: Actions as Rose-breasted Grosbeak. In flight, male shows orangeish upper rump, white primary bases and tail corners; underwing of male and female yellow. VOICE: Whistled warble, higher and faster than Rose-breasted Grosbeak. Call, a sharp *pik*. HABITAT: Open woodlands and forest edge. DISTRIBUTION: Summers in W USA and adjacent Canada.

5 INDIGO BUNTING Passerina cyanea 14cm FIELD NOTES: Skulking, except when singing. VOICE: A high-pitched *sweet-sweet - where-where - here-here - see-it-see-it*. Call, a sharp *tsick* or *spit*. HABITAT: Bushy pastures, wastelands, thickets and woodland edge. DISTRIBUTION: Summers in E USA and adjacent Canada; in the south extending west to the Rockies.

6 BLUE GROSBEAK Passerina caerulea 17cm FIELD NOTES: Often flares tail when perched. Shy, forages in dense cover. VOICE: Rapid warble with short, rising and falling phrases. Calls, a sharp *spink* or *chink* and a buzzy flight note. HABITAT: Bushy and weedy areas with scattered trees. DISTRIBUTION: Summers over most of the southern two-thirds of USA.

7 PAINTED BUNTING Passerina ciris 13cm FIELD NOTES: Forages on or near the ground. VOICE: A sweet continuous warble. Call, a loud *chip* or *pwich*. HABITAT: Thickets, weedy tangles, riverside brush and woodland edge. DISTRIBUTION: Summers in C S USA, and on the Atlantic coast, from North Carolina south to Florida. Winters in S Florida.

8 LAZULI BUNTING Passerina amoena 14cm FIELD NOTES: Forages on or near the ground in deep cover. VOICE: A rapid *see-see-sweert-sweert-sweert-zee-sweet-zeer-see-see*. Call, a sharp *tzip* and a dry buzz. HABITAT: Open woodland, thickets and chaparral. DISTRIBUTION: Summers in W USA and adjacent Canada, absent from S USA apart from SW California.

9 VARIED BUNTING Passerina versicolor 14cm FIELD NOTES: In dull light male can appear black. Shy, forages on or near the ground in cover. VOICE: Thin warbled notes. Call, a dry *spik*. HABITAT: Thickets in canyons and washes. DISTRIBUTION: Summers in S Arizona and SW Texas, a few winter in S Texas.

10 BLUE BUNTING Cyanocompsa parellina 14cm FIELD NOTES: 'Heavy' bill. Secretive, forages on or near the ground in cover. VOICE: A variable, sweet warble, often begins with 2 separate notes and fades at the end. Call, a metallic *chik*. HABITAT: Shrubby thickets, brushy forest, woodland and woodland edge. DISTRIBUTION: Rare vagrant along Gulf coast, from Mexico.

99 BOBOLINK, MEADOWLARKS AND AMERICAN BLACKBIRDS

1 BOBOLINK *Dolichonyx oryzivorus* 18cm FIELD NOTES: In flight, male shows white on rump and scapulars. Forages on or near the ground, among grasses and weeds. VOICE: A bubbling *bob-o-link bob-o-link link wink bob-o-link*, often given during flight display. Calls include a clear *pink* and a low *chuk*. HABITAT: Pastures, arable fields and open grassland. DISTRIBUTION: Summers over most of C North America.

2 EASTERN MEADOWLARK *Sturnella magna* 23cm FIELD NOTES: Forages on the ground; typically rests or sings from posts or wires. In flight shows much white in outer tail feathers. Winter birds have less distinct breast-band. VOICE: Slurred whistles *seeeeooaaa seeeeadoo* or similar. Call, a harsh *dziit*. HABITAT: Open grassland, agricultural fields and meadows. DISTRIBUTION: E USA and adjacent Canada. Northern birds move south in winter.

3 WESTERN MEADOWLARK *Sturnella neglecta* 23cm FIELD NOTES: Very similar to Eastern Meadowlark, best identified by voice. VOICE: Variable series of bubbling, gurgling and flute-like notes that accelerates at the end. Call, a bell-like *pluk* and a dull rattle. HABITAT: Grasslands, usually prefers dryer areas than Eastern Meadowlark. DISTRIBUTION: W North America, south from C Alberta and west of the Great Lakes, although only in winter CS USA. Northern birds move south in winter.

4 TAWNY-SHOULDERED BLACKBIRD *Agelaius humeralis* 19–22cm FIELD NOTES: Forages on the ground and in trees. May occur with other blackbird species. VOICE: A buzzy *preeee-whaaaaaaa*. Calls include a loud *chup-chup*, a nasal *whaap* and a metallic *pleeet*. HABITAT: Open areas with scattered trees, woodland edge and open woodlands. DISTRIBUTION: Very rare vagrant from Cuba.

5 RED-WINGED BLACKBIRD *Agelaius phoeniceus* 19–23cm FIELD NOTES: Often in very large flocks. Bicoloured blackbird A. *p. gubernator* (fig 5b) occurs in W California. VOICE: A bubbling, shrill *ok-a-leee*. Female song is a chattering *chit chit chit chit chit cheer teer teer teerr* or similar. Calls include a throaty *check* and a whistled *teeew* given when alarmed. HABITAT: Wet, brushy and marshy areas, winters in agricultural areas. DISTRIBUTION: North America, south of the sub-tundra areas. Northern birds move south in winter.

6 TRICOLOURED BLACKBIRD *Agelaius tricolor* 22–24cm FIELD NOTES: Regularly occurs in large flocks, often mixes with other blackbirds. Forages primarily on the ground. VOICE: A harsh *on-kee-kaaangh*. Calls like Red-winged Blackbird but lower-pitched. HABITAT: Marshes and dense thickets, winters in open agricultural areas. DISTRIBUTION: SW Oregon and W California.

7 YELLOW-HEADED BLACKBIRD *Xanthocephalus xanthocephalus* 24cm FIELD NOTES: In flight, male shows white primary coverts. Forages mainly on the ground. VOICE: Low, hoarse and rasping notes ending with a buzz. Call, a croaking *kruck*, *kack* or *ktuk*. HABITAT: Marshes and reed-beds, winters in open agricultural areas. DISTRIBUTION: Much of C North America, west from the Great Lakes. Winters from C California, along Mexican-US border to Texas.

8 RUSTY BLACKBIRD *Euphagus carolinus* 23cm FIELD NOTES: Forages on the ground, often with grackles or other blackbirds. If disturbed, retreats to nearby trees or bushes. VOICE: A squeaky *kush-a-lee* or *chuck-la-weeeee*. Call, a soft *chuck*. HABITAT: Wooded swamps, lake shores and open agricultural fields. DISTRIBUTION: Boreal Alaska, Canada and NE USA. Winters in E USA, apart from the north.

9 BREWER'S BLACKBIRD *Euphagus cyanocephalus* 23cm FIELD NOTES: Forages on the ground. Female usually dark-eyed; generally unmarked, dull greyish. VOICE: A short, buzzy, cackling *t-kzzzz* or *t-zherr*. Calls, a short *ket*, *chak* or *chuk*. HABITAT: Agricultural fields, grasslands, alpine meadows, beaches and urban areas. DISTRIBUTION: W USA and adjacent Canada, extending to the Great Lakes. Northern and eastern birds winter in CS USA.

100 AMERICAN ORIOLES

1 BLACK-VENTED ORIOLE *Icterus wagleri* 20–23cm FIELD NOTES: Arboreal, favours flowering trees or bushes. VOICE: A gurgling warble interspersed with nasal and squeaky notes. Calls include a *coo-nyah-ra* and a nasal *nyeh*, which is often repeated when alarmed. HABITAT: Dry scrub, open areas with scattered trees and riparian shrubs. DISTRIBUTION: Very rare vagrant from Mexico.

2 ORCHARD ORIOLE *Icterus spurius* 18cm FIELD NOTES: Arboreal, forages in trees and shrubs for insects and small fruits. VOICE: A lively warble with a distinctive, ringing *plit titi zheeeer* ending. Calls include a clear *tweeo*, a soft *chut*, a rasping *jarrsh* and a soft *yeeep* flight note. HABITAT: Woodlands, thickets and gardens. DISTRIBUTION: Summers in much of E USA and adjacent Canada.

3 HOODED ORIOLE *Icterus cucullatus* 20cm FIELD NOTES: Arboreal, with a liking for palms. First-summer male like female but with black throat and bib, very similar to first-summer male Orchard Oriole. VOICE: A rapid series of throaty whistles, trills and rattles. Calls, a hard *chairr*, a rising *wheet* and sharp *veek* flight note. HABITAT: Dry open woodland, parks and gardens. DISTRIBUTION: Summers in California and US-Mexican border states.

4 STREAKED-BACKED ORIOLE *Icterus pustulatus* 21cm FIELD NOTES: Arboreal, feeds on insects, seeds, nectar and fruit. VOICE: A whistled *to do teweeep yoo teewi*. Calls, a dry rattle and a rising *wheet* flight note. HABITAT: Riparian woods in desert, open woodland and dry scrub. DISTRIBUTION: Rare vagrant from Mexico.

5 SPOT-BREASTED ORIOLE *Icterus pectoralis* 23–25cm FIELD NOTES: Arboreal, forages in pairs or small groups; attracted to fruiting and flowering trees. VOICE: A rich melodious warbled whistling. Calls include a nasal *nyeh*, a sharp *whip* and a chattering *ptcheck*. HABITAT: Urban areas with flowering trees and shrubs. DISTRIBUTION: S Florida (introduced).

6 ALTIMIRA ORIOLE *Icterus gularis* 25cm FIELD NOTES: Arboreal, usually forages in pairs, feeding on insects, seeds, fruit and nectar. VOICE: A series of loud, clear whistles. Calls, a whistled *teeu*, or similar; in flight gives a hoarse, rising *griink*. HABITAT: Open arid woodlands. DISTRIBUTION: S Texas.

7 AUDUBON'S ORIOLE *Icterus graduacauda* 24cm FIELD NOTES: Shy and retiring, generally in pairs foraging in the dense shady parts of trees. VOICE: A melancholy, slurred *hooooo heeeowee heeew hewee*. Calls, a whistled *too* or *oooeh* and a husky, rising *jeeek jeeek....* HABITAT: Edges of dense forest and riparian thickets. DISTRIBUTION: S Texas.

8 BALTIMORE ORIOLE (NORTHERN ORIOLE) *Icterus galbula* 22cm FIELD NOTES: Arboreal, attracted to trees with colourful flowers or dense foliage. VOICE: Variable, consisting of clear whistled notes, transcribed as *pidoo tewdl tewdl yewdi tew tidew* or a simple series of *hew-li* notes. Call, a rattling *cher-r-r-r-r-r*; also a tinny *veeet* given in flight. HABITAT: Open woodland, orchards, parks and gardens. DISTRIBUTION: Summers in E USA, apart from the southern states; also in S Canada from C British Columbia east to S New Brunswick. Winters in Florida and on the Atlantic coast south from North Carolina.
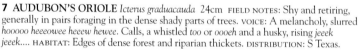

9 BULLOCK'S ORIOLE *Icterus bullockii* 23cm FIELD NOTES: Often combined with Baltimore Oriole when known as Northern Oriole. Hybridises with the latter where ranges meet. VOICE: Short and lively, transcribed as *cut cut cudut whee up chooup*, less melodic than Baltimore Oriole. Calls include a short rattle and a soft *chuk*. HABITAT: Deciduous open woodland, woodland edge and urban parks. DISTRIBUTION: Summers in W USA and adjacent Canada.
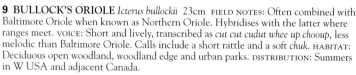

10 SCOTT'S ORIOLE *Icterus parisorum* 23cm FIELD NOTES: The black face on female variable, can be more or less than depicted. VOICE: A rich, mellow, fluty warble. Calls include a nasal *cheh-cheh...* or *chuhk* and a quiet *huit*. HABITAT: Dry hillsides, with yucca. DISTRIBUTION: Summers in SW USA.
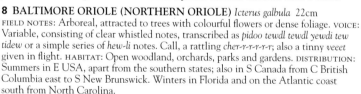

101 GRACKLES AND COWBIRDS

1 COMMON GRACKLE *Quiscalus quiscula* 32cm FIELD NOTES: Usually winters in large flocks, often alongside blackbirds. Variable; depicted are the nominate 'Florida Grackle' and the 'Bronzed Grackle' *Q. q. versicolor* (fig 1b), which occurs in the west and northern parts of the range. Female duller and smaller tailed. Juvenile generally brown. VOICE: A loud *chack* or *chuck*. Song is a screechy *readle-eek*, *re-lick* or *scudle-eek*. HABITAT: Almost any open areas, including woodland, bogs, farmland and urban parks and gardens. DISTRIBUTION: Most of North America east of the Rockies and south of Arctic areas. Northern and western birds move SE in winter.

2 GREAT-TAILED GRACKLE *Quiscalus mexicanus* Male 46–48cm; Female 38–40cm FIELD NOTES: Eastern females dark greyish-brown below. Often in large groups, especially after breeding. VOICE: Very varied, song starts with harsh notes followed by an undulating *cheweechewe*, more harsh notes then finally several loud *cha-wee* calls. Common call is a low, hard *chuk*. HABITAT: Open areas with scattered trees or bushes, including pastures, grassland, parkland and urban gardens. DISTRIBUTION: S half of USA, from SC Louisiana west to California. Northernmost birds move south in winter.

3 BOAT-TAILED GRACKLE *Quiscalus major* Male 42–44cm; Female 37–39cm FIELD NOTES: Gregarious at all times. Yellow-eyed race *Q. m. torreyi* (fig 3b) occurs on the Atlantic coast from New York to N Florida. VOICE: Very varied, song consists of high, ringing notes; also harsh notes mixed with rustling sounds and various rattling, trilling and whistled notes. Common call of male is a deep *chuk*; also a *kle-teet*. Female gives a low *chenk* or *chuup*. HABITAT: Saltwater and freshwater marshes. May spread to farmland in winter. DISTRIBUTION: Atlantic and Gulf coasts of USA.

4 SHINY COWBIRD *Molothrus bonariensis* 18–20cm FIELD NOTES: Forages on the ground, often seen around livestock. Gregarious, especially during the non-breeding season. VOICE: A rolling rattle. The song consists of several liquid purrs, followed by a high whistle. HABITAT: Woodland edge, open country and agricultural areas. DISTRIBUTION: Resident in S Florida.

5 BRONZED COWBIRD *Molothrus aeneus* 22–23cm FIELD NOTES: Red eyes. Ruffed rear neck give males a large-headed look. Gregarious. Females of SW race *M. a. loyei* (fig 5b) are generally paler. VOICE: Song transcribed as *ugh gub bub tse pss tseeeee*, the last note is far carrying. Calls include a harsh *chuck*; flocks give whistles in flight; females sometimes utter a rattling chatter. HABITAT: Woodlands, thickets, pastures and agricultural land. DISTRIBUTION: Summers along US-Mexican border states.

6 BROWN-HEADED COWBIRD *Molothrus ater* 19–20cm FIELD NOTES: Gregarious, often in large flocks mixed with blackbirds. Forages on the ground. Juveniles similar to pale female with streaked underparts. VOICE: A harsh *chuk* and a squeaky *weee-titi*, the latter often given in flight. Song; a bubbly *glug-glug-gleeee*, followed by thin, slurred whistles. HABITAT: Open woodland, pastures, farmland, parks and gardens. DISTRIBUTION: Virtually the whole of sub-tundra North America. Northern and western birds move south in winter.

102 FINCHES

1 CHAFFINCH *Fringilla coelebs* 15cm FIELD NOTES: Forages on the ground and in trees and bushes; also makes fly-catching sallies. Often mixes with other finches and sparrows. Winter birds have duller colours. VOICE: A short accelerating and descending musical *chip-chip-chip-tell-tell-cherry-erry-erry-tissi-cheweeo*. Calls include a *pink* or *pink-pink*, a loud *whit* and a wheezy *eeese*; in flight, gives a soft *tsup*. HABITAT: All types of woodland, farmland, parkland and gardens. In winter often occurs in stubble fields. DISTRIBUTION: Very rare vagrant from Europe.

2 BRAMBLING *Fringilla montifringilla* 15cm FIELD NOTES: In flight, both sexes show a white rump. Forages on the ground, regularly retreating to nearby trees and bushes. Often associates with sparrows. VOICE: A harsh, monotonous *zweeeeur* interspersed with weaker fluty notes and sometimes a rattling trill. Call, a nasal *tsweek* or *zweee* and a *chuk-chuk* given in flight. HABITAT: Various woodlands and forests, forest edge and scrub. In winter often occurs on stubble fields and on open weedy ground. DISTRIBUTION: Vagrant from Europe.

3 BULLFINCH (COMMON or EURASIAN BULLFINCH) *Pyrrhula pyrrhula* 16cm FIELD NOTES: Generally wary; often the first sign of bird's presence is the melancholy call or the flash of white rump as it flies into cover. Acrobatic feeder in bushes and trees. Juvenile birds lack the black cap and bib. VOICE: A weak, scratchy warble interspersed with soft whistles. Call is a low, melancholic, piping *peeu, pew, teu, due* or *due-due*. HABITAT: Coniferous and deciduous woodlands with dense undergrowth, hedgerows, thickets, orchards, parks and gardens. DISTRIBUTION: Very rare vagrant from Europe.

4 COMMON CROSSBILL (RED CROSSBILL) *Loxia curvirostra* 16cm FIELD NOTES: Sociable. Often feeds acrobatically, even upside-down, to extract pine seeds. Frequently drinks at small pools. Juvenile generally greyish brown, streaked darker above and below. VOICE: A series of call notes leading into a *cheeree-cheeree-choop-chip-chip-chip-cheeree*, which is combined with various twitters, trills and further call notes. Calls, a *chip-chip* and a softer *chuk-chuk*. HABITAT: Primarily conifer forests. DISTRIBUTION: Resident in SE Alaska, boreal Canada and in USA, in the W mountain regions and N parts of the east. During winter, irruptions may occur anywhere in USA.

5 WHITE-WINGED CROSSBILL (TWO-BARRED CROSSBILL) *Loxia leucoptera* 17cm FIELD NOTES: Habits and many actions similar to Common Crossbill. As well as pine seeds, feeds on berries and insects. Often mixes with Common Crossbills, Pine Grosbeaks and Evening Grosbeaks. VOICE: Rich and variable, with buzzing trills and harsh rattles. Calls, a metallic *glip-glip, kip-kip* or *chiff-chiff*. Flocks often utter a *chut-chut* or *chuch-chuch*. HABITAT: Coniferous forests, especially larch, hemlock and spruce. DISTRIBUTION: Resident over much of Alaska and Canada south of Arctic regions. Regularly makes irruptive movements to N USA and beyond.

6 HAWFINCH *Coccothraustes coccothraustes* 17cm FIELD NOTES: Wary, feeds mainly in treetops; also on the ground below trees. In flight shows white wing bar and broad white tail tips. VOICE: A bunting-like *deek-waree-ree-ree* or *tchee-tchee-turr-wee-wee*. Calls, an abrupt *tick* or *tzik* and a thin *seep* or *sreee*. HABITAT: Deciduous and mixed woodlands, orchards and parks. DISTRIBUTION: Very rare vagrant from Europe.

7 EVENING GROSBEAK *Coccothraustes vespertinus* 20cm FIELD NOTES: In flight, male shows white secondaries, female also shows a white patch on primaries and white on tail tip. Gregarious, forages in trees and frequently visits garden feeding stations. VOICE: A rambling, erratic warble, ending with a whistle. Call, a loud *clee-ip* or *cleer*. HABITAT: Coniferous and mixed forests and copses; in winter, often visits parks and gardens. DISTRIBUTION: Resident across S Canada, extreme NE USA and in the mountain regions of W USA. Winters over much of USA, apart from southern and central southern areas.

103 FINCHES

1 GREY-CROWNED ROSY-FINCH *Leucosticte tephrocotis* 14–18cm
FIELD NOTES: Variable. Bering Sea race *L. t. umbrina* (fig 1b) is the darkest of the
grey-faced races. Forages on the ground, in pairs or small parties. VOICE: Slow
descending series of *cheew* notes. Calls include a repeated *chew* or *cheew*, a dry *pert*
and a high-pitched *chirp*. HABITAT: Tundra, grassy maritime plains, mountains, scree
slopes. Winters in foothills, valleys, coastal plains, farmland and suburban areas.
DISTRIBUTION: W North America, from Bering Sea islands south to CE California.
Northern birds move south to winter from British Columbia to California and
N New Mexico.

2 BLACK ROSY-FINCH *Leucosticte atrata* 14–16cm FIELD NOTES: Female duller.
Often 'lumped' with the previous and following species as Rosy-finch. Actions of
all 3 very similar. VOICE: Similar to Grey-crowned Rosy-finch. HABITAT: Montane
and sub-montane tundra, open scree slopes, mountain lakesides. Winters at lower
levels in mountains usually near the snow-line, also in cultivation and forest edge.
DISTRIBUTION: WC USA, spreads to wider WC area in winter.

3 BROWN-CAPPED ROSY-FINCH *Leucosticte australis* 14–16.5cm FIELD NOTES:
Actions and habits as Grey-crowned Rosy-finch. VOICE: Similar to Grey-crowned
Rosy-finch. HABITAT: Montane tundra above the tree line, rocky areas and scree slopes.
Winters in high elevation meadows, grassy valleys and forest edge. DISTRIBUTION:
WC USA, S Wyoming south to N New Mexico.

4 PINE GROSBEAK *Pinicola enucleator* 22cm FIELD NOTES: Unobtrusive, often
staying relatively hidden as it clambers about in foliage. Often more conspicuous in
winter when small flocks feed on berry-bearing trees and shrubs. VOICE: Loud, musical,
fluty warble. Calls include a fluty *teu-teu-teu* or *pee-lee-jeh*; also a *pui-pui-pui* or *quid-
quid-quid* given in flight. HABITAT: Coniferous woods, moves to mainly deciduous trees
in winter. DISTRIBUTION: Boreal Alaska and Canada, N New England and south along
the Rockies. Northern birds move south, often in irruptions to N USA.

5 COMMON ROSEFINCH *Carpodacus erythrinus* 13–15cm FIELD NOTES: Forages
in bushes, trees or on the ground. Occasionally mixes with other finches or buntings.
VOICE: A repeated, fluty, rising and falling *sooee-teeew, weeeja-wu-weeeja, te-te-wee-chew*
or other variations. Calls include a rising, whistled *ooeet, weet* or *too-ee*; when alarmed
utters a sharp *chay-eee*. HABITAT: Various types of woodland, thickets or scrub; also
orchards and parks. DISTRIBUTION: Rare vagrant from Europe.

6 HOUSE FINCH *Carpodacus mexicanus* 13–15cm FIELD NOTES: Forages mainly on
the ground. Yellow morph more frequent in the SW. VOICE: A jumble of musical notes,
ending with a *whee-er*. Calls include a *cheet* or *queet* and a *chirp*. HABITAT: Towns and
villages, farmland, scrub and orchards. DISTRIBUTION: Virtually the whole of the USA
and adjacent Canada.

7 PURPLE FINCH *Carpodacus purpureus* 13.5–14.5cm FIELD NOTES: Forages on the
ground or in trees and bushes. In winter, often associates with other finches. Female
Pacific birds are duller below with more diffuse streaking. VOICE: A rising and falling
warble of rich bubbling notes. Calls include a sharp *pik, tick* or *pink* and a musical *char-
lee, chee-wee* or *whit whewe*. HABITAT: Open conifer forests, mixed woodland, parks and
gardens. DISTRIBUTION: Much of boreal Canada, Pacific coastal states of USA and
NE USA. Canadian birds move south to winter in E USA.

8 CASSIN'S FINCH *Carpodacus cassinii* 14.5–16.5cm FIELD NOTES: Forages on the
ground and in treetops. In winter often associates with other finch species. VOICE: A
high-pitched varied, jumbled warble. Calls include a dry *giddy-up, tee-dee-yip, kee-yup* or
cheedly-up, all often given in flight. HABITAT: Montane open conifer forests, in winter
occurs in conifer forests at lower levels. DISTRIBUTION: Mountain areas of W USA and
SE British Columbia. Northern birds move south to winter in interior of W USA.

1 REDPOLL (COMMON REDPOLL) *Carduelis flammea* 13cm
FIELD NOTES: Usually in pairs or small parties, larger groups in winter. Forages in trees, often acrobatically, and on the ground. Greenland race *C. f. rostrata* is generally darker and larger. VOICE: A high trilling, combined with rolling notes, often given in circular display flight. Calls, a metallic, twittering *chuch-uch-uch-uch* and a ringing *sooeet* or *djueee*. HABITAT: Birch and willow thickets, conifer and broadleaved woods. DISTRIBUTION: W and E Greenland, Alaska and N Canada. Northern birds winter in Canada and much of N USA.

2 ARCTIC REDPOLL (HOARY REDPOLL) *Carduelis hornemanni* 13cm
FIELD NOTES: Actions and habits similar to Redpoll, with which it often associates. VOICE: Similar to Redpoll, calls said to be more metallic or coarser. HABITAT: Stunted trees or bushes on tundra, birch and willow thickets. DISTRIBUTION: N Greenland, N Alaska and N Canada. Far northern birds move south to winter throughout Canada.

3 PINE SISKIN *Carduelis pinus* 13cm FIELD NOTES: Actions similar to Redpoll. Some birds are yellower on wing coverts and underparts. VOICE: A rambling series of nasal and chattering notes, ending with a rising *zzzhreeee*. Call, a hoarse *tee-ee*, *clee-ip* or *chlee-it*, a rising *sweeeet* and a short *tit* or *twit-it-tit*. HABITAT: Conifer and mixed woods, alder thickets and ornamental suburban trees. DISTRIBUTION: SE Alaska, boreal Canada, much of N and W USA. Alaskan and most W Canadian birds move south and east to winter throughout the USA.

4 SISKIN (EURASIAN SISKIN) *Carduelis spinus* 12cm FIELD NOTES: Actions similar to Redpoll. Wide, yellow wing bars. VOICE: A rapid, undulating series of twittering phrases interspersed with trills and wheezy notes, ending with a rasping *kree*. HABITAT: Coniferous and mixed woodland; after breeding spreads to streamsides, hedgerows and gardens. DISTRIBUTION: Very rare vagrant from Europe.

5 ORIENTAL GREENFINCH *Carduelis sinica* 14cm FIELD NOTES: In flight shows large yellow wing bar and yellow bases to outer tail feathers. Forages in trees and on the ground. VOICE: A nasal trill and a rising *teu-teu-teu-teu* interspersed with harsh notes such as *kirr, korr*. Calls include a nasal *dzweee* and a twittering *dzi-dzi-i-dzi-i* given in flight. HABITAT: Woodland edge, scrub, cultivations and gardens. DISTRIBUTION: Rare vagrant from the E Palearctic.

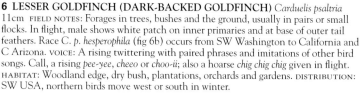

6 LESSER GOLDFINCH (DARK-BACKED GOLDFINCH) *Carduelis psaltria*
11cm FIELD NOTES: Forages in trees, bushes and the ground, usually in pairs or small flocks. In flight, male shows white patch on inner primaries and at base of outer tail feathers. Race *C. p. hesperophila* (fig 6b) occurs from SW Washington to California and C Arizona. VOICE: A rising twittering with paired phrases and imitations of other bird songs. Call, a rising *pee-yee*, *cheeo* or *choo-ii*; also a hoarse *chig chig chig* given in flight. HABITAT: Woodland edge, dry bush, plantations, orchards and gardens. DISTRIBUTION: SW USA, northern birds move west or south in winter.

7 AMERICAN GOLDFINCH *Carduelis tristis* 12cm FIELD NOTES: Actions similar to Lesser Goldfinch. VOICE: A lively series of twitters, trills and *swee* notes. Calls include a thin *toweeeowee* or *tweeee*, soft *tihoo*; in flight utters a soft, descending *ti di di di*. HABITAT: Open woodlands, thickets, weedy fields, orchards and gardens. DISTRIBUTION: Virtually throughout N USA and S Canada. Northern birds move south to winter over most of the USA.

8 LAWRENCE'S GOLDFINCH *Carduelis lawrencei* 12cm FIELD NOTES: Habits much as Lesser Goldfinch, although spends much time on the ground. VOICE: A tinkling twitter, incorporating mimicry of other bird songs. Calls include a *tink-oo* or *tink-il* and sharp *kee-yerr*. HABITAT: Chaparral, dry grassy slopes and oak savannah. DISTRIBUTION: Summers in California, winters in S California and S Arizona.

FURTHER READING

Alström, P. & Mild, K. (2003) *Pipits and Wagtails of Europe, Asia and North America.* Helm.

Beaman, M. & Madge, S. (1998) *The Handbook of Bird Identification for Europe and the Western Palearctic.* Helm.

Bond, J. (1960) *Birds of the West Indies.* Collins.

Byers, C., Olsson, U. & Curson, J. (1995) *Buntings and Sparrows.* Helm.

Clement, P., Harris, A. & Davis, J. (1993) *Finches and Sparrows.* Helm.

Clement, P. & Hathway, R. (2000) *Thrushes.* Helm.

Cramp, S., Simmons, K.E.L. & Perrins, C.M. (eds) (1977–94) *The Birds of the Western Palearctic.* Vols 1–9. Oxford University Press.

Curson, J., Quinn, D. & Beadle, D. (1994) *New World Warblers.* Helm.

Dickinson, E.C. (ed.) (2003) *The Howard and Moore Complete Checklist of the Birds of the World.* Helm.

Fry, C.H., Fry, K. & Harris, A. (1992) *Kingfishers, Bee-eaters and Rollers.* Helm.

Hancock, J. & Elliott, H. (1978) *Herons of the World.* London Editions.

Hancock, J., Kushlan, J.A. & Kahl, M.P. (1992) *Storks, Ibises and Spoonbills of the World.* Academic Press.

Harrison, P. (1983 & updates) *Seabirds: An Identification Guide.* Helm.

Hayman, P., Marchant, A.J. & Prater, A.H. (1986) *Shorebirds: An Identification Guide to the Waders of the World.* Helm.

del Hoyo, J., Elliott, A. & Sargatal, J. (eds) (1992–2009) *Handbook of the Birds of the World.* Vols 1–15. Lynx Edicions.

Jaramillo, A. & Burke, P. (1999) *New World Blackbirds.* Helm.

Madge, S. & Burn, H. (1988) *Wildfowl: An Identification Guide to the Ducks, Geese and Swans of the World.* Helm.

Madge, S. & Burn, H. (1991) *Crows and Jays.* Helm.

Madge, S. & McGowan, P. (2002) *Pheasants, Partridges and Grouse. Including Buttonquails, Sandgrouse and Allies.* Helm.

Mullarney, K., Svensson, L., Zetterström, D. & Grant, P.J. (1999) *Collins Bird Guide.* HarperCollins.

Olsen, K.M. & Larsson, H. (2004) *Gulls of Europe, Asia and North America.* Helm.

Olsen, K.M. & Larsson, H. (1997) *Skuas and Jaegers: A guide to Skuas and Jaegers of the World.* Pica Press.

Olsen, K.M. & Larsson, H. (1995) *Terns of Europe and North America.* Helm.

Onley, D. & Scofield, P. (2008) *Albatrosses, Petrels and Shearwaters of the World.* Helm.

Palmer, R.S. (ed.) (1962–88) *Handbook of North American Birds.* Vols 1–5. Yale University Press.

Peterson, R.T. (1990) *A Field Guide to Western Birds.* 3rd edn. Houghton Mifflin.

Peterson, R.T. (1980) *A Field Guide to the Birds.* 4th edn. Houghton Mifflin.

Raffaele, H., Wiley, J., Garrido, O., Keith, A. & Raffaele, J. (1998) *Birds of the West Indies.* Helm.

Sibley, D. (2000) *The North American Bird Guide.* Helm.

Terres, J.K. (1980) *The Audubon Society Encyclopedia of North American Birds.* Alfred A. Knopf.

Turner, A. & Rose, C. (1989) *Swallows and Martins of the World.* Helm.

Winkler, H., Christie, D.A. & Nurney, D. (1995) *Woodpeckers: A Guide to the Woodpeckers, Piculets and Wrynecks of the World.* Pica Press.

INDEX

ACCENTOR, SIBERIAN
152
Accipiter cooperii 60
  gentilis 60
  striatus 60
Acridotheres tristis 178
Acrocephalus schoenobaenus
166
Actitis hypoleucos 78
  macularia 78
Aechmophorus clarkii 34
  occidentalis 34
Aegolius acadicus 116
  funereus 116
Aeronautes saxatalis 120
Aethia cristatella 106
  pusilla 106
  pygmaea 106
Agelaius humeralis 208
  phoeniceus 208
  tricolor 208
Aimophila aestivalis 194
  botterii 194
  carpalis 194
  cassinii 194
  quinquestriata 196
  ruficeps 194
Aix sponsa 20
Ajaia ajaja 54
Alauda arvensis 152
ALBATROSS, BLACK-
    BROWED 36
  BLACK-FOOTED 36
  LAYSAN 36
  LIGHT-MANTLED 36
  LIGHT-MANTLED
    SOOTY 36
  SHORT-TAILED 36
  SHY 36
  SNOWY 36
  STELLER'S 36

WANDERING 36
WHITE-CAPPED 36
WHITE-WINGED 36
YELLOW-NOSED 36
Alectoris chukar 30
Alle alle 106
Amazilia beryllina 122
  rutila 122
  violiceps 122
  yucatanensis 122
Amazona viridigenalis 126
AMAZON, GREEN-
    CHEEKED 126
  RED-CROWNED 126
Ammodramus bairdii 198
  caudacutus 198
  henslowii 198
  lecontei 198
  maritimus 198
  nelsoni 198
  savannarum 198
Amphispiza belli 198
  bileneata 198
Anas acuta 18
  americana 16
  bahamensis 18
  carolinensis 18
  clypeata 18
  crecca 18
  cyanoptera 18
  discors 18
  falcata 16
  formosa 18
  fulvigula 16
  penelope 16
  platyrhynchos 16
  poecilorhyncha zonorhyncha
    16
  querquedula 18
  rubripes 16
  strepera 16
ANHINGA 48
Anhinga anhinga 48

ANI, GROOVE-BILLED
    112
  SMOOTH-BILLED 112
Anous stolidus 100
Anser albifrons 12
  anser 12
  brachyrhynchus 12
  caerulescens 14
  canagica 14
  erythropus 12
  fabalis 12
  rossii 14
Anthracothorax prevostii 122
Anthus cervinus 152
  gustavi 152
  hodgsoni 152
  pratensis 152
  rubescens 152
  spragueii 152
  trivialis 152
Aphelocoma californica 148
  coerulescens 148
  insularis 148
  ultramarina 148
Aphriza virgata 84
Apus apus 120
  pacificus 120
Aquila chrysaetos 56
Aramus guarauna 68
Aratinga holochlora 126
Archilochus alexandri 124
  colubris 124
Ardea alba 52
  cinerea 50
  herodias 50
Arenaria interpres 84
  melanocephala 84
Arremonops rufivirgatus 194
Asio flammeus 114
  otus 114
  stygius 114
Asturina nitida 60
Athene cunicularia 116

Atthis heloisa 124
AUK, LITTLE 106
AUKLET, CASSIN'S 106
  CRESTED 106
  KNOB-BILLED 106
  LEAST 106
  PARAKEET 106
  PYGMY 106
  RHINOCEROS 106
  WHISKERED 106
Auriparus flaviceps 160
AVOCET, AMERICAN 70
Aythya affinis 20
  americana 20
  collaris 20
  ferina 20
  fuligula 20
  marila 20
  valisineria 20

Baeolophus alticristatus 162
  bicolor 162
  inornatus 162
  ridgwayi 162
  wollweberi 162
BALDPATE 16
BANANAQUIT 192
Bartramia longicauda 78
Basileuterus culicivorus 190
  rufifrons 190
BEARDLESS-
  TYRANNULET,
  NORTHERN 134
BECARD, ROSE-
  THROATED 134
BITTERN, AMERICAN
  50
  CHINESE LITTLE 50
  LEAST 50
  LONG-NOSED 50
  YELLOW 50
BLACKBIRD 172
  BREWER'S 208

  EURASIAN 172
  RED-WINGED 208
  RUSTY 208
  TAWNY-SHOULDERED
  208
  TRICOLOURED 208
  YELLOW-HEADED 208
BLACKCAP 166
BLUEBIRD, EASTERN
  170
  MOUNTAIN 170
  WESTERN 170
BLUETAIL, RED-
  FLANKED 170
BLUETHROAT 170
  RED-SPOTTED 170
BOBOLINK 208
BOBWHITE, NORTHERN
  30
Bombycilla cedrorum 178
  garrulus 178
Bonasa umbellus 28
BONXIE 102
BOOBY, BLUE-FACED 46
  BLUE-FOOTED 46
  BROWN 46
  MASKED 46
  RED-FOOTED 46
  WHITE 46
Botaurus lentiginosus 50
Brachyramphus brevirostris
  104
  marmoratus 104
  perdix 104
BRAMBLING 214
BRANT 12
Branta bernicla 12
  canadensis 12
  hutchinsii 12
  leucopsis 12
Brotogeris versicolurus 126
Bubo scandiacus 114
  virginianus 114

Bubulcus ibis 52
Bucephala albeola 24
  clangula 24
  islandica 24
BUDGERIGAR 126
BUFFLEHEAD 24
BULBUL, RED-
  WHISKERED 178
BULLFINCH 214
  COMMON 214
  EURASIAN 214
Bulweria bulwerii 42
BUNTING, BLUE 206
  GREY 204
  INDIGO 206
  LAPLAND 202
  LARK 198
  LAZULI 206
  LITTLE 204
  McKAY'S 202
  PAINTED 206
  PALLAS 204
  PALLAS'S REED 204
  PINE 204
  REED 204
  RUSTIC 204
  SNOW 202
  VARIED 206
  YELLOW-BREASTED
  204
  YELLOW-BROWED 204
  YELLOW-THROATED
  204
Burhinus bistriatus 70
BUSHTIT 160
Buteo albicaudatus 62
  albonotatus 60
  brachyurus 62
  jamaicensis 62
  lagopus 62
  lineatus 62
  magnirostris 60
  platypterus 62

regalis 62
swainsoni 62
Buteogallus anthracinus 60
Butorides virescens 50
BUZZARD, ROUGH-
LEGGED 62

CAHOW 38
Cairina moschata 22
Calamospiza melanocorys
198
Calcarius lapponicus 202
mccownii 202
ornatus 202
pictus 202
Calidris acuminata 84
alba 84
alpina 88
bairdii 86
canutus 84
ferruginea 88
fuscicollis 86
himantopus 88
maritima 88
mauri 86
melanotos 84
minuta 86
minutilla 86
ptilocnemis 88
pusilla 86
ruficollis 86
subminuta 86
temminckii 86
tenuirostris 84
Callipepla californica 30
gambeli 30
squamata 30
Calliphlox evelynae 124
Calonectris diomedea 40
leucomelas 40
Calothorax lucifer 124
Calypte anna 124
costae 124

Campephilus principalis 132
Camptostoma imberbe 134
Campylorhynchus
brunneicapillus 164
CANVASBACK 20
Caprimulgus carolinensis 118
indicus 118
ridgway 118
vociferus 118
CARACARA, CRESTED
58
Caracara cheriway 58
Cardellina rubrifrons 190
CARDINAL, NORTHERN
204
Cardinalis cardinalis 204
sinuatus 204
Carduelis flammea 218
hornemanni 218
lawrencei 218
pinus 218
psaltria 218
sinica 218
spinus 218
tristis 218
Carpodacus cassinii 216
erythrinus 216
mexicanus 216
purpureus 216
CATBIRD, GREY 178
Cathartes aura 56
Catharus aurantiirostris 174
bicknelli 174
fuscescens 174
guttatus 174
mexicanus 174
minimus 174
ustulatus 174
Catherpes mexicanus 164
Centrocercus minimus 28
urophasianus 28
Cepphus columba 104
grylle 104

Cerorhinca monocerata 106
Certhia americana 162
CHACHALACA, PLAIN
26
Chaetura pelagica 120
vauxi 120
CHAFFINCH 214
Chamaea fasciata 168
Charadrius alexandrinus 74
collaris 74
dubius 74
hiaticula 74
melodus 74
mongolus 74
montanus 72
morinellus 72
semipalmatus 74
veredus 72
vociferus 72
wilsonia 74
CHAT, YELLOW-
BREASTED 190
Chen caerulescens 14
canagica 14
rossii 14
CHICKADEE, BLACK-
CAPPED 160
BOREAL 160
CAROLINA 160
CHESTNUT-BACKED
160
GREY-HEADED 160
MEXICAN 160
MOUNTAIN 160
Chlidonias hybrida 100
leucopterus 100
niger 100
Chloroceryle americana 126
Chondestes grammacus 196
Chondrohierax uncinatus 58
Chordeiles acutipennis 118
gundlachii 118
minor 118

Chroicephalus cirrocephalus 92
  philadelphia 92
  ridibundus 92
CHUCK-WILL, CAROLINA 118
CHUCK-WILLS-WIDOW 118
CHUKAR 30
Cinclus mexicanus 154
Circus cyaneus 58
Cistothorus palustris 164
  platensis 164
Clangula hyemalis 24
Coccothraustes coccothraustes 214
  vespertinus 214
Coccyzus americanus 112
  erythropthalmus 112
  minor 112
Coereba flaveola 192
Colaptes auratus 132
  chrysoides 132
Colibri thalassinus 122
Colinus virginianus 30
Columba livia 108
Columbina inca 110
  passerina 110
  talpacoti 110
CONDOR, CALIFORNIA 56
Contopus caribaeus 134
  cooperi 134
  pertinax 134
  sordidulus 134
  virens 134
CONURE, GREEN 126
COOT 68
  AMERICAN 68
  COMMON 68
  EURASIAN 68
Coragyps atratus 56
CORMORANT 48

BRANDT'S 48
DOUBLE-CRESTED 48
GREAT 48
NEOTROPIC 48
OLIVACEOUS 48
PELAGIC 48
RED-FACED 48
CORNCRAKE 66
Corvus brachyrhynchos 150
  caurinus 150
  corax 150
  corone 150
  cryptoleucus 150
  frugilegus 150
  imparatus 150
  monedula 150
  ossifragus 150
Coturnicops noveboracensis 66
COWBIRD, BRONZED 212
  BROWN-HEADED 212
  SHINY 212
CRAKE, LITTLE 66
  PAINT-BILLED 66
  SPOTTED 66
CRANE, COMMON 68
  EURASIAN 68
  SANDHILL 68
  WHOOPING 68
Creagrus furcatus 92
CREEPER, BROWN 162
Crex crex 66
CROSSBILL, COMMON 214
  RED 214
  TWO-BARRED 214
  WHITE-WINGED 214
Crotophaga ani 112
  sulcirostris 112
CROW, AMERICAN 150
  CARRION 150
  FISH 150

MEXICAN 150
NORTHWESTERN 150
TAMAULIPAS 150
CUCKOO 112
  BLACK-BILLED 112
  COMMON 112
  EURASIAN 112
  MANGROVE 112
  ORIENTAL 112
  YELLOW-BILLED 112
Cuculus canorus 112
  saturatus 112
CURLEW 80
  AUSTRALIAN 80
  BRISTLE-THIGHED 80
  COMMON 80
  EASTERN 80
  ESKIMO 80
  EURASIAN 80
  FAR-EASTERN 80
  LITTLE 80
  LONG-BILLED 80
  SLENDER-BILLED 80
  WESTERN 80
Cyanocitta cristata 148
  stelleri 148
Cyanocompsa parellina 206
Cyanocorax morio 148
  yncas 148
Cyclorrhynchus psittacula 106
Cygnus buccinator 14
  columbianus 14
  cygnus 14
  olor 14
Cynanthus latirostris 122
Cypseloides niger 120
Cyrtonyx montezumae 30

DARTER, AMERICAN 48
Delichon urbica 156
Dendragapus fuliginosus 26
  obscurus 26
Dendrocopus major 128

Dendrocygna autumnalis 12
  bicolor 12
Dendroica caerulescens 182
  castanea 186
  cerulea 186
  chrysoparia 184
  coronata 182
  discolor 186
  dominica 184
  fusca 184
  graciae 184
  kirtlandii 184
  magnolia 182
  nigrescens 184
  occidentalis 184
  palmarum 186
  pensylvanica 182
  petechia 182
  pinus 184
  striata 186
  tigrina 182
  townsendi 184
  virens 184
DICKCISSEL 202
Diomedea exulans 36
DIPPER, AMERICAN 154
DIVER, BLACK-
    THROATED 32
  GREAT NORTHERN 32
  PACIFIC 32
  RED-THROATED 32
  WHITE-BILLED 32
  YELLOW-BILLED 32
Dolichonyx oryzivorus 208
DOTTEREL 72
  EURASIAN 72
  MOUNTAIN 72
  ORIENTAL 72
DOVE, AMERICAN
    MOURNING 110
  COLLARED 108
  COMMON TURTLE 108
  EUROPEAN

COLLARED 108
EUROPEAN TURTLE
  108
INCA 110
MOURNING 110
NECKLACE 108
ORIENTAL TURTLE
  108
ROCK 108
RUFOUS TURTLE 108
SPOTTED 108
TURTLE 108
WHITE-FRONTED 110
WHITE-TIPPED 110
WHITE-WINGED 110
ZENAIDA 110
DOVEKIE 106
DOWITCHER, COMMON
  82
  LONG-BILLED 82
  SHORT-BILLED 82
Dryocopus pileatus 132
DUCK, AMERICAN
    BLACK 16
  BAHAMA 18
  BLACK 16
  BLACK-BELLIED TREE
  12
  CAROLINA WOOD 20
  FALCATED 16
  FLORIDA 16
  FULVOUS TREE 12
  HARLEQUIN 20
  LONG-TAILED 24
  MASKED 24
  MOTTLED 16
  MUSCOVY 22
  RED-BILLED TREE 12
  RING-NECKED 20
  RUDDY 24
  SPOT-BILLED 16
  TUFTED 20
  WOOD 20

Dumetella carolinensis 178
DUNLIN 88

EAGLE, BALD 56
  GOLDEN 56
  WHITE-TAILED 56
EGRET, CATTLE 52
  CHINESE 52
  GREAT 52
  GREAT WHITE 52
  LITTLE 52
  REDDISH 52
  SNOWY 52
  SWINHOE'S 52
  WESTERN REEF 52
Egretta caerulea 52
  eulophotes 52
  garzetta 52
  gularis 52
  rufescens 52
  thula 52
  tricolor 52
EIDER 22
  COMMON 22
  FISCHER'S 22
  KING 22
  SPECTACLED 22
  STELLER'S 22
ELAENIA, GREENISH
  134
  WHITE-CRESTED 134
Elaenia albiceps 134
Elanoides forficatus 58
Elanus leucurus 58
Emberiza aureola 204
  chrysophrys 204
  elegans 204
  leucocephalos 204
  pallasi 204
  pusilla 204
  rustica 204
  schoeniclus 204
  variabilis 204

Empidonax alnorum 136
 difficilis 136
 flaviventris 136
 fulvifrons 136
 hammondii 136
 minimus 136
 oberholseri 136
 occidentalis 136
 traillii 136
 virescens 136
 wrightii 136
Empidonomus aurantioatro-
  cristatus 134
 varius 134
Eremophila alpestris 152
Eudocimus albus 54
 ruber 54
Eugenes fulgens 122
Euphagus carolinus 208
 cyanocephalus 208
Euptilotis neoxenus 126
Eurynorhynchus pygmeus 88
Euthlypis lachrymosa 190

Falcipennis canadensis 26
Falco columbarius 64
 femoralis 64
 mexicanus 64
 peregrinus 64
 rusticolus 64
 sparverius 64
 subbuteo 64
 tinnunculus 64
 vespertinus 64
FALCON, APLOMADO
  64
 COLLARED FOREST
  64
 PEREGRINE 64
 PRAIRIE 64
 RED-FOOTED 64
 WESTERN RED-
  FOOTED 64

Ficedula albicilla 168
 mugimaki 168
 narcissina 168
FIELDFARE 174
FINCH, CASSIN'S 216
 HOUSE 216
 PURPLE 216
FLAMINGO, GREATER
  54
FLICKER, COMMON 132
 GILDED 132
 NORTHERN 132
 YELLOW-SHAFTED
  132
FLYCATCHER, ACADIAN
  136
 ALDER 136
 ASH-THROATED 138
 ASIAN BROWN 168
 BROWN 168
 BROWN-CRESTED 138
 BUFF-BREASTED 136
 CORDILLERAN 136
 CROWNED SLATY 134
 DARK-SIDED 168
 DUSKY 136
 DUSKY-CAPPED 138
 FORK-TAILED 142
 GREAT-CRESTED 138
 GREY 136
 GREY-SPOTTED 168
 GREY-STREAKED 168
 HAMMOND'S 136
 KISKADEE 142
 LA SAGRA'S 138
 LEAST 136
 MUGIMAKI 168
 NARCISSUS 168
 NUTTING'S 138
 OLIVE-SIDED 134
 PACIFIC-SLOPE 136
 PIRATIC 134
 RED-THROATED 168

SCISSOR-TAILED 142
 SIBERIAN 168
 SOCIAL 142
 SOOTY 168
 SPOTTED 168
 SULPHUR-BELLIED
  142
 TAIGA 168
 TUFTED 134
 VARIEGATED 134
 VERMILION 138
 WILLOW 136
 WRIGHT'S 136
 YELLOW-BELLIED 136
Fratercula arctica 106
 cirrhata 106
 corniculata 106
Fregata ariel 46
 magnificens 46
 minor 46
Fregetta tropica 44
FRIGATEBIRD, GREAT
  46
 LESSER 46
 MAGNIFICENT 46
Fringilla coelebs 214
 montifringilla 214
Fulica americana 68
 atra 68
FULMAR 36
 NORTHERN 36
Fulmarus glacialis 36

GADWALL 16
Gallinago gallinago 90
 stenura 90
Gallinula chloropus 68
GALLINULE, AMERICAN
  PURPLE 68
 AZURE 68
 PURPLE 68
GANNET 46
 NORTHERN 46

GARGANEY 18
Gavia adamsii 32
  arctica 32
  immer 32
  pacifica 32
  stellata 32
Gelochelidon nilotica 98
Geococcyx californianus 112
Geothlypis poliocephala 188
  trichas 188
Geotrygon chrysia 110
  montana 110
Geranospiza caerulescens 60
Glareola maldivarum 90
Glaucidium brasilianum 116
  californicum 116
GNATCATCHER,
  BLACK-CAPPED 166
  BLACK-TAILED 166
  BLUE-GREY 166
  CALIFORNIA 166
GODWIT, BAR-TAILED
  82
  BLACK-TAILED 82
  HUDSONIAN 82
  MARBLED 82
GOLDENEYE 24
  BARROW'S 24
  COMMON 24
GOLDFINCH,
  AMERICAN 218
  DARK-BACKED 218
  LAWRENCE'S 218
  LESSER 218
GON-GON 38
GOOSANDER 24
GOOSE, BARNACLE 12
  BEAN 12
  BLUE 14
  BRENT 12
  CACKLING 12
  CANADA 12
  EMPEROR 14

GREATER WHITE-
  FRONTED 12
GREYLAG 12
LESSER CANADA 12
LESSER WHITE-
  FRONTED 12
PINK-FOOTED 12
ROSS'S 14
SNOW 14
WHITE-FRONTED 12
GOSHAWK 60
  NORTHERN 60
GRACKLE, BOAT-TAILED
  212
  COMMON 212
  GREAT-TAILED 212
Gracula religiosa 178
GRASSQUIT, BLACK-
  FACED 192
  YELLOW-FACED 192
GREBE, BLACK-NECKED
  34
  CLARK'S 34
  EARED 34
  HORNED 34
  LEAST 34
  PIED-BILLED 34
  RED-NECKED 34
  SLAVONIAN 34
  WESTERN 34
GREENFINCH,
  ORIENTAL 218
GREENSHANK 76
  COMMON 76
GROSBEAK, BLACK-
  HEADED 206
  BLUE 206
  CRIMSON-COLLARED
  206
  EVENING 214
  PINE 216
  ROSE-BREASTED 206
  YELLOW 206

GROUND-DOVE,
  COMMON 110
  RUDDY 110
GROUSE, DUSKY 26
  GREATER SAGE 28
  GUNNISON SAGE
  28
  RUFFED 28
  SHARP-TAILED 28
  SOOTY 26
  SPRUCE 26
  WILLOW 26
Grus americana 68
  canadensis 68
  grus 68
GUILLEMOT 104
  BLACK 104
  BRÜNNICH'S 104
  PIGEON 104
GULL, AMERICAN
  HERRING 96
  BAND-TAILED 94
  BELCHER'S 94
  BLACK-HEADED 92
  BLACK-TAILED 94
  BONAPARTE'S 92
  CALIFORNIA 96
  COMMON 96
  COMMON BLACK-
  HEADED 92
  FRANKLIN'S 92
  GLAUCOUS 96
  GLAUCOUS-WINGED
  96
  GREAT BLACK-
  BACKED 94
  GREY-HEADED 92
  GREY-HOODED 92
  HEERMANN'S 94
  HERRING 96
  ICELAND 96
  IVORY 92
  JAPANESE 94

GULLS *continued*
  KELP 94
  LAUGHING 92
  LESSER BLACK-
    BACKED 94
  LITTLE 92
  MEW 96
  RING-BILLED 96
  ROSS'S 92
  SABINE'S 92
  SIMEON'S 94
  SLATY-BACKED 94
  SWALLOW-TAILED 92
  TEMMINCK'S 94
  THAYER'S 96
  WESTERN 94
  YELLOW-FOOTED 94
  YELLOW-LEGGED 96
Gymnogyps californianus 56
Gymnorhinus cyanocephalus
  148
GYRFALCON 64

Haematopus bachmani 70
  ostralegus 70
  palliatus 70
Haliaeetus albicilla 56
  leucocephalus 56
  pelagicus 56
HARRIER, HEN 58
  NORTHERN 58
HAWFINCH 214
HAWK, BROAD-WINGED
  62
  COMMON BLACK 60
  COOPER'S 60
  CRANE 60
  FERRUGINOUS 62
  GREY 60
  HARRIS 60
  RED-SHOULDERED 62
  RED-TAILED 62
  ROADSIDE 60

  ROUGH-LEGGED 62
  SHARP-SHINNED 60
  SHORT-TAILED 62
  SWAINSON'S 62
  WHITE-TAILED 62
  ZONE-TAILED 60
HAWK-OWL, BROWN
  114
  ORIENTAL 114
Heliomaster constantii 124
Helmitheros vermivorum 186
HERON 50
  GREAT BLUE 50
  GREEN 50
  GREY 50
  LITTLE BLUE 52
  LOUISIANA 52
  NIGHT 50
  TRICOLOURED 52
  WESTERN REEF 52
Himantopus himantopus 70
  mexicanus 70
Hirundapus caudacutus 120
Hirundo rustica 156
Histrionicus histrionicus 20
HOBBY 64
  EURASIAN 64
  NORTHERN 64
HOOPOE 112
  EURASIAN 112
HUMMINGBIRD,
  ALLEN'S 124
  ANNA'S 124
  BERYLLINE 122
  BLACK-CHINNED 124
  BLACK-THROATED
    122
  BLUE-THROATED 122
  BROAD-BILLED 122
  BROAD-TAILED 124
  BUFF-BELLIED 122
  BUMBLEBEE 124
  CALLIOPE 124

  CINNAMON 122
  COSTA'S 124
  FAWN-BRESTED 122
  LUCIFER 124
  MAGNIFICENT 122
  RIVOLI'S 122
  RUBY-THROATED 124
  RUFOUS 124
  VIOLET-CROWNED
    122
  WHITE-EARED 122
  XANTU'S 122
Hydrobates pelagicus 44
Hydrocoloeus minutus 92
Hylocharis leucotis 122
  xantusii 122
Hylocichla mustelina 174
Hyrdroprogne caspia 98

IBIS, AMERICAN WHITE
  54
  GLOSSY 54
  SCARLET 54
  WHITE 54
  WHITE-FACED 54
Icteria virens 190
Icterus bullockii 210
  cucullatus 210
  galbula 210
  graduacauda 210
  gularis 210
  parisorum 210
  pectoralis 210
  pustulatus 210
  spurius 210
  wagleri 210
Ictinia mississippiensis 58
Ixobrychus exilis 50
  sinensis 50
Ixoreus naevius 172

JABIRU 54
Jabiru mycteria 54

JACANA, NORTHERN 70
Jacana spinosa 70
JACKDAW 150
  EURASIAN 150
  WESTERN 150
JAEGER, LONG-TAILED 102
  PARASITIC 102
  POMARINE 102
JAY, BLUE 148
  BROWN 148
  CANADA 148
  GREEN 148
  GREY 148
  GREY-BREASTED 148
  MEXICAN 148
  PINYON 148
  STELLER'S 148
JUNCO, DARK-EYED 200
  YELLOW-EYED 200
Junco hyemalis 200
  phaeonotus 200
Jynx torquilla 128

KESTREL 64
  AMERICAN 64
  COMMON 64
  EUROPEAN 64
KILLDEER 72
KINGBIRD, CASSIN'S 140
  COUCH'S 140
  EASTERN 140
  GREY 140
  LOGGERHEAD 140
  THICK-BILLED 140
  TROPICAL 140
  WESTERN 140
KINGFISHER, BELTED 126
  GREEN 126
  RINGED 126

KINGLET, GOLDEN-CROWNED 168
  RUBY-CROWNED 168
KISKADEE, GREAT 142
KITE, AMERICAN SWALLOW-TAILED 58
  EVERGLADE 58
  HOOK-BILLED 58
  MISSISSIPPI 58
  SNAIL 58
  SWALLOW-TAILED 58
  WHITE-TAILED 58
KITTIWAKE 96
  BLACK-LEGGED 96
  RED-LEGGED 96
KNOT 84
  EASTERN 84
  GREAT 84
  GREATER 84
  LESSER 84
  RED 84

Lagopus lagopus 26
  leucurus 26
  mutus 26
Lampornis clemenciae 122
Lanius cristatus 142
  excubitor 142
  ludovicianus 142
LAPWING 72
  NORTHERN 72
LARK, HORNED 152
  SHORE 152
Larus argentatus 96
  belcheri 94
  californicus 96
  canus 96
  crassirostris 94
  delawarensis 96
  dominicanus 94
  fuscus 94
  glaucescens 96

glaucoides 96
  heermanni 94
  hyperboreus 96
  livens 94
  marinus 94
  michahellis 96
  occidentalis 94
  schistisagus 94
  smithsonianus 96
  thayeri 96
Latterallus jamaicensis 66
Legatus leucophaius 134
Leptotila verreauxi 110
Leucophaeus atricilla 92
  pipixcan 92
Leucosticte atrata 216
  australis 216
  tephrocotis 216
Limicola falcinellus 88
Limnodromus griseus 82
  scolopaceus 82
Limnothlypis swainsonii 186
Limosa fedoa 82
  haemastica 82
  lapponica 82
  limosa 82
LIMPKIN 68
Locustella lanceolata 166
  ochotensis 166
LONGSPUR, CHESTNUT-COLLARED 202
  LAPLAND 202
  McCOWN'S 202
  SMITH'S 202
LOON, ARCTIC 32
  BLACK-THROATED 32
  COMMON 32
  GREAT NORTHERN 32
  PACIFIC 32
  RED-THROATED 32
  YELLOW-BILLED 32
Lophodytes cucullatus 24

Loxia curvirostra 214
  leucoptera 214
Luscinia calliope 170
  cyane 170
  svecica 170
Lymnocryptes minimus 90

MAGPIE, BLACK-BILLED
  150
  YELLOW-BILLED 150
MALLARD 16
MANGO, GREEN-
  BREASTED 122
MARTIN, BROWN-
  CHESTED 156
  COMMON HOUSE 156
  CUBAN 156
  GREY-BREASTED 156
  HOUSE 156
  NORTHERN HOUSE
    156
  PURPLE 156
  SAND 158
  SOUTHERN 156
  WHITE-BELLIED 156
MEADOWLARK,
  EASTERN 208
Megaceryle alcyon 126
  torquata 126
Melanerpes aurifrons 128
  carolinus 128
  erythrocephalus 128
  formicivorus 128
  lewis 128
  uropygialis 128
Melanitta americana 22
  deglandi 22
  perspicillata 22
Melanotis caerulescens 176
Meleagris gallopavo 26
Melopsittacus undulatus 126
Melospiza georgiana 200
  lincolnii 200

melodia 200
MERGANSER, COMMON
  24
  HOODED 24
  RED-BREASTED 24
Mergellus albellus 24
Mergus merganser 24
  serrator 24
MERLIN 64
Micrastur semitorquatus 64
Micrathene whitneyi 116
Mimus gundlachii 176
  polyglottos 176
Mitrephanes phaeocercus 134
Mniotila varia 186
MOCKINGBIRD,
  BAHAMA 176
  BLUE 176
  NORTHERN 176
MOLLYMAWK, BLACK-
  BROWED 36
  SHY 36
  YELLOW-NOSED 36
Molothrus aeneus 212
  ater 212
  bonariensis 212
MOORHEN 68
  COMMON 68
Moras bassanus 46
Motacilla alba ocularis 154
  cinerea 154
  citreola 154
  flava 154
  tshutshensis 154
MURRE, COMMON 104
  THICK-BILLED 104
MURRELET, ANCIENT
  104
  CRAVERI'S 104
  KITTLITZ'S 104
  LONG-BILLED 104
  MARBLED 104
  SCRIPP'S 104

SHORT-BILLED 104
  XANTUS'S 104
Muscicapa daurica 168
  griseisticta 168
  sibirica 168
  striata 168
Myadestes townsendi 170
Mycteria americana 54
Myiarchus cinerascens 138
  crinitus 138
  nuttingi 138
  sagrae 138
  tuberculifer 138
  tyrannulus 138
Myioborus miniatus 190
  pictus 190
Myiodynastes luteiventris 142
Myiopagis viridicata 134
Myiopsitta monachus 126
Myiozetetes similis 142
MYNA, COMMON 178
  HILL 178
  INDIAN 178

NEEDLETAIL, WHITE-
  THROATED 120
Neocrex erythrops 66
NIGHTHAWK,
  ANTILLEAN 118
  COMMON 118
  LESSER 118
  TRILLING 118
NIGHT-HERON, BLACK-
  CROWNED 50
  YELLOW-CROWNED 50
NIGHTINGALE-
  THRUSH, BLACK-
  HEADED 174
  ORANGE-BILLED 174
NIGHTJAR, BUFF-
  COLLARED 118
  GREY 118
  JUNGLE 118

Ninox scutulata 114
NODDY, BLACK 100
   BROWN 100
   COMMON 100
   WHITE-CAPPED 100
Nomonyx dominica 24
Nucifraga columbiana 150
Numenius americanus 80
   arquata 80
   borealis 80
   madagascariensis 80
   minutus 80
   phaeopus 80
   tahitiensis 80
   tenuirostris 80
NUTCRACKER, CLARK'S
   150
NUTHATCH, BROWN-
   HEADED 162
   PYGMY 162
   RED-BREASTED 162
   WHITE-BREASTED 162
Nycticorax nycticorax 50
   violaceus 50
Nyctidromus albicollis 118

Oceanites oceanicus 44
Oceanodroma castro 44
   furcata 42
   homochroa 44
   hornbyi 42
   leucorhoa 44
   melania 44
   microsoma 44
   tethys 44
   tristrami 44
Oenanthe oenanthe 170
OLDSQUAW 24
Onychoprion aleutica 100
   anaethetus 100
   fuscata 100
Oporornis agilis 188
   formosus 188

   philadelphia 188
   tolmiei 188
Oreortyx pictus 30
Oreoscoptes montanus 176
ORIOLE, ALTIMIRA 210
   AUDUBON'S 210
   BALTIMORE 210
   BLACK-VENTED 210
   BULLOCK'S 210
   HOODED 210
   NORTHERN 210
   ORCHARD 210
   SCOTT'S 210
   SPOT-BREASTED 210
   STREAKED-BACKED
   210
Ortalis vetula 26
OSPREY 58
Otus asio 116
   flammeolus 116
   kennicottii 116
   sunia 116
   trichopsis 116
OVENBIRD 188
OWL, BARN 114
   BARRED 114
   BOREAL 116
   BURROWING 116
   ELF 116
   FLAMMULATED 116
   GREAT GREY 114
   GREAT HORNED 114
   HAWK 114
   LONG-EARED 114
   MOTTLED 114
   NORTHERN HAWK 114
   NORTHERN SAW-
   WHET 116
   SHORT-EARED 114
   SNOWY 114
   SPOTTED 114
   STYGIAN 114
   TENGMALM'S 116

Oxyura jamaicensis 24
OYSTERCATCHER 70
   AMERICAN 70
   AMERICAN BLACK
   70
   EURASIAN 70

Pachyramphus aglaiae 134
Pagophila eburnea 92
Pandion haliaetus 58
Parabuteo unicintus 60
PARAKEET, CANARY-
   WINGED 126
   GREEN 126
   GREY-BREASTED 126
   MONK 126
   QUAKER 126
   WHITE-WINGED 126
Pardirallus maculatus 66
PARROT, RED-
   CROWNED 126
PARTRIDGE 30
   GREY 30
PARULA, NORTHERN
   182
   TROPICAL 182
Parula americana 182
   pitiayumi 182
   superciliosa 182
Passer domesticus 202
   montanus 202
Passerculus sandwichensis
   198
Passerella iliaca 200
Passerina amoena 206
   caerulea 206
   ciris 206
   cyanea 206
   versicolor 206
Patagioenas fasciata 108
   flavirostris 108
   leucocephala 108
   squamosa 108

PAURAQUE 118
  COMMON 118
PEEWIT 72
Pelagodroma marina 42
PELICAN, AMERICAN
    WHITE 48
  BROWN 48
Pelecanus erythrorhynchos
    48
  occidentalis 48
Perdix perdix 30
PEREGRINE 64
Perisoreus canadensis 148
PETREL, BERMUDA 38
  BLACK 38
  BLACK-CAPPED 38
  BLUE-FOOTED 38
  BULWER'S 42
  CAPE VERDE 38
  CAPPED 38
  COOK'S 38
  DARK-RUMPED 38
  DIABLOTIN 38
  FEA'S 38
  FRIGATE 42
  GREAT-WINGED 38
  GREY-FACED 38
  HARCOURT'S 44
  HAWAIIAN 38
  LEACH'S 44
  MOTTLED 38
  MURPHY'S 38
  PARKINSON'S 38
  PEALE'S 38
  SCALED 38
  SOOTY 44
  STEJNEGER'S 38
  TRINIDADE 38
  WHITE-CHINNED
    38
Petrochelidon fulva 158
  pyrrhonota 158
Peucedramus taeniatus 180

PEWEE, CRESCENT-EYED
    134
  CUBAN 134
  GREATER 134
Phaethon aethereus 46
  lepturus 46
  rubricauda 46
Phaetusa simplex 100
PHAINOPEPLA 178
Phainopepla nitens 178
Phalacrocorax auritus 48
  brasilianus 48
  carbo 48
  pelagicus 48
  penicillatus 48
  urile 48
Phalaenoptilus nuttallii 118
PHALAROPE, GREY 90
  NORTHERN 90
  RED 90
  RED-NECKED 90
  WILSON'S 90
Phalaropus fulicaria 90
  lobatus 90
  tricolor 90
Phasianus colchicus 28
PHEASANT 28
  RING-NECKED 28
Pheucticus chrysopeplus 206
  ludovicianus 206
  melanocephalus 206
Philomachus pugnax 82
Phoebastria albatrus 36
  immutabilis 36
  nigripes 36
PHOEBE, BLACK 138
  EASTERN 138
  SAY'S 138
Phoebetria palpebrata 36
Phoenicopterus ruber 54
Phylloscopus borealis 166
  fuscatus 166
  inornatus 166

  proregulus 166
  sibilatrix 166
  trochilus 166
Pica hudsonia 150
  nuttalli 150
Picoides albolarvatus 130
  arcticus 130
  arizonae 130
  borealis 130
  dorsalis 130
  nuttallii 130
  pubescens 130
  scalaris 130
  villosus 130
PIGEON, BAND-TAILED
    108
  RED-BILLED 108
  RED-NECKED 108
  SCALY-NAPED 108
  SEA 104
  WHITE-CROWNED
    108
Pinicola enucleator 216
PINTAIL 18
  BAHAMA 18
  NORTHERN 18
  WHITE-CHEEKED
    18
Pipilo aberti 194
  chlorurus 194
  crissalis 194
  erythrophthalmus 194
  fuscus 194
  maculatus 194
PIPIT, AMERICAN 152
  BUFF-BELLIED 152
  MEADOW 152
  OLIVE-BACKED 152
  OLIVE TREE 152
  PECHORA 152
  RED-THROATED 152
  SPRAGUE'S 152
  TREE 152

Piranga bidentata 192
  flava 192
  ludoviciana 192
  olivacea 192
  rubra 192
Pitangus sulphuratus 142
Platalea leucorodia 54
Plectrophenax hyperboreus
    202
  nivalis 202
Plegadis chihi 54
  falcinellus 54
PLOVER, AMERICAN
    GOLDEN 72
  ASIAN GOLDEN 72
  BLACK-BELLIED 72
  COLLARED 74
  COMMON RINGED 74
  EASTERN GOLDEN 72
  EASTERN SAND 72
  EURSIAN GOLDEN
    72
  GOLDEN 72
  GREATER RINGED 74
  GREEN 72
  GREY 72
  LESSER GOLDEN 72
  LESSER SAND 74
  LITTLE RINGED 74
  MONGOLIAN 74
  MOUNTAIN 72
  ORIENTAL 72
  PACIFIC GOLDEN 72
  PIPING 74
  RINGED 74
  SEMIPALMATED 74
  SNOWY 74
  THICK-BILLED 74
  WILSON'S 74
Pluvialis apricaria 72
  dominica 72
  fulva 72
  squatarola 72

POCHARD 20
  COMMON 20
  EUROPEAN 20
Podiceps auritus 34
  grisegena 34
  nigricollis 34
Podilymbus podiceps 34
Poecile atricapilla 160
  carolinensis 160
  cincta 160
  gambeli 160
  hudsonica 160
  rufescens 160
  sclateri 160
Polioptila caerulea 166
  californica 166
  melanura 166
  nigriceps 166
Polysticta stelleri 22
Pooecetes gramineus 196
POORWILL 118
  COMMON 118
Porphyrio flavirostris 68
  martinica 68
Porzana carolina 66
  parva 66
  porzana 66
PRAIRIE-CHICKEN,
    GREATER 28
  LESSER 28
PRATINCOLE, EASTERN
    90
  LARGE INDIAN 90
  ORIENTAL 90
Procellaria aequinoctialis 38
  parkinsoni 38
Progne chalybea 156
  cryptoleuca 156
  elegans 156
  subis 156
  tapera 156
Protonotaria citrea 186
Prunella montanella 152

Psaltriparus minimus 160
PTARMIGAN 26
  ROCK 26
  WHITE-TAILED 26
  WILLOW 26
Pterodroma arminjoniana 38
  cahow 38
  cookii 38
  feae 38
  hasitata 38
  inexpectata 38
  longirostris 38
  macroptera 38
  phaeopygia 38
  ultima 38
Ptilogonys cinereus 178
Ptychoramphus aleuticus
    106
PUFFIN 106
  ATLANTIC 106
  COMMON 106
  HORNED 106
  TUFTED 106
Puffinus auricularis 42
  baroli 42
  bulleri 40
  carneipes 40
  creatopus 40
  gravis 40
  griseus 40
  lherminieri 42
  opisthomelas 42
  pacificus 40
  puffinus 42
  tenuirostris 40
Pycnonotus jocosus 178
PYGMY-OWL,
    CALIFORNIAN 116
  FERRUGINOUS 116
  NORTHERN 116
Pyrocephalus rubinus 138
Pyrrhula pyrrhula 214
PYRRHULOXIA 204

QUAIL, CALIFORNIA 30
  GAMBEL'S 30
  MONTEZUMA 30
  MOUNTAIN 30
  SCALED 30
QUAIL-DOVE, KEY WEST
  110
  RUDDY 110
QUETZAL, EARED 126
Quiscalus major 212
  mexicanus 212
  quiscula 212

RAIL, BLACK 66
  CLAPPER 66
  CRAKE 66
  KING 66
  SORA 66
  SPOTTED 66
  VIRGINIA 66
  WATER 66
  YELLOW 66
Rallus aquaticus 66
  elegans 66
  limicola 66
  longirostris 66
RAVEN 150
  CHIHUAHUAN 150
  NORTHERN 150
RAZORBILL 104
Recurvirostra americana 70
REDHEAD 20
REDPOLL 218
  ARCTIC 218
  COMMON 218
  HOARY 218
REDSHANK 76
  DUSKY 76
  SPOTTED 76
REDSTART, AMERICAN
  186
  PAINTED 190
  SLATE-THROATED 190

REDWING 174
REEVE 82
Regulus calendula 168
  satrapa 168
Rhodostethia rosea 92
Rhodothraupis celaeno 206
Ridgwayia pinicola 172
Riparia riparia 158
Rissa brevirostris 96
  tridactyla 96
ROADRUNNER,
  GREATER 112
ROBIN, AMERICAN 172
  CLAY-COLOURED 172
  ORANGE-FLANKED
  BUSH 170
  RUFOUS-BACKED 172
  SIBERIAN BLUE 170
  WHITE-THROATED 172
ROOK 150
ROSEFINCH, COMMON
  216
Rostrhamus sociabilis 58
ROSY-FINCH, BLACK 216
  BROWN-CAPPED 216
  GREY-CROWNED 216
RUBYTHROAT,
  SIBERIAN 170
RUFF 82
Rynchops niger 100

Salpinctes obsoletus 164
SANDERLING 84
SANDPIPER, BAIRD'S 86
  BROAD-BILLED 88
  BUFF-BREASTED 78
  COMMON 78
  CURLEW 88
  GREAT 84
  GREEN 76
  GREY RUMPED 78
  LEAST 86
  MARSH 76

PECTORAL 84
  PURPLE 88
  RED-BACKED 88
  ROCK 88
  SEMIPALMATED 86
  SHARP-TAILED 84
  SIBERIAN PECTORAL
  84
  SOLITARY 76
  SPOONBILL 88
  SPOON-BILLED 88
  SPOTTED 78
  STILT 88
  TEREK 78
  UPLAND 78
  WESTERN 86
  WHITE-RUMPED 86
  WOOD 76
SAPSUCKER, COMMON
  132
  RED-BREASTED 132
  RED-NAPED 132
  WILLIAMSON'S 132
  YELLOW-BELLIED 132
Saxicola torquatus 170
Sayornis nigricans 138
  phoebe 138
  saya 138
SCAUP 20
  GREATER 20
  LESSER 20
Scolopax minor 90
  rusticola 90
SCOPS-OWL, ASIAN 116
  EASTERN 116
  ORIENTAL 116
SCOTER, BLACK 22
  SURF 22
  WHITE-WINGED 22
SCREECH-OWL,
  COMMON 116
  EASTERN 116
  SPOTTED 116

WESTERN 116
WHISKERED 116
SCRUB-JAY, FLORIDA 148
ISLAND 148
WESTERN 148
SEA-EAGLE, STELLER'S 56
WHITE-SHOULDERED 56
WHITE-TAILED 56
SEEDEATER, WHITE-COLLARED 192
Seiurus aurocapilla 188
motacilla 188
noveboracensis 188
Selasphorus platycercus 124
rufus 124
sasin 124
Setophaga ruticilla 186
SHEARWATER,
AUDUBON'S 42
BLACK-VENTED 42
BULLER'S 40
CORY'S 40
FLESH-FOOTED 40
GREAT 40
GREATER 40
GREY-BACKED 40
MANX 42
NEW ZEALAND 40
NORTH ATLANTIC LITTLE 42
PALE-FOOTED 40
PINK-FOOTED 40
SHORT-TAILED 40
SLENDER-BILLED 40
SOOTY 40
STREAKED 40
TOWNSEND'S 42
WEDGE-TAILED 40
WHITE-FACED 40
SHOVELER 18
NORTHERN 18

SHRIKE, BROWN 142
GREAT GREY 142
LOGGERHEAD 142
NORTHERN 142
Sialia currucoides 170
mexicana 170
sialis 170
SILKY-FLYCATCHER, GREY 178
SISKIN 218
EURASIAN 218
PINE 218
Sitta canadensis 162
carolinensis 162
pusilla 162
pygmaea 162
SKIMMER, AMERICAN 100
BLACK 100
SKUA, ARCTIC 102
GREAT 102
LONG-TAILED 102
MacCORMICK'S 102
POMARINE 102
SOUTH POLAR 102
SKYLARK 152
SMEW 24
SNAKEBIRD 48
SNIPE 90
COMMON 90
JACK 90
PIN-TAILED 90
WILSON'S 90
SNOWCOCK, HIMALAYAN 30
SOLITAIRE, TOWNSEND'S 170
Somateria fischeri 22
mollissima 22
spectabilis 22
SORA 66
SPARROW, AMERICAN TREE 196

BACHMAN'S 194
BAIRD'S 198
BLACK-CHINNED 196
BLACK-THROATED 198
BOTTERI'S 194
BREWER'S 196
CASSIN'S 194
CHIPPING 196
CLAY-COLOURED 196
ENGLISH 202
EURASIAN TREE 202
FIELD 196
FIVE-STRIPED 196
FOX 200
GOLDEN-CROWNED 200
GRASSHOPPER 198
HARRIS'S 200
HENSLOW'S 198
HOUSE 202
LARK 196
LE CONTE'S 198
LINCOLN'S 200
NELSON'S SHARP-TAILED 198
OLIVE 194
RUFOUS-CROWNED 194
RUFOUS-WINGED 194
SAGE 198
SALTMARSH SHARP-TAILED 198
SAVANNAH 198
SEASIDE 198
SONG 200
SWAMP 200
TREE 202
VESPER 196
WHITE-CROWNED 200
WHITE-THROATED 200
WORTHEN'S 196

235

Sphyrapicus nuchalis 132
  ruber 132
  thyroideus 132
  varius 132
SPINDALIS, WESTERN
  192
Spindalis zena 192
Spiza americana 202
Spizella arborea 196
  atrogularis 196
  breweri 196
  pallida 196
  passerina 196
  pusilla 196
  wortheni 196
SPOONBILL 54
  EURASIAN 54
  ROSEATE 54
  WHITE 54
Sporophila torqueola 192
SPOTBILL, CHINESE 16
STARLING 178
  COMMON 178
  EUROPEAN 178
STARTHROAT, PLAIN-
  CAPPED 124
Stelgidopteryx serripennis 158
Stellula calliope 124
Stercorarius longicaudus 102
  maccormicki 102
  parasiticus 102
  pomarinus 102
  skua 102
Sterna dougallii 98
  elegans 98
  forsteri 98
  hirundo 98
  maxima 98
  paradisaea 98
  sandvicensis 98
Sternula antillarum 98
STILT, BLACK-NECKED
  70

BLACK-WINGED 70
STINT, LITTLE 86
  LONG-TOED 86
  RED-NECKED 86
  RUFOUS-NECKED 86
  TEMMINCK'S 86
STONECHAT 170
STORK, WOOD 54
STORM-PETREL 44
  ASHY 44
  BAND-RUMPED 44
  BLACK 44
  BLACK-BELLIED 44
  EUROPEAN 44
  FORK-TAILED 42
  GALAPAGOS 44
  GREY 42
  HORNBY'S 42
  LEAST 44
  MADEIRAN 44
  RINGED 42
  STEJNEGER'S 44
  TRISTRAM'S 44
  WEDGE-RUMPED 44
  WHITE-FACED 42
  WILSON'S 44
Streptopelia chinensis 108
  decaocto 108
  orientalis 108
  turtur 108
Streptoprocne zonaris 120
Strix nebulosa 114
  occidentalis 114
  varia 114
  virgata 114
Sturnella magna 208
  neglecta 208
Sturnus vulgaris 178
Sula dactylatra 46
  leucogaster 46
  nebouxii 46
  sula 46
SURFBIRD 84

Surnia ulula 114
SWALLOW 156
  AMERICAN CLIFF 158
  BAHAMA 158
  BANK 158
  BARN 156
  CAVE 158
  CLIFF 158
  MANGROVE 158
  NORTHERN ROUGH-
    WINGED 158
  TREE 158
  VIOLET-GREEN 158
SWAN, MUTE 14
  TRUMPETER 14
  TUNDRA 14
  WHISTLING 14
  WHOOPER 14
SWIFT 120
  ANTILLEAN PALM 120
  BLACK 120
  CHIMNEY 120
  COLLARED 120
  COMMON 120
  DUSKY-BACKED 120
  EUROPEAN 120
  FORK-TAILED 120
  NEEDLE-TAILED 120
  NORTHERN WHITE-
    RUMPED 120
  PACIFIC 120
  VAUX'S 120
  WHITE-COLLARED 120
  WHITE-THROATED
    120
Sylvia atricapilla 166
  curruca 166
Synthliboramphus antiquus
  104
  craveri 104
  hypoleucus 104

Tachornis phoenicobia 120

Tachybaptus dominicus 34
Tachycineta albilinea 158
  bicolor 158
  cyaneoviridis 158
  thalassina 158
TANAGER, FLAME-
    COLOURED 192
  HEPATIC 192
  SCARLET 192
  STRIPE-HEADED 192
  SUMMER 192
  WESTERN 192
Tarsiger cyanurus 170
TATTLER, GREY-TAILED
  78
  POLYNESIAN 78
  SIBERIAN 78
  WANDERING 78
TEAL 18
  BAIKAL 18
  BLUE-WINGED 18
  CINNAMON 18
  COMMON 18
  EURASIAN 18
  FALCATED 16
  FORMOSA 18
  GREEN-WINGED 18
TERN, ALEUTIAN 100
  AMERICAN LITTLE 98
  ARCTIC 98
  BLACK 100
  BRIDLED 100
  BROWN-WINGED 100
  CASPIAN 98
  COMMON 98
  ELEGANT 98
  FORSTER'S 98
  GULL-BILLED 98
  KAMCHATKA 100
  LARGE-BILLED 100
  LEAST 98
  ROSEATE 98
  ROYAL 98

  SANDWICH 98
  SOOTY 100
  WHISKERED 100
  WHITE-WINGED 100
  WHITE-WINGED
    BLACK 100
  WIDEAWAKE 100
Tetraogallus himalayensis 30
Thalassarche cauta 36
  chlororhynchos 36
  melanophris 36
THICK-KNEE, DOUBLE-
    STRIPED 70
THRASHER, BENDIRE'S
  176
  BROWN 176
  CALIFORNIA 176
  CRISSAL 176
  CURVE-BILLED 176
  LE CONTE'S 176
  LONG-BILLED 176
  SAGE 176
THRUSH, AZTEC 172
  BICKNELL'S 174
  CLAY-COLOURED 172
  DUSKY 172
  EYE-BROWED 172
  GREY-CHEEKED 174
  HERMIT 174
  NAUMANN'S 172
  RUFOUS-BACKED 172
  SONG 174
  SWAINSON'S 174
  VARIED 172
  WHITE-THROATED
    172
  WOOD 174
Thryomanes bewickii 164
Thryothorus ludovicianus 164
Tiaris bicolor 192
  olivaceus 192
TIT, SIBERIAN 160
TITMOUSE, BLACK-

  CRESTED 162
  BRIDLED 162
  JUNIPER 162
  OAK 162
  TUFTED 162
TITYRA, MASKED 142
Tityra semifasciata 142
TOWHEE, ABERT'S 194
  CALIFORNIA 194
  CANYON 194
  EASTERN 194
  GREEN-TAILED 194
  SPOTTED 194
Toxostoma bendirei 176
  curvirostre 176
  dorsale 176
  lecontei 176
  longirostre 176
  redivivum 176
  rufum 176
Tringa brevipes 78
  erythropus 76
  flavipes 76
  glareola 76
  incana 78
  melanoleuca 76
  nebularia 76
  ochropus 76
  semipalmatus 78
  solitaria 76
  stagnatilis 76
  totanus 76
Troglodytes aedon 164
  hiemalis 164
TROGON, COPPERY-
    TAILED 126
  EARED 126
  ELEGANT 126
Trogon elegans 126
TROPICBIRD, RED-
    BILLED 46
  RED-TAILED 46
  WHITE-TAILED 46

Tryngites subruficollis 78
Turdus assimilis 172
  grayi 172
  iliacus 174
  merula 172
  migratorius 172
  naumanni 172
  obscurus 172
  philomelos 174
  pilaris 174
  rufopalliatus 172
TURKEY, WILD 26
TURNSTONE 84
  BLACK 84
  RUDDY 84
Tympanuchus cupido 28
  pallidicinctus 28
  phasianellus 28
Tyrannus caudifasciatus 140
  couchii 140
  crassirostris 140
  dominicensis 140
  forficatus 142
  melancholicus 140
  savana 142
  tyrannus 140
  verticalis 140
  vociferans 140
TYSTIE 104
Tyto alba 114

Upupa epops 112
Uria aalge 104
  lomvia 104

Vanellus vanellus 72
VEERY 174
VERDIN 160
Vermivora bachmanii 180
  celata 180
  chrysoptera 180
  crissalis 180
  luciae 180

  peregrina 180
  pinus 180
  ruficapilla 180
  virginiae 180
VIOLET-EAR, GREEN 122
  MEXICAN 122
VIREO, BELL'S 144
  BLACK-CAPPED 146
  BLACK-WHISKERED 146
  BLUE-HEADED 144
  CASSIN'S 144
  GREY 144
  HUTTON'S 146
  PHILADELPHIA 146
  PLUMBEOUS 144
  RED-EYED 146
  SOLITARY 144
  THICK-BILLED 144
  WARBLING 146
  WHITE-EYED 144
  YELLOW-GREEN 146
  YELLOW-THROATED 144
  YUCATAN 146
Vireo altiloquus 146
  atricapillus 146
  bellii 144
  cassinii 144
  crassirostris 144
  flavifrons 144
  flavoviridis 146
  gilvus 146
  griseus 144
  huttoni 146
  magister 146
  olivaceus 146
  philadelphicus 146
  plumbeus 144
  solitarius 144
  vicinior 144
VULTURE, AMERICAN
  BLACK 56

  BLACK 56
  TURKEY 56

WAGTAIL, ALASKAN
  YELLOW 154
  CITRINE 154
  EASTERN YELLOW 154
  GREY 154
  SWINHOE'S WHITE 154
  WHITE 154
  YELLOW 154
  YELLOW-HOODED 154
WARBLER, ARCTIC 166
  BACHMAN'S 180
  BAY-BREASTED 186
  BLACK-AND-WHITE 186
  BLACKBURNIAN 184
  BLACKPOLL 186
  BLACK-THROATED BLUE 182
  BLACK-THROATED GREEN 184
  BLACK-THROATED GREY 184
  BLUE-WINGED 180
  CANADA 190
  CAPE MAY 182
  CERULEAN 186
  CHESTNUT-SIDED 182
  COLIMA 180
  CONNECTICUT 188
  CRESCENT-CHESTED 182
  DUSKY 166
  FAN-TAILED 190
  GOLDEN-CHEEKED 184
  GOLDEN-CROWNED 190
  GOLDEN-WINGED 180
  GRACE'S 184

HERMIT 184
HOODED 190
KENTUCKY 188
KIRTLAND'S 184
LANCEOLATED 166
LUCY'S 180
MacGILLIVRAY'S 188
MAGNOLIA 182
MIDDENDORFF'S
   GRASSHOPPER 166
MOURNING 188
MYRTLE 182
NASHVILLE 180
OLIVE 180
ORANGE-CROWNED
   180
PALLAS'S 166
PALLAS'S LEAF 166
PALM 186
PINE 184
PRAIRIE 186
PROTHONOTARY 186
RED-FACED 190
RUFOUS-CAPPED 190
SEDGE 166
SWAINSON'S 186
TENNESSEE 180
TOWNSEND'S 184
VIRGINIA'S 180
WILLOW 166
WILSON'S 190
WOOD 166
WORM-EATING 186
YELLOW 182
YELLOW-BROWED 166
YELLOW-RUMPED 182
YELLOW-THROATED
   184
WATERTHRUSH,
   LOUISIANA 188
NORTHERN 188
WAXWING 178
BOHEMIAN 178

CEDAR 178
WHEATEAR 170
   NORTHERN 170
WHIMBREL 80
   LITTLE 80
WHIP-POOR-WILL 118
   RIDGWAY'S 118
WHISTLING-DUCK,
   BLACK-BELLIED 12
FULVOUS 12
WHITESTART, PAINTED
   190
   WHITE-THROATED
   190
WHITETHROAT, LESSER
   166
WIGEON 16
   AMERICAN 16
   EURASIAN 16
WILLET 78
Wilsonia canadensis 190
   citrina 190
   pusilla 190
WOODCOCK 90
   AMERICAN 90
   EURASIAN 90
WOODPECKER, ACORN
   128
   AMERICAN THREE-
   TOED 130
   ARIZONA 130
   BLACK-BACKED 130
   BROWN-BACKED 130
   DOWNY 130
   GILA 128
   GOLDEN-FRONTED
   128
   GREAT SPOTTED 128
   HAIRY 130
   IVORY-BILLED 132
   LADDER-BACKED 130
   LEWIS'S 128
   NUTTALL'S 130

PILEATED 132
   RED-BELLIED 128
   RED-COCKADED 130
   RED-HEADED 128
   STRICKLAND'S 130
   WHITE-HEADED 130
WOOD-PEWEE,
   EASTERN 134
   WESTERN 134
WOODSTAR, BAHAMA
   124
WREN, BEWICK'S 164
   CACTUS 164
   CANYON 164
   CAROLINA 164
   HOUSE 164
   MARSH 164
   ROCK 164
   SEDGE 164
   WINTER 164
WRENTIT 168
WRYNECK 128
   EURASIAN 128

Xanthocephalus
   xanthocephalus 208
Xema sabini 92
Xenus cinereus 78

YELLOWLEGS, GREATER
   76
   LESSER 76
YELLOWTHROAT 188
   COMMON 188
   GREY-CROWNED 188

Zenaida asiatica 110
   aurita 110
   macroura 110
Zonotrichia albicollis 200
   atricapilla 200
   leucophrys 200
   querula 200